Masculinities
and Violence

RESEARCH ON MEN AND MASCULINITIES SERIES

Series Editor:
MICHAEL S. KIMMEL, SUNY Stony Brook

Contemporary research on men and masculinity, informed by recent feminist thought and intellectual breakthroughs of women's studies and the women's movement, treats masculinity not as a normative referent but as a problematic gender construct. This series of interdisciplinary, edited volumes attempts to understand men and masculinity through this lens, providing a comprehensive understanding of gender and gender relationships in the contemporary world. Published in cooperation with the Men's Studies Association, a Task Group of the National Organization for Men Against Sexism.

Volumes in this Series

1. Steve Craig (ed.)
   MEN, MASCULINITY, AND THE MEDIA
2. Peter M. Nardi (ed.)
   MEN'S FRIENDSHIPS
3. Christine L. Williams (ed.)
   DOING WOMEN'S WORK: Men in Nontraditional Occupations
4. Jane C. Hood (ed.)
   MEN, WORK, AND FAMILY
5. Harry Brod and Michael Kaufman (eds.)
   THEORIZING MASCULINITIES
6. Edward H. Thompson, Jr. (ed.)
   OLDER MEN'S LIVES
7. William Marsiglio (ed.)
   FATHERHOOD
8. Donald Sabo and David Frederick Gordon (eds.)
   MEN'S HEALTH AND ILLNESS
9. Cliff Cheng (ed.)
   MASCULINITIES IN ORGANIZATIONS
10. Lee H. Bowker (ed.)
    MASCULINITIES AND VIOLENCE

Masculinities and Violence

Edited by
Lee H. Bowker

Published in cooperation with the Men's Studies Association,
A Task Group of the National Organization for Men Against Sexism

SAGE Publications
International Educational and Professional Publisher
Thousand Oaks   London   New Delhi

For information:

SAGE Publications, Inc.
2455 Teller Road
Thousand Oaks, California 91320
E-mail: order@sagepub.com

SAGE Publications Ltd.
6 Bonhill Street
London EC2A 4PU
United Kingdom

SAGE Publications India Pvt. Ltd.
M-32 Market
Greater Kailash I
New Delhi 110 048 India

Printed in the United States of America

Library of Congress Cataloging-in-Publication Data

Masculinities and violence / edited by Lee H. Bowker.
    p. cm.—(Research on men and masculinities series ; v. 10)
    Includes bibliographical references and index.
    ISBN 0-7619-0451-4 (cloth: acid-free paper).—ISBN 0-7619-0452-2
(pbk.: acid-free paper)
    1. Men. 2. Masculinity. 3. Violence. I. Bowker, Lee H.
II. Series: Research on men and masculinities series; 10.
HQ1090.M379 1997
303.6′081—dc21   97-33904

    99 00 01 02 03 04 10 9 8 7 6 5 4 3 2

Acquiring Editor:	Peter Labella
Editorial Assistant:	Corinne Pierce
Production Editor:	Michele Lingre
Production Assistant:	Denise Santoyo
Typesetter/Designer:	Marion Warren
Cover Designer:	Candice Harman
Print Buyer:	Anna Chin

Contents

Acknowledgments

My profound thanks to Richard Gelles for the original suggestion that I edit a volume on masculine violence and to Michael Kimmel for his encouragement and wise advice throughout the development of the book. I greatly appreciate the willingness of the staff at Sage to delay the publication schedule while I dealt with numerous medical problems. It has been a vast pleasure to be associated with the authors of the chapters, who are on the cutting edge of the understanding of the masculinities-violence nexus. They have, without exception, been a delight to work with. I could not have completed the task without the typing and organizational assistance provided by Linda Hall-Martin and Gwendolyn Alice Bowker. Finally, I hope that my loving partner and our wonderful daughters will consider the finished product to have been worth the loss of family time that was necessary to produce it.

Introduction

Living masculine is a yin and yang experience. Much of what is good in the world, whether in terms of philosophy, art, music, literature, medical advantages, or technological improvements, has been contributed by masculine role players. In contrast, an extremely high proportion of the negative forces in human experience also are the product of masculine role players. These negativities include environmental destruction and pollution, war, property crime, family violence, religious persecution, sexual allure, fraud and other forms of exploitation by corporations, and numerous additional categories of human rights violations. For an unavoidably masculine role player like myself, how shall I regard the masculine legacy of the ages to which I am inextricably tied through my genes as well as the social conventions (norms, values, and beliefs) that define the content and boundaries of the multiple masculine roles I play in diverse circumstances and settings? If I look back over my shoulder in one direction, I can relish masculine achievements but if I look back in the other direction, I wonder how I ever can begin to make up for the depredations of my masculine ancestors (to say nothing of my contemporaries).

Historical contradictions in masculine roles are mirrored in my experiences with men in my own life. I have known a considerable number of exceptionally fine men, many of whom have served as ego ideals for my own development as a caring human being. These men evinced a variety of intellectual abilities and artistic talents, never in the same combination. As near as I can discern, what they all shared was a sensitivity to social situations and human needs, a dedication to helping and supporting others, and an unwillingness to victimize their fellow human beings. An example of this behavior is a vivid memory I have from my days as an undergraduate student. The deadline for one fee or another was upon me and I was in a panic because I had not brought much cash to campus with me that morning. For some reason, I was audacious enough to seek help from my mathematics professor. Eschewing small talk, I opened with a request for a loan. To my amazement, he had his wallet out of his back pocket before I finished my first sentence. He asked me how much money I needed, and gave me a handful of bills. His generosity in helping me will never be forgotten, but his sensitivity in divining my need and putting me at ease set a standard of behavior that I have admired even more then his generosity.

How did my mathematics professor know what I wanted? Was it his awareness of institutional rhythms, so that he had the fee deadline in mind when I entered his office? Or was it something about the way I phrased my opening sentence? Perhaps I betrayed my stress in the tone of my voice or on my face. I have no idea how he did it, but his simple act of kindness was a virtuoso performance of sensitivity to social situations and human needs.

Masculinities and Violence is not a book about the positive contributions that masculine role players have made to human existence. There are no mentors to be found in its pages. Instead, this is a volume of research reports, essays, and literature analyses about the negative side of masculine behavior. It is not kindness and sensitivity that are showcased, but rather selfishness and insensitive rapaciousness. Since I have offered a personal story about the positive side of masculine role performance, I will balance it with an equally personal example of the dark side of masculinity before turning to the contents of the 11 chapters that follow.

While working myself up through the professional ranks, I served as a volunteer administrator of the Social Therapy Program at the Washington State Penitentiary. We created the program to cull the most violent drug abusers out of the prison's general population and offer them membership in an isolated therapeutic community that featured daily therapy groups with a mixture of prisoners and trained volunteers from the college. My story begins as I finished escorting the evening group of volunteers out to the front gate. There, I received a message that there had been a violent incident back on the tier and I immediately went to the prison hospital.

Our most antisocial program member was stretched out on a table with a deep knife wound just an inch from his heart. Two other prisoners from the program were working on him. No physicians were on duty, nor were any called by prison officials. Three times his heart stopped beating and three times the two prisoners, who had extensive past experience assisting physicians, brought him back. Then he stabilized, eventually recovered, and was released after serving the rest of his sentence.

The man who stabbed him was in another room with several correctional officers. From him and some of the other members of the program, I learned what had transpired during the few minutes that I spent escorting the volunteers out of the prison. The dying prisoner was a white racist who objected to having African American prisoners in the program. It would have been a violation of the local convict code to have made trouble while any outsiders were on the tier, so he waited until we left. Then he took out the two hammers that he had somehow smuggled into his cell and went after the African American in a nearby cell. The cells had not yet been locked down for the night. He got in one hard blow to the skull of his intended victim, who then produced his smuggled knife and abruptly ended the encounter by inflicting the near-fatal chest wound.

The prison administration contained its own racist elements. As I remember it, the white aggressor had no time added to his sentence and the African American served additional time for having dared to defend himself. In a later incident, the white prisoner, then fully recovered, threatened to kill me when he was released because I wouldn't give him a positive Parole Board recommendation. He never did get around to carrying out that threat, instead journeying to California after release and, I was told, dying in a street fight with another criminal.

Having experienced the high and low points of masculine role performance both as a culture consumer and as a participant in interaction with other masculine role players, I apologize to readers for having brought together a set of chapters that portray only the dark side of masculine role performance. This unbalanced portrayal is necessitated by the ways in which knowledge is segmented as it is organized into meaningful topic areas for cultural dissemination. Lest you become too depressed as you read on, I recommend that you medicate yourself by obtaining some of the other looks in the Research on Men and Masculinities series under the general editorship of Michael Kimmel. Recent volumes issued in this series by Sage Publications include: *Masculinities in Organizations* by Cliff Cheng, *Men's Health and Illness* by Donald Sabo and David Gordon, and *Fatherhood* by William Marsiglio.

Masculinities and Violence portrays masculinities negatively not just because of the book's focus on violence, but also because violence is dominated by masculine role players in all modern, complex societies. Choose a form of violence and examine international statistics on the gender of its perpetrators. You always will find a severely unbalanced sex ratio, generally with 90% to 100% of the violence being perpetrated by men and less than 10% being perpetrated by women. From time to time, a small number of violent acts committed by woman gain newspaper headlines and perhaps even a few scholarly articles on the rise in female crime. The reality behind this is that female violent crime is so rare that some states have managed to survive for a century without any prison for women. The few female criminals who needed to be incarcerated were shipped off to larger adjacent states and paid for via a per diem rate.

When somebody trumpets about a sharp rise in female violent crime of 50%, they usually are creating a statistical distortion by using a very low base rate of female violent crime to start with. In a town with 20 female and 200 male violent crimes in 1995, a rise of 10 violent crimes by each gender in 1996 to 30 and 210 crimes, respectively, can be represented as a 50% increase in female crime. This female "crime wave" can then be compared with a "minuscule" 5% increase in male crime so as completely to obscure the fact that the absolute rise in crime was the same for both genders, 10 crimes each.

After all the confusion is stripped away, we are left with the realization that violence is a major contradiction of the variety of masculine roles that have been socially embroidered around the biological male of the human species. The chapters in *Masculinities and Violence* advance the perspective that masculine violence must be identified, revealed, and understood if it is ever to be diminished.

This book is divided into four parts, containing a total of 11 chapters. The parts are titled "Learning Violence," "Men Victimizing Women and Children," "Men Victimizing Men," and "Masculinities and Organizational Violence." The first section begins with my chapter, "On the Difficulty of Eradicating Masculine Violence: Multisystem Overdetermination." In this essay, I attempt to convince readers that intervention schemes designed to interrupt masculine violence at a single system level of action are doomed to failure. I argue that violence is simultaneously determined at multiple system levels of action and suggest that there are five system levels that are relevant to masculine violence: the cultural, social, economic, personality, and biological systems. The more system levels that are attacked in an intervention scheme, the greater the impact of the intervention will be in reducing masculine violence. We learn about violence at a very early age. Sarah Sobieraj demonstrates the contribution made to masculine violence by Saturday morning toy commercials. Even if boys and girls were born with equal propensities for violence, the immense and intense socialization differences between the two genders soon would cause them to behave very differently. While boys are being socialized toward a conception of masculinity that subsumes a willingness to employ aggression to achieve desired goals, girls are not left in a vacuum. Sobieraj shows that they are taught to attend to a different focus for personality organization: personal attractiveness.

Chapter 3 is a chilling revelation about "Bureaucratizing Masculinities Among Brazilian Torturers and Murderers" by Martha Huggins and Mika Haritos-Fatouros. These researchers divide the Brazilian torturers and murderers they studied into lone wolves and institutional functionaries. The lone wolves maintained their independence from the political system, evincing an inner-directed masculinity. Other police torturers felt enveloped by the police bureaucracy, which carried out the polices of the political system. They were willing to subordinate their masculine role performance to the requirements of the organization, thus becoming other-directed "rational" agents of police culture and the desires of political elites.

Part II of *Masculinities and Violence* begins with a broad research synthesis by Neil Websdale and Meda Chesney-Lind on the victimization of women. They summarize what has been discovered by social scientists about diverse forms of men's violence against women, including murder and assault by intimates, mass murder, sexual victimization, the abuse of prostitutes, sexual harassment, and the (over)incarceration of women. Websdale and Chesney-Lind understand that women are exposed to so many forms of violence because of the disadvantaged situations in which they live.

Chris O'Sullivan continues in the comparative mode of analysis with "Ladykillers: Similarities and Divergences of Masculinities in Gang Rape and Wife Battery." She concludes that gang rapists and batterers share some common patriarchal beliefs about women, but differ fundamentally in the nature and purpose of their violence against women. Whereas gang rape is a public performance that solidifies the perpetrators' masculinity and enhances the public social control of men over women by fear, battering is usually a private act that has nothing to so with solidifying group masculinity. It enhances the private control of one man over his woman instead of the generalized social control of men by women.

In Chapter 6, I develop a preliminary topology of sexual and nonsexual aspects of the coaching abuse of junior and senior high school girls by their male coaches and trainers. This predatory behavior is made possible, and sometimes easy, by a customary social setting in which the coach has tremendous power over his players and there are few checks and balances to limit his abuse so long as he maintains a winning record. The examples I have gathered from victims of coaching abuse communicate the suffering caused by abusive coaches to those on whom they focus their attentions and other players who are disadvantaged because they are not successful in meeting their coach's nonathletic needs.

Men are not less likely to be victimized then women just because women have a much lower rate of violence. The male victimization of other men more than makes up for the low rate of violence against men by women. This topic is explored in the third section of *Masculinities and Violence,* beginning with James Messerschmidt's study of lynching between 1865 and 1900. His painstaking analysis of historical and sociological materials leads to the conclusion that lynching and castration simultaneously maintained gender and racial hierarchies. During the Reconstruction, white men were challenged on both the gender and the racial fronts. African American men became the legal equals of white-supremacist men when they were freed from slavery. At the same time, there arose a new female role in American society, the "New Woman" who declared herself to be autonomous and happy with professional and social welfare concerns instead of marriage. Lynching and castration warned these women that they needed the protection of white men while simultaneously signaling African American men that any attempt to undermine white male hegemony would be met with mob violence.

In "Frat Boys, Bossmen, Studs, and Gentlemen," John Hagedorn describes the ways in which drug dealing gang men experience their masculinity. His research brings these gang men to us as multidimensional personalities, not stereotypes. He has good reasons to believe that frat boys, bossmen, and studs all can become gentlemen. The social settings and the content of the roles played by the gang men are constantly changing. This fluidity in the lives of gang men gives us hope that there could be rapid changes in their lifestyles in response to improved economic and social circumstances for central cities.

The final chapter on the victimization of men by men is "Hypermasculinity and Prison Violence" by Hans Toch. In prison, the concentration of men whose sense of self-worth has been diminished by unfavorable life chances produces a reliance on the equation: hypermasculinity equals status, self-worth, and diminished risk of victimization. Toch details a number of prisoner social roles and relates each of them to its hypermasculine content. He argues that hypermasculinity is bankrupt as the central organizing ideology of a social system and points out that it and its baggage of overt violence decline in salience as men age. This provides an opportunity for rehabilitation that rarely is noticed in American punishment-oriented prisons. He closes with a brief description of a therapeutic community program developed by the Scottish Prison Service that directly confronts hypermasculinity prior to the release of long-term segregated prisoners. This program sounds very much like the Social Therapy Program at the Washington State Penitentiary in the 1970s in which the violent incident I described earlier in this introduction took place. In support of Toch's observations about the relationship between hypermasculinity and age, all of the violence potential we dealt with in the Social Therapy Program was by young men. The older men in the program (in prison, over 30 is "older") lent stability and suppressed the violence potential of the younger prisoners.

"Masculinities and Organizational Violence" concludes the book with three chapters that illustrate how masculine destructiveness can be multiplied through bureaucratic organization. The Holocaust is probably the "ideal type" of the extreme extension of violence through bureaucratic rationalization. Our examples are less violent, but much closer to home. The first of these is Constance Chapple's examination of corporate crime against women, "Dow Corning and the Silicone Breast Implant Debacle." In the tradition of the thalidomide mutations and the Dalkon Shield, Dow Corning suppressed negative information about the defects and dangers of its silicone breast implants. Whether merely socially irresponsible or fraudulent and illegal, these actions by Dow Corning's masculine role-playing executives caused physical injuries to many thousands of women.

Tracy Karner directs our attention away from corporate crime to institutionalized violence in the military, concluding our tour of the many ways in which masculinities and violence are intertwined. "Engendering Violent Men: Oral Histories of Military Masculinity" is based on a series of interviews conducted with Vietnam War combat veterans who had entered a midwestern Veterans Administration hospital for the treatment of post-traumatic stress disorder. The organizational violence into which these men fit was not devoid of precursors in the men's earlier lives, for all but one of them remembered being abused by their fathers and they

xviii   MASCULINITIES AND VIOLENCE

had extensive experiences with childhood war games, schoolyard violence, and organized aggression through competitive sports. Only one man was drafted; the others enlisted and welcomed military training as an extension of their masculine development. Karner describes how the military bureaucracy substituted a homosocial "family" of buddies and squads for the heterosocial families the men had experienced in their civilian lives. Unfortunately for them, the excesses of violence that were produced by the conditions of the battlefield in Vietnam proved toxic to the men's well-being. The hypermasculinity that was necessary for survival in Vietnam left these veterans unable to adjust to postwar civilian life by adapting less virulent forms of masculine role playing.

PART ONE

LEARNING VIOLENCE

1

On the Difficulty of Eradicating Masculine Violence

Multisystem Overdetermination

LEE H. BOWKER

Violent men are notoriously difficult to socialize into prosocial lifestyles. Recidivism rates for prison releasees are high, and criminal careers typically involve hundreds or thousands of victims before the criminals grow old enough to retire from the stress of committing crimes. Male-dominated corporations that begin patterns of environmental destruction and consumer victimization repeat these patterns for decades unless forced to change by legal intervention. In my own research on woman-battering, not one of the 1,000 battered women in my study reported that her batterer spontaneously reformed, giving up his violent ways once he understood the effects of his violence on his partner (Bowker, 1986a). Attempts to reform batterers through a variety of community-based programs also have experienced great difficulty in extinguishing the men's violence (Bowker, 1994).

My thesis in this chapter is that individuals, programs, and institutions generally fail to extinguish masculine violence because their ameliorative efforts usually focus on a single system level of action, whereas masculine violence has roots in multiple system levels. In this sense, masculine violence is overdetermined rather than merely caused. Unisystemic interventions may be useful within the system on which they are focused, but they cannot suppress masculine violence that has its roots in multiple systems of action.

Consider these rather unsuccessful interventions: anger control for batterers, fines as penalties for corporate crime, and castration for sex offenders. The first hopes to reform batterers through a psychological system intervention alone. The second attacks corporate crime via only the economic system, and the third limits its intervention to the biological system. Some batterers have problems with anger control, yet most are clearly in control when assaulting loved ones. Indeed, increased control is intrinsic to intimate violence. Corporations treat fines as a cost of doing business and externalize the expense by raising consumer prices. Castrated sex offenders find that they still have strong urges to repeat the sexual rituals that have given them so much satisfaction in the past. While the testosterone engine is on idle, other system influences on sexual predation are unaltered.

System Levels of Action

What do I mean by a "system level of action?" This is, in turn, based on definitions of the key terms, *system* and *action*. By system, I refer to collections of elements that interact more with each other than with other elements nearby. I assume that some, but not necessarily all, of these elements are alive. The interaction of these elements can be observed to be in the service of reaching one or more goals, the most general of which is system survival.

One of the essential tasks for system survival is dividing the world into two groups of elements, system elements and nonsystem elements. The system utilizes an internal division of labor among its elements: a functional differentiation to meet system needs. Boundary maintenance is a characteristic of all systems. A system's boundary separates organized system elements from less organized nonsystem elements, which may be termed the system's environment.

A system cannot exist totally segregated from its environment, so it develops input and output mechanisms for interaction with the environment in ways that are favorable to its survival as a system. A system also must have some sort of feedback subsystem through which it gathers information about the environment and modifies itself to adapt to environmental changes. A system without an adequate feedback loop soon will be ineffective in dealing with the environment, and eventually will collapse. The feedback subsystem differs from the input-output process in that it is information about the environment that is gathered, whereas input activity brings elements from the environment into the system for processing. A second difference is that information gained through a feedback subsystem results in system change, in contrast with the processing of input elements where it is the elements that change rather than the system.

Systems are inherently acquisitive, in the sense that they seek both feedback information and input elements from the external environment. They take on a predatory cast when it is realized that environmental elements must be coerced or captured to be inputted into a system, and that system processing means destruction for most inputted elements. Many social theorists have ignored this aspect of system functioning, perhaps because of their involvement and investment in their own social systems. In his early survey, "Representative Biological Theories of Society," Harry Elmer Barnes (1925) differentiated between the classic social theorists, such as Herbert Spencer, who had a positive view of the social process and those, such as Ludwig Gumplowicz, who emphasized the role of "struggle," conflict, and destruction in system survival.

Action is what happens as a living system goes about its work. Action is the way in which living systems attempt to reach their goals. Parsons and Shils (1959) define action as behavior that is "oriented to the attainment of ends in situations, by means of the normatively regulated expenditure of energy" (p. 53). They are interested in three categories of human systems: social systems, personality systems, and cultural systems. Although analytically distinct, these three systems interact to influence human behavior (action). Parsons and Shils hold that not only are social systems impossible without personality systems, but also that the two systems "*interpenetrate* in the sense that no personality system can exist without *participation* in a social system" (p. 109).

Talcott Parsons occasionally recognized that other systems codetermined human action. In 1975, he published a paper in which he identified a fourth action-relevant system as the behavioral organism, but he did not maintain this system in his analytic scheme for long (Bierstedt, 1981). For the purpose of understanding masculine violence, I believe it is essential to retain something like this system, which I shall label the biological system.

To these four systems—social, cultural, personality, and biological—I will add the economic system. Parsons included the economic system in his scheme only as a subsystem of the social system, a mere footnote. This had the political advantage within academia of subordinating economics to sociology, Parson's particular field. I prefer to separate the economic system from the social system because, in practice, it is a major factor in much human behavior in general and masculine violence in particular. When examining masculine violence in the field, economic system elements are easily identified and are distinct from elements that are part of any other system.

In fact, it is often easier to separate economic system influences from social system influences than to separate personality system influences from cultural system influences. Take, for example, my system for evaluating battering and related forms of intimate abuse. I use this system when acting as an expert witness in the legal system. The five dimensions in my evaluative frame are psychological/cultural, physical, sexual, social, and economic. When I began the development of this system, I had six dimensions, with the psychological and cultural categories being separate. As I accumulated cases in my research file, I realized that I could not separate the psychological from the cultural, so closely were they intertwined.

Consider the abuser who calls his partner a "fat slob," a "stupid bitch," and a "whore." He is psychologically abusing his partner in forcefully affixing these labels to her. At the same time, these labels are cultural inventions. Cultural elements consist of norms (standards of behavior), values (desired states), and beliefs (representations of reality). Norms, values, and beliefs are all involved in the creation and maintenance of the degrading images called forth by sexist epithets. Psychological abuse would have little value as a mechanism for enhancing an abuser's domination of his victim without incorporating cultural elements. Take the cultural out of the psychological and all you have left is, "Do this or I'll hit you." My research with battered women indicates that psychological/cultural abuse with a minimum of physical violence is much more effective in reaching batterers' goals than is a substantial amount of violence without the incorporation of cultural elements.

The interpenetration of the cultural and personality systems can be approached from the opposite direction. How could a demeaning cultural stereotype come to life without first being processed through many different personality systems? A pornographic story line is created by the personality systems of only a few writers before it is written up, published, and distributed as a cultural artifact to a much larger number of personality systems. To further complicate things, the publication and distribution of the cultural artifact is accomplished via the social and economic systems, and there is copious evidence that it is a causal factor in subsequent biological system damage.

In contrast to the difficulty of separating psychological and cultural system effects in practice, it is relatively easy to distinguish between economic and social system effects. The discipline of accounting has rationalized numerous aspects of economic elements and transactions. When an abuser uses economic elements to increase the domination of his victim, there usually is evidence of his actions. A few examples are (a) selling the victim's car and buying a new car in his name only, (b) having a joint checking account with no checks ever being signed by the victim, (c) always accompanying the victim to the bank to cash her checks or having her sign all of them over to him so he can cash them himself, and (d) making the victim responsible for certain categories of expenses, such as food and all of the children's needs, giving her an allowance that is far too small to cover these expenses, and then making her account in writing for every penny spent.

The economic strategies that batterers employ to dominate their victims use social system elements only as a background to the action, which is almost exclusively between batterer and victim. Social system strategies for domination begin in a more complex social arena. Both abuser and victim have friends and acquaintances. Over time, the batterer eliminates his victim's friends and acquaintances, leaving her with no source of social and emotional support with which to resist him. Many of these strategies involve interaction between the batterer and the victim's friends, such as when he (a) interrupts and abruptly terminates phone calls, (b) is openly discourteous to friends who come to visit, (c) damages friends' property, and (d) deliberately verbally abuses his partner severely in front of friends to make them so uncomfortable that they leave and do not return. Thus, while a victim's testimony about economic systems abuse usually is supported by written evidence, her testimony about enforced social isolation is supported by interviews with the people who were her friends and acquaintances before her abuser cut them off.

This is not to say that economic and social system elements are unrelated. Economic deprivation has social consequences and social isolation has economic consequences. "Fresh tuna is in at the dock for only $1.25 a pound." "Judy, down at the Emporium, is looking for an evening employee who can stay late and close up." "There's an apartment available for $50.00 less than the usual price, but the owner will raise the price if she has to advertise to fill it." These quotes are examples of economic advantages in food, employment, and housing that individuals acquire by word of mouth rather than through personal experience and advertising. When victims of masculine violence are cut off from the normal flow of social contacts, they gradually become less economically competitive. How can we estimate the value of the economic losses suffered by a battered woman who has suffered enforced social isolation for 7 years? I know of no standard methodology for making this calculation. Looking at it from the other direction, economic deprivation has social system consequences. Reduced discretionary income, lack of easy access to a vehicle, and a prohibition on spending money on friends (or to go out with friends) are ways in which economic elements in a dominance-enhancing control system can have social system consequences.

To summarize this section, I recognize five analytically distinct but empirically interacting systems that are relevant to the category of human action formed by the intersection of masculinities and violence: the social, cultural, biological, personality, and economic systems. For use in the legal system, I modify this list because of the difficulty I experience in separating psychological from cultural phenomena at the microsocial level of analysis, and I separate biological into sexual and physical (nonsexual) because different laws apply to these two categories of biological system abuse.

Readers may wonder why I use the term *system levels* instead of just *systems* in the title of this section. This is based on the notion that the five systems influencing masculine violence are not of equal generality, nor are they equally close to the scene of a violent act. I see the cultural system as the most general of the five systems of action, followed by the social, economic, personality, and biological systems in that order. In contrast, I see the biological system as closer to the scene of a violent act than the other systems. The personality system is obviously also very close to phenomenal violence, but the economic system is much farther away. The social and cultural systems drift farther into the fog of causal confusion. The farther a system is from the scene of a violent act, the harder it is to prove that system elements "caused" the event in some way. This is as true in the world of science as it is in the worlds of civil and criminal law. Whether the cultural system or the biological system is at the top of the list is arbitrary. What I take to be clear is that there is an element of hierarchy in the relations among the five systems. If we place the most general influence first, then the five system levels, in order, are the cultural, social, economic, personality, and biological systems.

Three caveats are in order for this discussion. First, the examples given are taken from the viewpoint of the victim rather than the aggressor. They could just as easily have been taken from the viewpoint of the batterer. Second, I have designated the batterer as male and the victim as female because that is the focus of much of my research, and it is from my research that I have drawn the examples provided above. However, it is possible under unusual conditions to reverse the customary scenario with the woman becoming an abuser and the man being her victim. Alternatively, intimate violence in same-sex couples finds men assaulting men and women assaulting women, and either a man or a woman might assault children of either sex. One could repeat the set of possibilities for nonintimate violence, meaning violence among strangers, acquaintances, and relatives too distant for the relationships to have a familial character.

The third caveat is that I am not really writing about biological men when I associate masculinities with violence. Anyone can play a masculine role, and it appears that heightened violence potential is associated with the masculine role (a property of the social system as I define it) roughly as much as with masculine biological system elements (running from muscle bulk to hormones). Whatever the biological composition of an intimate adult dyad, if one member of the dyad plays a significantly more masculine role than the other member, the first person is also more likely to be the aggressor (and the second person to be the victim) in any violence that occurs between them. I would only predict equal violence propensity if the dyad were truly unisex, in that both members played roles that had the same balance of masculine and feminine characteristics.

Overdetermination in Action

The model I am proposing is that forces influencing masculine violence occur in all five system levels of action. It is impossible to conceive of a violent act that is related to just a single system level. To illustrate the problem, let us suppose that a fly lands on my leg and in a split second, I slap it with my hand. The fly, as you might expect, is too fast for me. It gets away and lands on another leg. Yet my act is no less violent because it fails to achieve its objective. My intent was murderous. Had the fly been dozing, it would have been a dead fly. Can we say that this was an instinctual act? We cannot, for not all human beings swat flies. I am the only flyswatter in my household. My wife and two daughters take a live-and-let-live attitude toward insects. If they find a spider in the house, the only action they might take if sufficiently annoyed would be to pick up the spider carefully and move it outside.

The idea that my slap at the fly is a mindless and culture-free reaction to a physical annoyance is hopelessly shortsighted. To begin with, "flyness" is not intrinsic to any specific group of insects. We learn criteria for identifying certain insects as "flies" from the cultural system, via delivery mechanisms that are part of the social system. Among the sensory cues leading me to label the bothersome insect as a fly are (a) the noise it makes before landing, (b) the force with which it lands, (c) how it feels after it lands, and (d) what it looks like. Appearance and noise are heavily loaded with cultural system influences, whereas landing force and crawling sensations depend more on previous personal experiences with similar insects. Cultural system influences extend beyond recognition cues to beliefs (flies carry germs), values (flies are worthless), and norms (when a fly bothers you, kill it). These are embodied in what might be termed the lore of the flies, images of flies and stories about them. Monster movies about giant mutated flies are an example of how social system elements such as movie studios, theaters, and advertising agencies work together to expose people to new cultural elements about flies.

The gradations in the cultural interpretation of common insects are precise. Add *dragon* (not a particularly positive cultural image until Puff the Magic Dragon came along) to *fly* and you get *dragonfly,* still an insect, but one that calls forth a very different set of beliefs (dragonflies are an important part of the aquatic food chain), values (dragonflies are beautiful), and norms (enjoy watching dragonflies hover over the water; never hurt them when they persist in landing on your fishing pole) from flies that are not joined to dragons.

Some people tend more than others to respond to annoyance with violence. This presumably is a personality system influence on whether to try to kill a fly, or at least on how vigorously to slap at it. Other possible personality system influences on attempted fly killing include (a) a neurotic fear of flying insects, (b) aversions to dirt and germs believed to be carried by flies, (c) so rigid a sense of personal space that an insect's touch is perceived as invasive, and (d) a heightened state of arousal, which increases sensitivity to environmental cues. On this last point, who would not join me in becoming hypervigilant while walking through a cloud of mosquitoes in the Wisconsin woods or fighting off biting flies on the shorelines of Canadian lakes?

This leaves biological and economic system influences on fly slapping. Perhaps people whose nerve endings are closer to the surface of the skin or whose skin is microscopically thinner feel the fly more than other people and so feel a greater urgency to do something about it. The same could be said for people whose hearing of fly flight noises is more acute than average. It is possible that men who have higher than average testosterone levels are more fatal to flies than average. On the other hand, this tendency might be countered by a cultural system influence in which macho men are defined as being beyond annoyance from something as inconsequential as a fly. If men with higher than average testosterone gravitate toward hypermasculine ideologies, then there would be a conflict between the cultural and biological system influences on the fly-slapping behavior of macho men.

The biological system and the personality system meet in the human brain, as is illustrated by the recently coined term *brain sex*. It is very difficult to untangle biological and personality system influences on specific incidents of violence. Even when an undeniable biological abnormality, such as the XYY chromosome syndrome, is present, experts in science and law differ as to the influence of the abnormality on violent behavior. I will have more to say on biological system interactions with other systems in the next section.

Economic system influences on fly swatting are the weakest of the five systems. Many insects have economic value in some countries. Chocolate covered ants sold as a gourmet food item in upscale department stores is one American example of the economic value of insects. Others are selling ant farms to young children and collections of rare butterflies to wealthy adults. Flies, as we think of them in Western societies, seem to have no positive economic value at all. However, they are believed to have considerable potential for negative economic impact. Notions that flies strike at one's pocketbook by contaminating food and at one's livelihood by spreading dangerous diseases are part of the cultural lore that justifies the shoddy treatment that most people accord to the common housefly, the deer fly, the horsefly and, in the tropics, the tsetse fly. It is fair to say that the economic system is a remote influence on fly swatting in North America and that this influence is exerted indirectly through the cultural system.

There are few conceivable violent acts that are more simple than slapping a fly. If this minor act of destruction can be shown to have roots in all five system levels of action, how much stronger can this argument be made for human violence against strangers? Violence against long-term intimates is the most complex of all categories of violence, with conceptually rich ties to the cultural, social, economic, personality, and biological system levels of action. It is overdetermined to an even greater extent than is violence against strangers, just as violence against strangers is overdetermined to a greater degree than violence against insects.

Biological System Interactions
With Other Action Systems

The behavioral and social sciences of anthropology, sociology, economics, and psychology grew out of the bedrock academic disciplines of history, philosophy, and biology. In their haste to differentiate their emerging fields from more developed disciplines, most theorists in the behavioral and social sciences ignored or minimized the interactions among disciplines. It is difficult to believe that so many learned scholars were able to ignore their daily phenomenological experiences of multisystem interactions and the overdetermination of human behavior for so many decades. As behavioral and social science scholars become more professionally and economically secure, multisystem analyses began to creep into their scholarly work. Anthropology had always had links to biology through archaeology and physical anthropology. Neuropsychology (or physical psychology) has become part of most college psychology curricula. Biosocial theorists began to write in sociological journals after Edward O. Wilson's *Sociology: The New Synthesis* appeared in 1975. The first issue of the journal *Human Nature: An Interdisciplinary Biosocial Perspective* appeared in 1990. Recent publications evincing a multisystem approach to human action have titles that include terms such as *psychobiology* (Hillbrand & Pallone, 1994; Maryanski, 1994), *evolutionary psychology* (Wright, 1994), and *evolutionary sociology* (Maryanski, 1994). A few years earlier, these writers might have felt constrained to use more descriptive terminology such as biosocial foundations (Udry, Talbert, & Morris, 1986), human nature and biocultural evolution (Lopreato, 1988), wedding social and autonomic components (Kemper, 1987), and biological predispositions (Udry, 1988).

Aside from taking biological system measurements from the actors in a violent incident (see Hillbrand & Pallone, 1994, for many illustrations), biological system variables appear in historical analyses of how men and women have come to possess certain identifiable tendencies. These analyses tend to be theoretical and speculative, but there is a trend toward the use of social and behavioral science data to confirm hypotheses derived from biosocial evolutionary theory. For example, in a recent issue of

Human Nature: An Interdisciplinary Biosocial Perspective, researchers
found evidence in support of evolutionary hypotheses about modern mate
selection (Pérusse, 1994) and the effect of psychosocial stress on infertility (Wasser, 1994). Biosocial evolutionary understandings of masculine
violence are important because in showing why the violence was useful
in ancestral ecological settings, it is possible to extrapolate to contemporary ecological settings and posit methodologies for reducing violence in
these settings (Tracy & Crawford, 1992). They also have the advantage
of moving the analysis from the moral condemnation of violence to a less
value-laden evolutionary perspective. The notion that violence is a biosocial survival from ancestral times may be easier for violent men to accept
than the blanket of moral condemnation that denies what many men feel
in themselves and hinders the development of motivation for change.
Because the other chapters in *Masculinities and Violence* provide numerous examples of social and cultural system influences on masculine
violence plus modest coverage of personality and economic system influences, I will balance these perspectives just a bit by briefly summarizing
the evolutionary biosocial perspective as it might be profitably applied to
masculine violence.

Biosocial evolutionary perspectives claim importance because of an
irregularity in the rate of change experienced by human societies. This is
that we humans have lived in small hunting and gathering groups for 99%
of our history. Nearly all of what we think of as "progress" has occurred
in the most recent 1% of human development (Symons, 1981). The speed
of social and cultural system change until recently was similar to the speed
of biological system change. When social and cultural system change
became too rapid for biological system change, a condition of biosocial
lag began to develop. The degree of biosocial lag has continued to
increase up to the present, and the rate of the increase has been acceler-
ating for many centuries.

What does "biosocial lag" imply about human behavior? It implies that
the biosocial system equipment on which human life depends is, in some
ways, less adequate for survival in modern complex societies than it was
in hunting and gathering groups. Certain biological elements that once
were useful and adaptive now are problematic sources of maladaptation
and psychosocial stress. Few people would argue with simple biosocial
lags of the "sweet tooth" variety. The classic example of this group of
biosocial lags is that humans developed a preference for sweets as a way
of recognizing and consuming large quantities of edible fruits. With the
invention of refined sugar, to say nothing of chocolate candy, the human

preference for sweets became problematic. People now consume monumental amounts of "empty calories" in the form of sugar-laden foods that have few nutrients, and the incidence of numerous illnesses rises as a result.

The rub comes when this same logic is applied to areas of human behavior that are more intimate, more controversial, or subject to strict moral judgment. Masculine violence, particularly violence against women and children, joins sexual expression as prime examples of behavior about which people are unusually sensitive. Of course, there is no reason why masculine violence would be either more or less subject to biosocial lag than the taste for sweets.

The basic approach to understanding masculine violence under the theory of biosocial lag is to try to determine how men benefited from violence in ancestral hunting and gathering societies through the analysis of archaeological remains, surviving hunting and gathering societies, and social behavior in nonhuman primate species. Masculine violence in ancestral times doubtless was an important factor in hunting success, and therefore in maximizing food supply, health, and social status. Reproduction was aided by violence in that females could be acquired through violence, retained as mates through violence, and motivated to be sexually compliant by their awareness of masculine violence potential. Violence also was useful in competing with other men for sexual access to women of child-bearing age.

With a relatively static environment and natural selection favoring an association between violence and masculinity over tens of thousands of generations, it is easy to understand why this association became part of the biological system level of action among men. This does not imply "magical" or as yet undiscovered genetic differences between men and women, and it also does not rely exclusively on hormonal sexual differences. Sexual dimorphism in size and muscle mass is a major product of natural selection among men. It is likely to be the most important biological influence on women battering today, just as it was in ancestral hunting and gathering societies. Among humans, men average 7% taller and 20% heavier than women (Nicholson, 1993).

Modern complex societies are environments in which the benefits of masculine violence are much more limited than was the case in ancestral hunting and gathering societies. Yet men continue to be influenced to engage in violence by biological system elements, just as they are selected by cultural, social, economic, and personality system elements in the United States.

Modern complex societies differ from ancestral hunting and gathering societies in another way. They lack the social control mechanisms that acted as a brake on masculine violence in ancestral times. Hunting in ancestral groups was necessarily cooperative, at least in the killing of large animals. If the dominant male in a group killed or injured other males, the flow of food to the group would be diminished. If his dominance was too severe by local standards, weaker men and women might form a coalition against him. There is evidence from primate groups that violence is used to enforce cultural norms of reciprocity, leading to reconciliation and violence cessation (Tracy & Crawford, 1992). This limiting mechanism does not function nearly as well in modern societies as in ancestral societies.

> While norms of reciprocity between husband and wife may have been relative-ly simple and clear to both spouses in the context of the ancestral hunter-gatherer band, these norms are not always clear in more modern settings [where] cultural diversity is so great and cultural change is so rapid that individual husbands and wives may frequently hold different expectations about what behaviors are appropriate for themselves and their partners in order to maintain an equitable situation within a marriage. (Tracy & Crawford, 1992, p. 28)

I am willing to speculate that masculine violence against other humans was lower in ancestral hunter-gatherer societies than it is in the United States today. Although ancestral societies had no police, no law, and no correctional systems, they had a unity and a strength of social control that we lack in contemporary America. Masculine violence has probably been decreasing in the United States from the extremely high levels experienced during the chaotic expansion of the western frontier and the vast immigrant floods that rapidly increased American cultural diversity without any corresponding increase in nonviolent social control mechanisms. Still, violence levels and related phenomena remain high enough for some scholars to conclude that *Men Are Not Cost-Effective* (Stephenson, 1995).

Eradicating Masculine Violence

The comprehensive research agenda needed to make significant progress toward eradicating masculine violence begins with a recognition that no violent act is determined at one system level of action. The preliminary categorization of causes of violence into cultural, social, economic, personality, and biological system influences is no more than a signpost on the road of violence diminution. The next step is to develop a full taxonomy of causal influences within each of the five general categories.

Intervention strategies and rehabilitation modalities then can be associated with groups of influences that are found to be morphologically similar in their mechanisms of violence activation.

Communities can make the best use of their limited existing resources by continuing to strengthen methods of cooperation among programs and agencies so that interventions with violent men become increasingly multidimensional. Psychotherapy can be useful in addressing certain personality system influences on violent behavior, but it is unlikely significantly to reduce or eradicate masculine violence without being coordinated with other interventions. The Alcoholics Anonymous model is not primarily a counseling intervention, instead owing much of its success in fighting alcoholism to intervention at the social and cultural system levels. It replaces pro-drinking friends with anti-drinking friends (a social system intervention) and pro-drinking norms, values, and beliefs with anti-drinking norms, values, and beliefs (a cultural system intervention). The likely result of closely coordinating both kinds of intervention models when applied to masculine violence would be not merely additive, but multiplicative due to synergistic interaction effects.

The same argument can be made for other pairs of system interventions. Adopting an integrated community approach will require the shedding of self-serving professional prejudices that currently separate system groups. Thus, criminal justice system personnel will have to be willing to work closely with psychotherapists, who will, in turn, have to give up prejudgments such as rejecting electronic monitoring as part of a suite of simultaneous interventions. Correctional institutions, which are limited to a prosocial biological system intervention at present (incapacitation), will have to be combined with other system-level interventions to create therapeutic communities dedicated to violence eradication, and so on.

Our current failure to decrease masculine violence significantly is not based on lack of knowledge about behavior change interventions as much as it is on the (a) lack of coordination among interventions, (b) inadequate funding for the implementation or expansion of existing interventions and emerging innovations, and (c) political opposition to violence control by masculine elites who benefit from the violence in some way. It is not our science but our will that is lacking.

2

Taking Control

Toy Commercials and the
Social Construction of Patriarchy

SARAH SOBIERAJ

Children and their parents are constantly bombarded with cultural messages that establish the boundaries of socially desirable behavior. Movies, television programs, and advertisements are powerful agents of socialization. Television commercials, though delivered in small doses, have a substantial cumulative effect. This research focuses on the content of television commercials that are directed toward children. "In a three hour sitting, which is common, a youngster will be subjected to around thirty minutes of advertising. This amounts to 20 to 40 ads an hour, depending on their length" (McNeal, 1987, p. 63). This 3-hour sitting is an optimistic estimate; the average American family leaves the television on more than 7 hours each day (Gerbner, 1994, p. 549).

The gender imagery in television commercials is relentlessly stereotyped. Boys are strong, independent, athletic, in control of their environments, adventurous, and aggressive. Girls are giggling, gentle, affectionate, fixated on their physical appearance, and extremely well behaved. Eiss (1994) observed that "variations of any sort from a strict gendering of boys and girls are rarely represented in advertising; and the exceptions are rarely more than slight aberrations of appearance, which often unintentionally reconfirm gender stereotypes" (p. 257). These rigid depictions oversimplify and exaggerate issues of gender identity, limiting children in their options. This chapter uses content analysis to explore children's toy commercials as agents that contribute to the reproduction of traditional gender roles, specifically the reproduction of violence and domination as standard components of masculinity.

Theory and Literature

From a social construction of reality perspective, gender roles are a product of society rather than biology. These clearly defined sex roles constitute part of a shared reality that is digested as factual and natural, despite its contrived foundations. People create and maintain this reality in a dialectic fashion: "people create society and that society comes to be an objective reality which, in turn, creates people" (Ritzer, 1992, p. 413).

Berger and Luckmann (1966) describe this dialectic in three stages that serve as a useful lens through which to examine the reproduction of gender ideology. Biologically, women and men have physical differences. In the externalization stage, humans use their creative power to extend the gender distinctions beyond those that are biologically defined. For example, men and women do not have a genetic propensity to dress differently or to select cutting the lawn over doing the laundry. Similarly, Lorber (1994) provides an excellent illustration:

> When little boys run around noisily, we say, "Boys will be boys," meaning that physical assertiveness has to be in the Y chromosome because it is manifest so early and so commonly in boys. But are boys universally, the world over, in every social group, a vociferous, active presence? Or just where they are encouraged to use their bodies freely, to cover space, take risks, and play outdoors at all kinds of games and sports? (p. 39)

These extended gender identities are assumed or produced for a variety of reasons, but when the habitualized actions and interactions lead to typifications, these historically specific trends are absorbed into social institutions.

In the next stage, this manufactured reality is interpreted as objectively factual, beyond human regulation. Because people accept this artificial reality as genuine, the perceived reality has consequences for the actor. Berger and Luckmann (1966) call this *objectivation*. When others expect gender-typed behavior from an individual because of their sex-category, the person is being impacted by a human creation.

The last stage is internalization. In this stage people adopt what is perceived to be the objective reality as their own by agreeing to conform to its standards. When women and men engage in gender-typed behaviors, they are conforming to the social norms and hence reproducing the social institution (Wallace & Wolf, 1995, pp. 264-268). "As Berger and Luckmann sum it up: 'society is a human product' (externalization); 'society is an objective reality' (objectivation); 'man [sic] is a social product' (internalization)" (Wallace & Wolf, 1995, p. 267).

Toy manufacturers and advertisers externalize when they choose to market a product in a gender-stereotyped manner. An impression is created that happy, loved, and admired children play with one another and with specific toys in certain ways. The children exposed to these advertisements then understand this creation as objectively factual. For these children, the advertisements provide cues about how they should behave and consume. This process is objectivation. If and when the children choose to mimic the portrayals, they have internalized the advertisements' cues about what is expected of them. In this dialectical process, humans create and then are created by advertisements.

Content analyses have been used sporadically to investigate the messages that children are receiving about gender-appropriate behavior. Young (1990) describes the embellishment typical of commercials created for children:

> there is a sharpening of social categories where the definition is heightened and the differences are clarified. The classic roles of gender with their associated stereotypes become well defined and clearly distinguished in the child who watches television advertising . . . where characterization tends toward caricature and the brush strokes used to paint the performers are bold. (p. 304)

Boys are stereotyped as active and rough. Three content analyses have examined male aggression in advertisements. Verna (1975), Welch, Huston-Stein, Wright, and Plehal (1979), and Macklin and Kolbe (1983, p. 39) indicate that commercials positioned toward males are more likely to contain aggression than either neutral advertisements or those positioned toward females. More than a decade has passed since these studies were conducted. Smith (1994) examines active and passive behavior, but does not separate the distinctly antisocial acts. Therefore, to reevaluate the presence of physical and verbal aggression in children's advertising, the following hypothesis is tested:

H_1: Toy advertisements featuring only boys depict aggressive behavior more often than toy advertisements featuring only girls.

The previous research and hypothesis H_1 explore aggression as a rigidly gendered, exclusively male, quality. Milkie's (1994) research on mass media and adolescents illustrates that excessive aggression is depicted as gendered, rather than positive or negative. Violence is associated with the "good guys" as well as the "bad guys" (p. 357). Despite the negative impact that physical and verbal aggression have on their recipients, these actions are often depicted in a value neutral or disturbingly positive context. For boys, aggression is almost exclusively depicted as positive. Jason Katz (1994) explains that advertising imagery equates masculinity with violence (p. 137). For boys this means that aggression is instrumental, it enables them to establish their masculinity. Based on the propensity for aggression to be depicted as free of negative consequences, the following hypothesis is tested:

H_2: Aggressive actions in toy advertisements are shown to have positive consequences more often than negative consequences.

The social construction of gender is a construction of difference, but also of domination. The social construction of patriarchy is established in a culture that creates and institutionalizes male dominance. Lee Bowker (1986b) explores the link between power and violence as components of the masculine ideal-type in his work on domestic violence. He describes the culture that encourages this dangerous coupling:

The abuse . . . continues to be encouraged and sustained by a masculine culture of dominance and violence which devalues women at the same time it glorifies masculine values such as toughness, emotional repression, and dominance enhancing behavior . . . much exposure to the masculine culture comes through everyday life, but we find it in its most concentrated form in segregated environments like violent sports, the armed forces, fraternities, barber shops, and bars. (p. 39)

This masculine culture does not spontaneously erupt in adulthood. Toughness, emotional repression, and dominance enhancing behavior are learned traits. The masculinization of control educates children that boys should strive for power. As an attempt to better understand how patriarchy is reproduced, the following hypothesis is tested:

H3: Toy commercials featuring only boys contain verbal references to domination more often than toy commercials featuring only girls.

The social construction of femininity is distinct from that of masculinity and illustrates the rigidity of gender-typed behaviors. During a preliminary viewing of the toy commercials in the sample, the emphasis on female physical attractiveness was unmistakable. This aspect of children's advertising was not addressed in the reviewed literature. Eiss (1994) briefly describes the tendency for girls' toys to promote being physically attractive (p. 260). England and Farkas (1980) list physical attractiveness last in their description of female gender roles (p. 87). These tangential references seem inadequate for the voluminous allusions to beauty. Although some merchandise is explicitly designed to enhance physical attractiveness, references to beauty appear to be in most of the commercials, regardless of the product's intended use. Guber and Berry (1993) note a growing number of cosmetic products on the market for girls. They also describe the demand: "More than one-half of six- to eight-year old girls said they wanted to buy makeup" (p. 79). To quantify this perceived emphasis on beauty, and to illustrate the polarity of gender depictions in advertising, the following hypothesis is tested:

H4: Toy advertisements featuring only girls include verbal references to physical attractiveness more often than toy advertisements featuring only boys.

The Study

In this study, toy commercials are distinguished as those advertisements featuring products that can be purchased at most large toy stores, including video games. Toys advertised with food products (e.g., cold cereal or fast food) are not included, because it is the food product, not the toy, that is actually being advertised. Although movies on videotape can be purchased at some toy stores, advertisements for taped movies are excluded because they tend to show only film clips with narration. Coding these commercials might illustrate gender construction in film, but not in toy advertisements.

The sample consists of Saturday morning toy advertisements aired between 7:00 a.m. and 1:00 p.m. Data was collected for 3 consecutive weeks on three of the major television networks: ABC, CBS, and NBC. The commercials were taped on November 18th, November 25th, and December 2nd, 1995. Because toy commercials dramatically increase before the winter holidays, a sizable sample was attained. This trend for toy commercials is well supported in the literature. Toy advertisements have been found to make up 55% of commercials during the Christmas season (see McNeal, 1987, p. 70, citing work by Bohuslav, Egan, & Morgan). This contrasts to the 23% found in Macklin and Kolbe's (1984) mid-June sample (p. 35). In addition, Smith (1994) cites the Nielsen Media Research of 1992 to illustrate that children watch television more during the winter (p. 329).

The research team was provided with 105 different commercials. This sample is sizable in comparison to previous content analyses. Smith (1994, p. 333) sampled 82 different advertisements. Other sample sizes in the literature include: Macklin and Kolbe (1985), 64; Moncrief and Landry (1982), 153; Welch et al. (1979), 60; and Doolittle and Pepper (1974), 49. Bretl and Cantor (1988) and Schuetz and Sprafkin (1978) had considerably larger samples with 397 and 372 different advertisements, respectively.

Analysis of the data is conducted in two ways. First, the four hypotheses are tested with each advertisement counted once, in keeping with Bretl and Cantor (1988) and Smith (1994, p. 330). The second analysis is conducted with each advertisement weighted for repetition; the data set for each commercial is multiplied by the number of times the commercial aired during the sample. The goal of this approach, which yields a total of 374 commercials, is to assess the cumulative effect on the viewer.

How to discern boys from girls without relying on gender stereotypes was a serious concern in creating the research instrument. It would be preferable to rely on gender-laden words describing familial relations or gender-specific pronouns to determine objectively whether a child actor is male or female. Body shape and voice are not viable indicators with child performers. Unfortunately, coders were confronted with only rigid gender stereotypes on which to judge. West and Zimmerman (1987) describe this classification issue: "Placement in a sex category is achieved through the application of sex criteria, but in everyday life, categorization is established and sustained by socially required identificatory displays that proclaim one's membership in one or the other category" (p. 127). Style of dress, activity, length of hair, and so on, are poor indicators because they are mired in the socially constructed gender ideology that this study searches to demystify. Nevertheless, these are the indicators this study uses due to the utter absence of alternatives.

Each commercial was coded with a standardized research instrument developed for this study. Some advertisements showed only male children, some only female, some both, and some did not show any children. Where no children were present it was tempting to rely on the gender of the narrator because the gender of the narrator usually matches the gender of the commercial's target audience (Smith, 1994, p. 327). However, because this tendency is not a rule, its application may have biased the research. Therefore, where no children were pictured, the only data collected were the product name, the manufacturer, and the number of repetitions. Two coders measured the following variables:

1. Type of toy, official name, and manufacturer
2. Number of male and female adults and children
3. Number of aggressive acts depicted (categorized)
4. Information about the context and outcome of each aggressive act
5. Verbal references to dominance in commercials containing aggression
6. Number of verbal references to physical attractiveness (categorized)

One coder was male, the other was female. Each coder evaluated half of the prerecorded tapes. In addition, 20 commercials were separately coded by each researcher to determine the interrater reliability. The coding instrument contained 61 possible answers. All answers were checked for intercoder reliability, except for the first question on "type of toy." This question was included strictly for recall purposes. It was not intended for classification or analysis. Of the 1,220 possible answers, there was only one discrepancy, yielding 99.9% agreement.

Results

Hypothesis H1, *toy advertisements featuring only boys depict aggressive behavior more often than toy advertisements featuring only girls*, is confirmed. As Table 2.1 illustrates, with all the commercials equally weighted, 61.2% of the commercials featuring only boys show at least one type of physical or verbal aggression.[1] The cumulative effect of all the commercials indicates that 68.6% of the commercials positioned toward boys contain incidents of verbal aggression, physical aggression, or both. There is no cross-gender display of aggressive behavior. Not one single-sex commercial featuring girls shows any act of aggression.

Table 2.1   Tendency for Toy Commercials Depicting Only One
Gender to Contain Verbal or Physical Aggression

Sex	Unweighted N	Unweighted % of Total	Weighted N	Weighted % of Total
Female	0	0	0	0
Male	19.0	61.2	67.0	68.6

Aggression is very clearly coded as male behavior. Macklin and Kolbe
(1984) also found male-oriented advertisements to display aggression
(although only 16.6%) and an absence of female-oriented commercials
containing aggression (p. 39).

The commercials contain several different forms of aggression. The
most common aggressive behavior is the imitation of violence using toys
($n = 16$).[2] This activity is especially common with action figures. Actors
are shown manipulating action figures to shoot guns at one another, fight
with knives, punch and kick, and inflict harm in various other ways. One
advertisement shows a boy using an action figure to launch a missile at
another action figure. The victim is knocked into a wall that crumbles
down on top of him. The boys in the commercials are also shown crashing
cars ($n = 4$). In one of these commercials, the narrator encourages the
viewer to play violently with the advertised car, saying, "Drive it like you
hate it!" as the actor simultaneously crashes the car against a wall,
breaking it into several pieces.

Almost as common as mimicking violence with toys are verbal threats
of violence ($n = 11$). These two activities are often shown together. In
most instances the threat comes indirectly, from an actor through a toy,
but verbal threats are also given directly from one actor to another. One
commercial shows a group of boys with toy guns approaching another
boy as the leader of the group says, "Come any closer and we'll use you
for target practice!"

Other forms of aggression in the sample include teasing, yelling,
wrestling or "rough housing," pushing, chasing, and intentionally scaring.
Hitting and kicking, although noticeable, occur indirectly. These actions
are performed by action figures that are controlled by children, but not by
the children directly. Only one advertisement shows direct person-to-
person violence. This advertisement is for a wrestling video game. The
commercial flips back and forth between live wrestlers throwing, jumping

on, and choking one another and the video game versions of these actions, while the narrator praises the realistic graphics in the game. Weapons are most commonly used in the aforementioned indirect fashion, but there is one exception where boys are shown launching toy missiles at one another.

The second hypothesis, *aggressive actions in toy advertisements are shown to have positive consequences more often than negative consequences,* is upheld. Nineteen different commercials featuring actors of only one sex contain aggressive actions. Seventeen of these advertisements depict aggressive acts as having positive consequences. One commercial shows negative consequences and in the remaining advertisement, no consequences are shown. Positive consequences include congratulatory remarks from other actors, congratulatory gestures from other actors (e.g., "high fives" or "thumbs up"), outright victory, and satisfied smiles, laughter, or both, on the part of the aggressor. The most common consequence for aggressive behavior is receiving positive feedback from others. Through all the pretend knife fighting and missile launching there are no concerns expressed over the make-believe injured people. No child ever castigates another for acting inappropriately. On the contrary, when a villain is defeated by a violent act, there is cause for celebration. Male aggressive behavior in children's advertising is not only abundant, it is revered.

The one advertisement that shows the negative consequences of aggression is a commercial for a city play set. One boy causes two cars to collide and then brings in a toy ambulance and rescue helicopter to help deal with the consequences of the crash. The message in this commercial is considerably different than that of the others. The underlying theme is that aggression hurts people and there is enjoyment in helping rather than in causing harm.

The third hypothesis, *toy commercials featuring only boys contain verbal references to domination more often than toy commercials featuring only girls,* is confirmed. As illustrated in Table 2.2, only 2.2% of the commercials positioned toward girls (2.7% when weighted for repetition) contain verbal references to domination. In marked contrast are the commercials containing exclusively boys. In these advertisements, 51.6% of the commercials (44.1% when weighted for repetition) contain at least one verbal reference to domination.

The references to domination in the commercials positioned toward boys are overt. One advertisement for toy cars describes their "exhilarating, unstoppable power" and "extraordinary control that makes you the

Table 2.2 Tendency for Toy Commercials Containing Only One Sex
to Contain Verbal References to Domination

Sex	Unweighted N	Unweighted % of Total	Weighted N	Weighted % of Total
Female	1.0	2.2	5.0	2.7
Male	16.0	51.6	45.0	44.1

boss!" Other advertisements contain verbal cues such as, "universal domination," "take control," "powerful," "use their power," and "you're in command." One commercial advertises an action figure as "the ultimate hero." The narrator describes the hero as "an eternal warrior . . . with power and friends by his side," and closes with, "ready to go, ready to win!" Competition is consistently at the center of each advertisement positioned toward boys, whether it is competition to win a football game or competition against the "enemy" or "evil forces."

The advertisements positioned toward girls rarely allude to competition. When games are played, the girls talk about how much fun they are having or how much they love their toys. The one advertisement positioned toward girls that contains a verbal reference to domination is more subtle than the references in advertisements positioned toward boys. The commercial advertises a remote control doll that performs gymnastics. The narrator describes the doll competing in "the championships" and "going after the medal," the implication being that she is attempting to win. However, there is no opponent shown and no outright mention of trying to defeat anyone else. When the doll (Jennie™) wins, the actress says, "*We* did it Jennie!" (emphasis added). Even this claim of victory is communal.

Domination was operationalized into verbal references in order to improve reliability and reduce bias. Coders searched for words such as *control, power, boss, command, in charge,* and so on. Using these concrete verbal references facilitated coding and improved consistency; however, there were also several nonverbal cues that were not included in this study. For example, winning is often understood, but not articulated. Victory can be depicted by showing a child acting triumphantly or an opponent acting downtrodden manner. Because these innuendoes are invisible in this data set, the number of references to domination are underestimated.

Table 2.3 Tendency for Toy Commercials Depicting Only One
Gender to Contain Verbal References to Physical
Attractiveness

Sex	Unweighted N	Unweighted % of Total	Average Number of References	Weighted N	Weighted % of Total	Weighted Average Number of References
Female	25.0	55.6	4.8	102.0	55.1	4.6
Male	0	0	0	0	0	0

One serendipitous finding is that the commercials positioned toward boys that contain aggression and those that contain domination are not mutually exclusive. Commercials positioned toward boys that contain acts of aggression are slightly more likely to contain verbal references to domination than those without aggression. In the unweighted analysis, 51.6% of all commercials positioned toward boys contain at least one verbal reference to domination. This rises to 57.8% among only those commercials that contain aggression.

The fourth hypothesis, *toy advertisements featuring only girls include verbal references to physical attractiveness more often than toy advertisements featuring only boys,* is strongly supported by the data. As Table 2.3 illustrates, with each commercial weighted equally, 55.6% of all single-sex advertisements positioned toward girls included verbal references to physical attractiveness. When the advertisements were weighted for repetition, the percentage decreased slightly, to 55.1%. Of the single-sex commercials positioned toward boys, none contained verbal references to physical attractiveness. Furthermore, the commercials positioned toward girls that contained verbal references to physical attractiveness had an average of 4.8 *separate* references *per advertisement.* This average decreased to 4.6 when the commercials were weighted for repetition.

Much like domination, physical attractiveness was operationalized into verbal references to enhance the structure of the coding process and reduce bias. Coders searched specifically for words such as *gorgeous, pretty,* and *beautiful,* as well as expressions like *looking good* and slang words such as *hot.* They were further instructed to search for verbal references to clothing and physique. This measure helped to increase reliability. However, the data reported include only the spoken references.

Countless additional references were transmitted in the form of posturing before mirrors, admiring glances from others, gasping or sighing over clothing, combing hair, and applying cosmetics. These powerful messages are invisible in this data set, although they may be analyzed in further work.

Discussion and Conclusions

The results demonstrate that rigid gender dichotomies continue to be depicted in children's toy advertisements. Girls and only girls are shown fawning over physical appearance. Boys and only boys are shown exhibiting aggressive behaviors. West and Zimmerman (1987) explain how boys and girls have different gender expectations:

> Little boys appropriate the gender ideal of "efficaciousness," that is, being able to affect the physical and social environment through the exercise of physical strength or appropriate skills. In contrast, little girls learn to value "appearance," that is, managing themselves as ornamental objects. (p. 141)

Eighteen of the reviewed commercials contained no children. All of these advertisements had male announcers. Other researchers have found that the narrators' gender tends to match the gender of the target audience.[3] If this is an accurate assumption, then all of the commercials without children in this sample should be positioned toward boys, which means that all of the female-positioned commercials contain actresses. This seemingly mandatory physical presence in commercials targeting females may be linked to the overwhelming emphasis on physical attractiveness that permeates these advertisements.

Perhaps the most alarming finding in this study is the overwhelming emphasis on domination as a male gender ideal. Coupled with the more commonly acknowledged association between violence and masculinity, this socialization encourages men to seek domination and simultaneously teaches that aggression is an effective avenue of goal attainment. Lee Bowker (1986b) acknowledges how dangerous this pairing is within the family:

> When escalated to a more severe level, male dominance-enhancing activity includes many related phenomena, including severe and frequent wife-beating, child abuse, marital rape, violence-induced miscarriages, sadistic torture,

psychological abuse, punitive economic deprivation, coerced social isolation, and threats of femicide and infanticide. (p. 40)

Dominance does not have to be coupled with violence to be problematic. Oppressive behavior hinders women who attempt to move up the corporate ladder, impedes women who strive to gain access to traditionally male arenas, and perplexes women who struggle for self-determination. The reproduction of patriarchy is often considered insidious, yet in the context of this study it is alarmingly overt.

Children construct their gender identities based on input from the world around them. "Children perceive the world as an objective reality; that is it was there before they were born and it will be there after they die" (Ritzer, 1992, p. 390). By the time an average child viewer reaches the age of 17, he or she has seen an estimated 350,000 commercials (Bretl & Cantor, 1988, p. 596). The messages contained in these advertisements help to make up the social construction of gender. Girls are not biologically obsessed with their looks, predisposed to cleaning house, or enthusiasts of the color pink. When boys emerge from the womb they do not instinctually seek validation through superordination or intimidation. These ideas are externally imposed and consumed by children at face value. Stephen Kline (1993) explains that children's preferences can be sought out and successfully altered through advertising (p. 168). If advertising did not influence human action, it would not be an effective means of promoting merchandise. Advertising abounds precisely because of its influence. Television is capable of creating a desire for something and providing directions on how to behave. The culmination of this constant bombardment is social control. However, as Eiss (1994) explains, the blame does not rest solely with the media:

> What gets communicated to parents about their kids encourages them to reproduce a rather limited range of gender-stereotyped appearances and reinforce a rather limited range of gender-bound behaviors . . . parents encourage the gender-differentiated play preferences of even very young children. (p. 259)

Parents learn not only to accept, but also to value the stifling social norms for gender. They become facilitators, rewarding their children for behaving in ways that conform to this ideology. As Berger and Luckmann (1966) specified, the social order is created by past human behavior and can be maintained only if humans participate in its reproduction. The media, parents, and other agents of socialization help maintain the facade of objectively real, mutually exclusive, gender differences.

The human ability to take subjective meanings and convert them into institutions that are digested as objectively factual is simultaneously voluntaristic and deterministic. This powerful force would be a valuable component of learning if the ideologies were not restricting. When gender ideology successfully corrals women into the lowest-paying jobs and demands a second job be fulfilled in the home, women are limited. When women are taught to be more preoccupied with appearances than reality, that is also a limitation. When men are taught that their relations with others are first and foremost power relationships, they are restricted. When men are stigmatized for crying, cooking, or caring for their children, that also is a limitation. Men who learn that aggression is an acceptable means of goal attainment lack appropriate problem-solving skills, which jeopardizes their own success and endangers those around them. These preexisting narrow definitions of identity are insidious. Michele Barrett (1980) aptly emphasizes that

> the struggle over the meaning of gender is crucial. It is vital for our purposes to establish its meaning in contemporary capitalism as *not simply* "difference," but as division, oppression, inequality, internalized inferiority for women. Cultural practice is an essential site of this struggle. (p. 113)

The social construction of gender in this manner must be acknowledged as something grander than the definition of masculinity and femininity; it is nothing less than the social construction of patriarchy.

Notes

1. Measures of verbal and physical aggression include teasing, threatening, yelling at someone, chasing, wrestling or "rough housing," mimicking violence with toys, crashing toys together, pushing, hitting, kicking, pulling hair, poking, and intentionally scaring or tricking someone.

2. n = The number of commercials.

3. Researchers who have found a correlation between the narrator's gender and the gender of the target audience include Smith (1994), Doolittle and Pepper (1974), and Welch et al. (1979).

3

Bureaucratizing Masculinities Among Brazilian Torturers and Murderers

MARTHA K. HUGGINS
MIKA HARITOS-FATOUROS

In 1964 the Brazilian military successfully overthrew elected President João Goulart, ushering in 21 years of military rule. Yet while the Brazilian Government's "dirty war" (1969-1979) against subversion did not kill proportionally as many people as in the Southern Cone—Argentina, Chile, and Uruguay—or Central America—Guatemala and El Salvador— Brazil's national security state did carry out massive repression, employing torture, murder, and "disappearances." Indeed, just between 1969 and 1974,

> institutional violence [was so much] a part of everyday life [in Brazil that] it was difficult to meet a Brazilian who had not come into direct or indirect contact with a torture victim or been the target of a [violent] search-and-arrest operation. (Alves, 1985, p. 125)

The violence was carried out by police and the military.

This study[1] focuses on male police who had been in Brazil's social control system during the military period (1964-1985), to learn how they talk about themselves and the violence they committed. From such dis-

AUTHORS' NOTE: This study was made possible by generous support from the Hamburger Stiftung zur Förderung von Wissenschaft und Kultur and from the first author's (Martha K. Huggins) Roger Thayer Stone Endowed Chair in Sociology at Union College.

course we have derived two modal masculinities associated with carrying out state-sponsored torture and murder in Brazil. Yet this was initially puzzling because the terms *torturer* and *murderer* do not suggest any but the most classical "masculine" image—an extreme version of "normal" masculine aggressiveness, where coldness, brute force, and pleasure in aggression dominate male gender role behavior. The labels "torturer" and "killer" are less likely to evoke an image of a professionally competent, formally trained, and "rational" person, or of an empathetic and "feeling" man. In fact, these terms are so gender-specific that they almost never conjure up a female image, although we know that female guards in Nazi concentration camps were equally as violent as male guards (Cohen, 1954), and Stanley Milgram's (1969) landmark experiments on obedience report no differences between his female and male subjects when asked by a person in authority to administer pain. In any case, obviously, the assumption that one unchanging masculinity carries out torture and murder needs to be examined in terms of the literature on masculinity and violence.

"Masculinities"

Much theorizing on the relationship of masculinity to violence has been deterministic; it has assumed that masculine gender role socialization intrinsically fosters aggression and violence. One argument is that "masculinism"—"an ideology that justifies and naturalizes male domination" (Brittan, 1989, p. 4)—shapes aggressive, controlling, competitive, power-oriented, rationalistic, instrumental behaviors in men. These characteristics are thought to promote male aggression and a predisposition toward violence.

Such an image of masculine violence does not acknowledge the varied Western and non-Western masculinities that diverge from this admittedly hegemonic form. Not all masculinities demonstrate the same degree and mode of competitiveness, aggressiveness, control, and domination. Indeed, according to Messerschmidt (1993), "diverse forms of [hegemonic] masculinity arise, depending on prevalent structural potentials and constraints" (p. 83). Recent scholarship points to a range of "masculinities," with no single one characterizing all Western male gender role behavior. We need to know more about these alternative configurations of Western masculinity.

We propose that if masculinity varies in form and content, then masculinities—even those specifically aggressive, competitive, controlling, and
dominating—express themselves differently in relation to violence. We
further propose that masculinities can change in relation to shifts in the
structure of states, with such changes in masculinity reflected in discourse
about violence. These propositions are explored in an initial study of
seven Brazilian police torturers and murderers in their differing relationships to masculinity and violence.

Centuries of Masculinity

Hegemonic Western—indeed, patriarchal—masculinity is "supported
[by] the range of practices and institutions that collectively constitute . . .
the all-embracing system of male domination [in] . . . patriarchal society"
(Jefferson, 1996, p. 339). Yet although such masculinity involves "domination through control over weaker persons, such practices and their
control may differ due to historical, cultural, and situational causes"
(Kersten, 1996, p. 383). Even Western masculinities vary according to
changing macro-sociostructural conditions (e.g., changes in state structure and type), and in their interaction with dominant hegemonic masculinity, and according to race and class hierarchies, and in relation to the
immediate situation (see Adler & Polk, 1996; Jefferson, 1996; Kersten,
1996; Liddle, 1996; Messerschmidt, 1993). Yet the standards of hegemonic masculinity provide a social ideal against which these various
subordinated masculinities are measured, judged, and must compete
(Jefferson, 1996, p. 339).

Beginning with how structural conditions influence masculinity, Liddle
(1996) argues that state making in England was associated with changing
masculinities and gender relations as the state shifted from medieval to
bourgeois. According to Liddle (1996), English "state-building" involved
"not just a deepening sexual division of labor [between men and women]
. . . , but also a 'differentiation of masculinities'—most notably between
aristocratic and bourgeois masculinities . . . , between 'warrior masculinities' and more rational/calculative [ones]" (p. 362). According to
Liddle (1996, pp. 370-371), aristocratic masculinities focused on a
man's relationship to family and blood line and on his duty to honor
others through "praiseworthy" acts. With the rise of the capitalist state,
bourgeois masculinities emphasized individualism, scientific nationality,

control, and a subdivision of psyche into public and private spheres—with a separate and distinct persona for each (Liddle, 1996). Just as masculinities are shaped by state structures, they are also influenced by existing racial and class hierarchies. Jefferson (1996) maintains that "men's positions in the various hierarchies of class [and] race vary, [and this determines] . . . their resources for accomplishing masculinity" (p. 340). In other words, within a range of masculinities shaped by race, class, and organizational and state structures, a hierarchy of masculinities develops, with hegemonic masculinity subordinating all others to itself. Situational factors also influence how masculinities are acted out. James Messerschmidt (1993), for example, argues that certain kinds of violence are merely public representations of certain masculinities, particularly those placing a premium on situational control. For example, when a situation arises in which male control is directly or indirectly challenged, violence may be expected to follow. Adler and Polk (1996, p. 409) point out that male violence can be situationally motivated by "emotionality" accompanied by "righteous fury," where violence is a reaction to a perceived affront to "personal integrity, [to male] pride, and [to male] mastery of the social environment" (p. 399).

Such past research suggests that a range of masculinities exists in any particular culture and during different historical periods. This study builds upon such scholarship, demonstrating that one single masculinity is not associated in Brazil with torture and murder. Indeed, we demonstrate that at least two masculinities are common among the torturers and killers within this sample without making the claim that certain masculinities are more prone than others to carry out violence for the state.

Locating and Interviewing Torturers and Murderers

This discourse analysis of seven Civil and Militarized Police is part of a larger study of 27 police who had been in service during Brazil's military period (1964-1985). Besides coming from Brazil's two main police organizations—the Civil Police, a nonuniformed investigative ("judicial") police force, and the Military (i.e., militarized) Police, a uniformed police for first-response street policing—the study also included a Militarized Policeman[2] from a hybrid military and police internal security organization, the DOI/CODI.[3]

Since Brazil's torturers and killers had very little to gain and much to lose from participating in a study about their past (see Huggins &

Haritos-Fatouros, 1995), we had to design a sampling strategy that would have a high probability of netting former torturers and killers. After locating police who had been in service during Brazil's military period, we sought men from police units known to have engaged in extensive violence—the Civil Police's DOPS political police and its Department of Criminal Investigations Division (DEIC); the Civil and Militarized Police motorized patrols and SWAT teams; the Militarized Police intelligence unit (S-2) and its Reserved Service; and the hybrid Military and Militarized and Civil Police DOI/CODI, a countrywide internal security organization infamous for torture and murder (BNM, 1986). We reasoned that if someone had been in one of these police units or divisions, they would have either themselves committed extensive violence or been present when it was taking place, in either case becoming desensitized to carrying out violence themselves (Grossman, 1995). In the words of Robert J. Lifton (1986), some organizations are "atrocity-producing . . . so structured . . . institutionally that the average person entering . . . will commit or become associated with atrocities" (p. 425). All of the interviewees in this subsample came from one or another of these "atrocity-producing" police units or organizations.

To further ensure having former torturers and murderers in our sample, we sought interviewees from regions known to have experienced the greatest political repression: The Center-South cities of São Paulo and Rio de Janeiro, Southern Porto Alegre, Northeastern Recife, and Brasilia—the Federal Capital, in Brazil's North Central region. Among this subsample's interviewees, two each had worked in Brasilia, in Rio de Janeiro, in São Paulo, and one had worked in Porto Alegre City.

Finally, we sought interviewees at a special Rio de Janeiro prison for Militarized and Civil Police, assuming that police incarcerated for committing crimes while on duty might talk more openly about police life. Among four of such interviews, one was translated in time for this study.

We ultimately secured interviewees from the categories identified above through a nonrandom "snowball" sampling technique. In each targeted city, the snowball began with an interview obtained through one of Huggins's prior contacts with local police or by referral from an interviewee elsewhere. Once one interview had been secured, that person was asked to suggest a colleague who might also agree to be interviewed. Just securing an interview took up to 2 hours, as the interviewer discussed the interview itself, the provisions for ensuring anonymity, and gave the interviewee a chance to "size her up." The interview lasted at least 3 hours, with questions about torture and murder not coming until at least

2 hours into the interview. After each interview, the audiotape was transcribed, translated,[4] and then analyzed for what police discourse about violence communicated about masculinities.

Masculine Identities and Violence

The interviews disclosed two modal masculinities within the seven-man sample. One set of Brazilian police interviewees, the "lone wolf," was so labeled because of their elective or enforced marginality to the police system and because of the way they carried out police work and violence. Looking more closely at the characteristics of this interviewee, he is a passionate "true believer" (Hoffer, 1966) driven by a purely internal commitment to a cause; he feels answerable ultimately only to himself. The lone-wolf policeman distanced himself from formal organization, presenting himself as a lone actor, either because the system could not or would not work with him, or because—given a particular police-man's professional position within an organization—the "buck stopped" with him. The lone-wolf policeman's masculinity came before and sub-ordinated his ties to the bureaucracy. According to David Riesman's (1950) framework, the lone-wolf police were "inner-directed."

By contrast, the "institutional functionaries" in the Brazilian police considered themselves enveloped by police "professional" bureaucracy, their masculinity subordinated to its expectations. Professionalism and loyalty to organization shaped their view of themselves and how they treated others. In contrast to the individualist "true-believers," the insti-tutional functionaries were first and foremost organization men—"ra-tional" agents of the organization. So the institutional functionaries were Riesman's (1950) "other-directed," in this case to the bureaucratic organi-zation.

In the analysis to follow, we illustrate how these selected police tortur-ers and murderers presented themselves and talked about the violence in which they participated. Through their discourse we can see their rela-tionship to the government itself, to the larger police system, and to their varied masculinities. Yet although their masculinities fell into two distinct types within each of the two broad masculine identity categories, there was no single unitary masculine mode. The lone wolves varied from one another, just as the institutional functionaries varied among themselves. The variation between these two broad masculinity groupings was greater than within each of them separately, however, suggesting that even among those who have carried out the most brutal acts of violence, there is no one unvarying "masculinity," as the following testimonies suggest.

Lone-Wolf Police

Julio, a Civil Police patrolman who entered police service in 1971 to "fill the blanks in [my] life," actually began police work informally some years earlier under his cousin's guidance. Julio was then in his cousin's Civil Police operations squad; the squad made liberal use of violence during night rounds. Julio says that this period was "very, very exciting . . . because . . . some nights we had three shootings."

After a few years of carrying out police work informally, Julio entered the Civil Police as an investigator; his cousin continued to mentor him, teaching Julio "how to see things and keep quiet [and] to avoid working with some . . . guys: 'That guy is a special policeman, [that one] is a very dirty one.' " Julio made a reputation for himself very early in his career as "a fighter." A black-belt in karate, Julio credits it with giving him focus, discipline, and control: "It very much trains the mind. I don't become ineffective when [things go] wrong." Julio was encouraged to use this skill in his police work: "My companions knew that I [would not] hurt [criminals] too much, and I was not going to shoot them; so they wanted to see a fight."

In fact, with his karate, Julio was frequently involved in fights with alleged criminals, but he maintains that this was merely to "demobilize" them. Julio argues that this was not violence: Fighting "is . . . a skill." Moreover, Julio claims he never "over-dominated" a suspect, even though he frequently "beat them up." Such fights were fair and square, he claims, because he gave criminals a fair fight. Julio reports that one criminal told him, "I fought many times in prison, . . . but never with both hands free [and] both feet free. You choked me in a way that I couldn't lift my hands." Julio believes that karate earned him criminals' respect: "All the [criminals] called me 'sir.' "

Julio seems not to have felt any camaraderie with other police, apart from his cousin, who died of cancer early in Julio's police career. Julio describes other police negatively: They are "stupid guys," "corrupt," "cruel," "dirty." Julio explains that, "Policemen are insecure, very insecure; when they are alone they are . . . cowards. [Only when] they are in the company of a guy that fights well, [who] knows how to fight, [do] they feel brave." Julio just once mentions "a few very good workers" among the police, noting that they were in the DOPS political police, the homicide divisions, and those dealing with robbery.

In any case, Julio describes himself as having been a "good policeman"—different from those who worked in "political repression." Claiming that he completely disbelieved the military government's national security ideology, Julio maintains that it was "an invention to allow cruelty against people." To the extent that Julio actually held such a view, he was an outsider to a police system that during the military period was subordinated to the military and its national security ideology. Yet Julio was identified by the head of his state's police amnesty organization[5] as having carried out a good deal of violent repression against alleged subversives.

Julio has an intellectual system for justifying police (and by implication his own) violence. For example, while Julio was involved in shoot-outs— which he found exciting—he says, "I haven't killed anybody. Some guys died, but I don't know who killed them. There were many guys shooting and . . . I don't know who hit the guy . . . I just knew that people died. Fortunately it was the other side." Julio thus neutralized his role in killings by claiming that the particular agent of death was unknown.

Julio maintains that he "never agreed with torturing people." For Julio, karate fighting "is different than torturing; tying someone's hands up, I never liked it." But although Julio "thought [torture] . . . was terrible," he did not leave the room when it was going on. When asked how he could remain a room where torture was taking place, and even snap pictures of it,[6] Julio preferred instead to explain why police torturers did not find his presence troubling: It was because "nobody talks" about such violence.

Julio disclosed five overlapping and at times incompatible explanations for police torture: (a) Torture was carried out by young, "stupid," "showoff" cops; (b) it was performed only by higher police officials (who are not usually young); (c) "it's one job within the many jobs" in the criminal justice system; (d) criminals brought it on themselves by refusing to divulge information in interrogation; and (e) it's a part of Brazil's heritage: "In Brazil we are used to . . . torture . . . because the Catholic Church tortured people for the Inquisition, [for] years and years, centuries and centuries."

Julio's justifications for torture and murder omit those that place responsibility for this violence within the police organizational structure itself, a discourse characteristic of the institutional functionaries. Julio, a lone wolf within his police system, does not claim that organizational, "professional," and institutional structures motivated and justified torture and murder. But Julio, who sees police violence in instrumental terms, never did address his own contradictory positions on violence. In any case, his alienation from the larger police organization and its national security rationale set Julio apart and reinforced his chosen lone-wolf status.

Isadoro, a lone wolf among Civil Policemen, entered the police in 1959 as an investigator. He is still an investigator. Isadoro describes police work as "a calling"—something you do with passion and commitment 24 hours a day. For Isadoro, good police work begins with a good partner. One scopes out a good partner through "conversations" in the police car, this "gives you security because you find out your colleague's reaction—if he's likely to defend you [in an emergency]. It's . . . conversations in the car, almost always at dawn, that teach you [these] things, [that] give you security [on the job]." Isadoro cannot find that kind of camaraderie today. He searches constantly "for the ideal partner, . . . one who even likes to work late; . . . who doesn't [say it's not] . . . a workday if he's called out on . . . the weekend." A good partner is "a humble person, . . . [with] purity in him." The younger police work by the clock, so Isadoro cannot find enough "true cops" to associate with.

For Isadoro, the roots of this problem date to the military period: He was "revolted" by the military's bringing men into the Civil Police who "weren't policemen by calling, they were 'just policemen.' " Today, most young Civil Policemen are on the job just for "the salary; they do not want to . . . go into a slum to arrest someone dangerous, they don't want to search anybody, because they're afraid of being attacked." Isadoro believes that police must "hangout" in slums in order to do their jobs effectively.

In the "old days," police frequently used "favors" to create loyal informants in slums: This makes slum dwellers "eternally bound, obligated by that favor." For example, on Saturday and Sunday, Isadoro

puts on Bermuda shorts and a t-shirt to go into [the slums] to drink a beer, because that's where you get information. You're not going to find it in your office. You go to the streets. Somebody comes along and asks you for money, you buy milk for his kid. He comes back and says, "I want to tell you something."

Yet the younger police "are afraid of the administration, [which sees] something wrong with that kind of [police] behavior." According to Isadoro, police officials discourage associating with poor communities.

Isadoro believes that if a policeman has "affection" for poor slum dwellers, and they "respect" him, he doesn't need "to beat anyone to find things out." For Isadoro, "personal satisfaction is greatest when you discover things by investigating, when you overpower someone with your intelligence. This person folds in front of you, and you wind up discovering things." Isadoro contrasts this philosophy of interrogation with the Brazilian military's procedures during its dictatorship: "They used much more physical force than [was] diligent . . . because they thought that the person wasn't going to withstand a beating." According to Isadoro, such physical coercion as torture—in contrast to "a beating"—does not work, because a suspect in great fear will confess to anything, and that confession will be worthless. Isadoro believes that, "You can't trust anybody's tears, because . . . [in particular] those involved in crimes against property—theft and robbery—have a great ability to cry."

At the same time, Isadoro maintains that not all criers are liars. Isadoro remembers "cry[ing] with a crook—he moved me so much that I cried with him." Isadoro's partner's response was that Isadoro "ought to be arrested along with that guy because . . . you're crying with him." Isadoro argued that he was crying because his own background in poverty led him to pity poor people who engaged in petty theft out of need: "I learned compassion for the poor from conversations with my parents at home." But Isadoro is very severe with the criminal who steals out of greed: "I don't cry with someone who pulls a gun to steal your tennis shoes, your bicycle, your watch. . . . I'm hard on them," rich or poor.

Isadoro's calculus for his own violence is fairly simple: When a certain type of criminal—the thief or the assassin—uses "crocodile tears and . . . the evidence is so obvious and they deny things . . . cynically," this criminal deserves violence. In such cases, "if a policeman working with them doesn't have a certain balance he'll slap him around a little"—Isadoro's euphemism for torture. Isadoro explains that he himself would torture a criminal who "want[s] to make a fool out of me." Under such circumstances, "we're going to spin him" on the "Parrot's Perch," rotating him "as if he were [a pig] on a barbecue spit, turning him while giving him electric shocks."

In deciding to use violence against a criminal, Isadoro considers simultaneously the extent of a criminal's affront to Isadoro's own intelligence, the reason for the crime committed—for greed or need—and the criminal's social class. For example, Isadoro caught the nephew of a socially prominent appellate court judge committing a robbery. Isadoro explains that, "I was arresting him—he knew karate—and he kicked me in the face."

I overpowered him and slugged him." Isadoro had to defend himself "from the beating he was giving me." Isadoro explains that he was even "proud of . . . slugging [the judge's nephew]," whom Isadoro almost beat to death. Yet, at the same time, Isadoro argues that "when you see someone poor who is stealing, you have to tell him that it's wrong, that he has to be arrested. . . . But inside you don't have to be that tough. You have to be tough on the outside and humble on the inside."

Perhaps because of these and other such "old fashioned" police values, Isadoro constantly runs afoul of police administrators. During the military period he was stripped of his political rights for 10 years (*cassação*) and simultaneously lost his police job for attempting to create a Civil Police union. In the past 5 years, with his rights and his job restored, Isadoro has been transferred frequently from one police station to another; he has faced much internal and external criticism of his work. His brand of policing, his belief that police work is "a calling," and his populist policing style all violate emergent "modern" bureaucratized policing. This leaves Isadoro marginalized from most police colleagues and from increasingly dominant corporate-style police administrators.

Isadoro, who values connections with the "right kinds" of police (e.g., others with his own old-fashioned police values), and with the community he polices, is a lone-wolf policeman. The lack of suitable police partners has left Isadoro emotionally isolated; administrative pressure against police socializing in poor neighborhoods subjects Isadoro to censure and criticism. Thus, it is ironic that Isadoro, who leans toward collective approaches to policing and defines himself through connections with other police, ends up a lone wolf within his Civil Police organization.

Sergio entered Civil Police service in 1957 as a *Delegado*—a police chief with a law degree. According to Sergio, in the early days of his career "the police *Delegado* was highly respected, . . . even more [so] than the judge or district attorney." According to Sergio, such respect was necessary because, in the rural backlands where he was posted, the "cowboy" had to fear the *Delegado*—"and unfortunately, we exploited that fear [because it] restrain[ed] certain men's aggressive impulses." According to Sergio, no such respect is given to the *Delegado* today.

After several years as a rural *Delegado,* Sergio was transferred to the state capital's political police secret service section where he quickly became the governor's trusted operative. Sergio says that most of what he learned in political police DOPS intelligence, "they don't teach you . . . anywhere. You only learn . . . from on-the-job experience: You have to work a long time to acquire that . . . quickness of thought, that mistrust." Sergio now believes that, "It's terrible to live permanently mistrusting" others, although at the time Sergio saw this as an asset. His work in the political police initially gave him great satisfaction. It was

> interesting, provocative—everything . . . had to be kept secret. I . . . thought it was very absorbing; I slept four hours a night—Saturdays, Sundays and holidays included. The man in the secret service is very important to the state. We kept in touch with . . . [American] Consuls—[particularly] those who were CIA Agents.

In DOPS intelligence service, Sergio was his own boss. He was answerable only to the governor: "I didn't [even] go through the Governor's secretary, I went directly to the Governor."

Sergio's eventual alienation from political police intelligence grew out of his isolation and necessary marginality from other police. His work was "intense and permanent":

> You sleep, wake up, dream [the work]. You couldn't transfer it [to someone else]. The final decision belonged to only one man [—me]. Sometimes I wouldn't sleep for three nights [in a row]. I took [a stimulant] to keep from falling asleep. You can't afford to [sleep]. It reached a point where . . . everything was piling up . . . my youth was worth something too.

Thinking back on it, Sergio now believes that being such a "true believer" was a big mistake: He was "totally absorbed" by his work, and this "was stupid . . . [because] there has to be a limit." As alienation from himself and his work increased, Sergio requested that the governor release him from DOPS secret service: "I was fed up, couldn't take any more . . . , exhausted, I didn't have any time for myself, any friends, nothing." But the governor instead promoted him to Director of DOPS Political Police, an even more responsible position within the state's internal security apparatus. Sergio argued with the governor about his promotion: " 'You want someone you can absolutely trust and there's no such thing as [being] absolute[ly] trustworthy under orders.' " But the governor insisted, so on top of his administrative duties, Sergio conducted sensitive intelligence work, handled difficult interrogations, and "dealt with the Governor's personal affairs." Speaking about his promotion to DOPS political police chief, Sergio says that it was purely political: The state governor knew that Sergio could be "absolutely trusted" to carry out his wishes. As DOPS chief, Sergio was "more trusted [by the governor] than any other [state official]," but this carried a heavy burden of responsibility.

Sergio's extensive use of the personal pronoun to describe activities that clearly involved a group effort demonstrates his perception that he alone could make things happen within the state's internal security system. Because Sergio did not trust his subordinates, he would not delegate important decisions and operations to them. In Sergio's words, when labor and student strikes were illegal, "There was only one man [—himself—] who would [know] whether there was going to be a strike or not." If Sergio's intelligence indicated that a strike was not in the offing, then no police would be sent to the site. If a strike did in fact occur, and caused damage, Sergio would be held responsible. Sergio points out that during this period, "There was a strike every two, three days. It was crazy. I'd say that I'd infiltrated literally everywhere. I had to pick up on everything." If there were any slipups in internal security, Sergio felt it solely his fault. In Sergio's mind, "you couldn't transfer [this kind of work]. The final decision belonged to only one man"—Sergio himself. Thus, Sergio felt isolated and alone—solely responsible for the success or failure of his police organization.

It was not long before Sergio had again become really "fed up, . . . I couldn't take it any more. . . . I didn't want anything to do with it any longer. [After a while] you don't think any more, you don't sleep. . . . You become totally absorbed by the problem." Sergio says that during this phase of his life he was "very aggressive" against subversives. In fact, because of the violence he perpetrated during Brazil's military period, Sergio has been condemned by Brazilian human rights groups for torture and murder. At the very least, he ordered his operatives to carry out this violence. Yet Sergio believes that a good policeman does not need to use extreme violence: Intelligence and planning can get him what he wants and this is preferable in most situations to torture.

Sergio's discourse about violence suggests his interstitial position between lone wolf and institutional functionary, the next group of police we will examine. As with most other lone-wolf police, Sergio sees some police violence as caused by personal outrage against "criminals" and "subversives," and some as instrumentally explained by the perpetrator's "misbehavior." However, like the institutional functionaries, Sergio sees some police violence as explained by pressures of the profession.

Sergio, speaking of situational outrage, says that he "almost beat [a student] to death" because this alleged perpetrator had been "uppity." The student's behavior was "so . . . cynical, so uncalled-for." In an example of instrumental violence, Sergio explained, "If I arrest someone who has kidnapped a little girl who might be killed in four hours, I'm not going to waste time by questioning [the alleged perpetrator] for two or three days. . . . I'll hang that guy up, work him over and he'll tell me in five minutes." Torture is presumably more expedient than interrogation. Besides, if the perpetrator just "talks, [he] can keep [his torture] from happening."

Pointing to institutional influences on police violence, Sergio says that police authorities can influence whether their subordinates' violence reaches beyond "normal" bounds. For example, after leaving DOPS, while heading his state's criminal investigations unit, DEIC, Sergio assembled an informal death squad to eliminate criminals. He had men in this squad "who were dangerous to control," but Sergio could regulate them by saying " 'Okay, slow down.' " Without such control, these police would "kill people as coldly as you'd kill a chicken."

It was exactly these "hard-nosed" police that Sergio selected for his informal death squad: "They liked . . . staying up all night, doing all those things you see in the movies." These men "got pleasure out of killing [a crook]. When one or two bullets were enough to kill someone, [the policeman] would wind up taking five rounds, pow, pow, pow."

Sergio maintains that some of the men in his death squad were not inherently aggressive; they had gotten that way after many years of carrying out violence. According to Sergio, appealing to an emotional explanation for their violence, the "policeman who's outraged because [the perpetrator has] already killed ten women—strangled them with a cord"—will commit murder if he has "the opportunity—since [the policeman is] . . . already bestialized." Sergio believes that such men "began in police work just like we all began," but in the process of carrying out violence they became more brutal: "Certain type[s] of police work bestialize men horribly. . . . They . . . do things they wouldn't have ever done after ten years in the routine of [ordinary police] violence."

Here, Sergio demonstrates what the institutional functionary, Marcio, labels a standard of "proportionality": Meeting violence with violence by using hard-nosed "bestialized" cops against the most hardened criminals. In Sergio's words, he would "find out where the [criminal] was and set a place for an ambush, [so that] even if [the criminal] didn't resist [arrest] they were going to kill him." Sergio "wouldn't be sad about [this] either [he'd] even say that it was a good thing . . . better than maintaining [the criminal] in [jail]." Besides, his team wasn't really a death squad, it "didn't go out *just* to kill." These men were "trained, skillful, and ha[d] the courage to go in under fire."

Although Sergio was a lone wolf within his state's internal security system, he was, far more than the two previous cases, embedded within police bureaucracy. This was so even though his need to control personally every aspect of his police division's operations meant that he kept himself out of its internal web of relationships. Because of the secrecy required by his work, Sergio was of the internal security system and yet on its margin—isolated from subordinate police, invisible to most other police officials, and in touch with only one superior—the governor.

On balance, therefore, Sergio is much more of a lone wolf than an institutional functionary. He describes his work in individualistic and personalistic terms; he does not see himself as part of a team. He micromanaged every aspect of his police organization. Control and systemic regularity were absolutely necessary. In fact, Sergio held himself so personally responsible for his state's internal security system that he rarely delegated authority to others. Because of his hands-on style of police administration, his work in intelligence, where isolation and secrecy were the rule, and his position at the top of his police organization, Sergio was a lone wolf.

Institutional Functionaries

Marcio, a quintessential institutional functionary, entered the Civil Police as a *Delegado* in 1956. His first post was in a Brazilian rural area, where Marcio felt "socially isolated, [because] if you [got] very friendly with one group, the other [group's] political boss [would] say that you're favoring the [first] political group." Marcio had to select very carefully his social support network very carefully, taking friends only from other career professionals—they had to be people who "exercise[d] more or less similar jobs [such as] the Finance Ministry Inspector, because he's also an . . . authority." Marcio sought out such people as friends because "career civil servants don't like laymen." Marcio "like[d to associate with] career *Delegados* [because they have] the spirit of the institution." But the closest that he could come to this ideal was through connections with a statewide network of *Delegados* that passed on important information, as "a duty, a moral obligation," to *Delegados* in isolated rural areas.

According to Marcio, *Delegados* "in the past were different from what they are today. Back then, they reminded you . . . of a judge . . . a venerable elder. They were deliberate, ritualistic, . . . they knew they were the incarnation of public authority. We had to do everything slowly in order to do it right. We had to discuss it, study [it], examine the [alleged criminal's] files." Today, "the faster [*Delegados*] act, the better [and] the more highly they're valued."

In the old days, "you'd only make an arrest when you'd reached the conclusion that there was a reasonable suspicion for detaining [the perpetrator]. The . . . *Delegado* would call for his arrest record, look it over, see if [the perpetrator] was or wasn't employed." But as the *Delegado's* work load increased, control by the chief disappeared. In locking people up, there weren't "detailed criteria for each case . . . and improper things began to happen . . . physical violence, torture."

Pointing to how Marcio views his relationship to the written and unwritten rules of his organization, this Civil Police *Delegado* argues that in the old days when police acted outside the law "they did so within a relatively narrow margin: There were criteria for . . . acting outside the law . . . [because] there was some proportionality between resources and the job." In contrast, today, "there is no proportionality"—roughly a relationship between the number of criminals and the number of *Delegados* to process them—because there are so many criminals and so few *Delegados*. For example, the *Delegado* cannot effectively do his job when, first "a patrol car arrives with three policemen and three prisoners, [and then] another arrives with three [police] bringing in three more criminals, [and then] another three [police] bring in six [more prisoners]. . . . If the *Delegado* were to do what he should in each of those cases," he could not get anything accomplished on any one of them, "so he starts resolving them with his eyes . . . [without] get[ting] their records" and through violence. Torture follows from public pressure on police to solve crimes quickly and at the lowest possible cost. As Marcio explains, "If you're going to do an operation against one man, you will literally use five men to [catch and interrogate the man]. Two hours [of torture] takes care of all that"—a presumably much cheaper and faster solution.

Marcio explains that recently a lack of "proportionality" has given rise to "an expanded margin" for acceptably carrying out police violence. Apparently, here, a lack of proportionality points to poor congruence between the seriousness or importance of a crime and the amount of violence necessary to investigate it. For example, Marcio explains that in the past, "if the police caught a thief who had stolen 200 watches, and 20 were in his possession, [the police would ask] where are the other 180 [watches]?" If the robber said, "I'm not going to tell you where the other 180 are, then he [was] tortured to tell where they are." But in more recent times, "when there was a loss of control [over police administration by the *Delegados*], they'd torture whoever had twenty, or whoever didn't have any [at all], on the supposition that he had some." This illustrates that, today, the "margin" or leeway for justifying torture is too broad; such torture, for Marcio, is illegitimate; it is not "rational" because there is no "proportionality" between the crime and the amount of violence used to investigate it.

It follows that, for Marcio, there are two kinds of torturers—the rational and moral ones, and the irrational and immoral ones. The rational torturer has "a view of the common good." He "thinks that torturing will gather more evidence so there are greater possibilities of indemnifying the victim, as well as of convicting the thief or murderer." In contrast, the irrational, abnormal torturer only "wants to . . . find out [any] . . . evidence and extort [gain from others]." Marcio believes that the police "who [are] apparently normal—controlled in their torture—ha[ve] limits"; they respect the "philosophy behind torture [—that it] must cause suffering, but must not cause injuries" and should only be used "[to] . . . discover evidence." Torture has "to . . . make the suffering compatible with a lack of injuries." This can be accomplished if "the policeman who is . . . torturing [is] . . . completely aware of what he is doing, so [that] he'll know [his] limit."

An integral part of Marcio's philosophy of torture is that authorities can and should influence subordinates' violence. According to Marcio, young police do not have autonomy on the job; they "have no choice" about their actions: "When we belong to a machine, we may or may not [torture] according to who is . . . materially or morally directing us." Consequently, when the highest police official "doesn't keep his eye on things, there is [irrational] torture." Yet, as "we get older, [we] start reaching another conclusion, [namely, that] the law prohibits torture and the law is the product of the popular will; so if I torture, I'm doing something that people don't want done."

Marcio places his justifications for torture within the context of his professional position and within the system's "legal-rational" (rule-based) operation. He speaks in the third person—of "the *Delegado*," "the policeman"—using status categories to refer to himself and others. Actors and their actions are placed within an organizational, rule-based context. A good "professional" subordinates personality, identity, and self to the organization's rules, procedures, and hierarchy. Marcio was the quintessential "institutional functionary": Integrated into the police bureaucracy, which was subordinated to the larger political system, Marcio defined himself and worked through an organic whole that embraced him.

Fernando entered his state's Militarized Police in 1961, as a rank-and-file street policeman, then becoming commander of a Shock Battalion, then commanding an elite SWAT team, and finally becoming an officer in Militarized Police intelligence service (P-2). Fernando looks back on his period in the Shock Battalion as "the happiest . . . of [his] life in professional terms." He admired his men because they "had backbone." They were a "group of determined people . . . , well trained and friends with one another." The Battalion was strong because "we suffered [together]": This period in Brazil's history "was . . . a bloody war, so violent. . . . [There were] atrocities committed by our side, and . . . atrocities, . . . mistakes and crimes committed by the other side." But as Fernando reports, "our group [wasn't] going to lose this war."

Fernando attributes his men's strength under fire to training at the Militarized Police Academy: They learned "humility"—"you must be humble." Humility was inculcated primarily through hazing: "You're going to polish my boots, . . . to do what we order. . . . You have to know how to obey [orders]." According to Fernando, hazing "is a type of value-building [activity]. . . . It creates respect."

Militarized police training also built strength and courage: In a sophisticated commando course, where physical punishment was used to "attract a man's will to fight, we had to go into the woods and get beaten on the knees, on the back." This taught "[us] to look for [our] limits." Such training eliminated those "who have fragile spirits, the men who shouldn't be there." Fernando explains that if there were "exaggerations" in training—where too much violence was used—this was the result of a particular trainer's bad "upbringing": Some trainers had "character disorders."

The key to a Militarized Policeman's success, according to Fernando, is knowing that "if . . . [the policeman] is a professional, if he tries, he [will be successful]. . . . If [he is] not [a professional], he may be the victim of his very own stupidity." Fernando maintains that "it doesn't do any good to have systems, . . . plans, if the man is fragile. When a man doesn't feel like a professional, . . . he's vulnerable . . . to corruption, to deserting . . . , to getting killed, . . . to putting others at risk." Moreover, if a man is "frightened, [and] he doesn't want to die . . . , during the first gun battle, he'll take off shooting and . . . kill someone who doesn't have anything to do with anything."

Fernando has been cited by Brazilian human rights groups for involvement in torture and murder during Brazil's military period. He denies these charges, maintaining that his street units only carried out "operations"—for example, such street repression as riot and strike control, street sweep dragnets, and other forms of violent population control. Fernando maintains that this did not include interrogation and torture: "We didn't work in the intelligence area [where torture occurred]; we were an operations group." In fact, Fernando argues that it is "completely unprofessional" for someone to interrogate who took part in a "capture": "The person who is operational is operational and the person who works in information works in information." Fernando's bureaucratically compartmentalized view of his own and other police behavior, justified by an ideology of "professionalism," is one of the characteristics of the institutional functionaries, as the next cases illustrate as well.

João entered police service in 1967, serving first as a Militarized Police intelligence and operations agent, then as a Federal Police censor of books, films, and magazines, and then as a Civil Police *Delegado*. As a young Militarized Policeman, João worked in intelligence and operations; his work was highly secret and he was usually isolated from other police. João spent long periods away from home. Up to 20 of his "missions" were "dangerous," but João "wasn't afraid [or] concerned, [because] when you're young, it seems that you have more courage." In those early days, João's work was so secret—(he often wore disguises and worked at night)—that even the chief of João's intelligence section did not know his operatives' real identities. Indeed, according to João, the only way an operative knew that he had performed well on a mission was that his superior gave him "another mission that had a certain importance." Yet for João, approval from superiors was not necessary, because he "believed in what [he] was doing. . . . [He was] a soldier fighting for his country, for internal control of that [subversive] movement . . . [that was] agitating the country."

As "part of an institution whose mission it was to maintain law and order," João, although a Catholic, had no problem "entering a Catholic Church and arresting everyone there." According to João, the people in the church were "violating a principle of God, having a meeting that had nothing to do with religion." While João himself claims never to have used "excess violence" in such operations, and "never tortured anyone," he headed police units that tortured and murdered. As a former officer of such units, João maintains "that there are certain situations where [the torturer] is needed": If the "higher-ups want the job done, don't do anything [to prohibit torture], and let [the policeman] do it," then torture will occur time after time. João believes that the torturer has "to be controlled, not to go overboard, not to commit unnecessary accidents."

According to João, torturers are likely to come from the already very aggressive policemen: If anyone "analyze[s] their psychological profile," it will be obvious that they have a higher tendency for aggressiveness—a very high degree." According to João, these police "are soon identified" by superiors as appropriate for carrying out the most violent policing. They are easily found "in the ... judicial police area, in ... grand larceny [control], [and in units pursuing] large-scale drug trafficking"; these divisions have "more aggressive policeman to be able to deal with a certain type of delinquent." Yet João maintains that such police are "really exploited by their bosses, by those who [just] want to get the job over quickly."

Although João maintains that some police violence is a necessary part of professional police practice, he recognizes that there are officials who are not beyond "exploiting" those who have a propensity for aggressiveness. Yet because such violent police are sectioned off into specialized units where their services are seen as unavoidably "necessary," João need not feel directly responsible for their committing torture and murder. He can claim no involvement in such violence because it has been carried out by aggressive, specialized police who are merely doing what the system wants, needs, and asks for.

Jorge, a former Militarized rank-and-file policeman, was the kind of violent, aggressive policeman that João and Sergio selected for their torture and murder squads. Jorge was reared in violence as an "orphan" in FUNABEM, a state-run orphanage for poor parentless children, after his father, a French citizen, had been arrested and deported as a "subversive." Jorge and his siblings were taken from his mother, also a suspected subversive. According to Jorge, "They beat us, cursed us, spanked us ... punished ... everything. ... The conditions at FUNABEM were terrible." "Unruly" children were subjected to "the needle"—having to "lean ... [against] the wall [holding yourself up with your] fingers [until] your fingers couldn't take [the weight] any more. If someone fell they'd put a heavy weight around his neck" and make him assume the needle position again. Jorge says that this treatment "revolted" him and contributed to his aggressiveness.

Jorge was "funneled" very early into violent police work, when soon after entering Militarized Police service in the mid-1970s, he began working undercover in one of DOI/CODI's "bust" (murder) squads. Jorge says that police training contributed to his violence: "They taught us terrible things—torture, how to torture, how to kill ... [that] everybody was the enemy." His personal background and training were good preparation for his police work because, according to Jorge, DOI/CODI only wants "objective, cold" people with the capacity "to obey orders." Jorge describes his real self as "different" from other DOI/CODI operatives: He was "softer, really softer . . . very sentimental."

Nevertheless, Jorge says that he "accounted for eighty deaths" between 1980 and 1982, a euphemism for his having murdered 80 people. Jorge's career in violence began when 15 poor people were caught in a cemetery that the military had filled with land mines to keep the poor from seeking a place to live there. After having been loaded onto the back of a Military Police truck, "screaming [and] asking for help," a police captain ordered his men to "take care of [the fifteen captives]," first passing his gun to the lieutenant, who passed it to the corporal, who passed it to Jorge. Ordered to shoot the prisoners, Jorge, who had "never shot anybody in [his] life," was obliged to "hold the heads of the people and kill them." Next, the captain ordered Jorge to "put [the bodies] in the garbage truck." But Jorge refused, telling his superior "to do your own dirty work."

Just the same, Jorge was promoted after this operation to Militarized Police "Reserved Service," where, according to Jorge,

you don't do anything but kill. They'd detect a person who was involved in a certain crime and the Reserved Service would go in, pick him up, "Ta, Ta, Ta" . . . waste the criminal, whether he was civilian or policeman. . . . The police [even] used their own men to kill [a policeman own who was] out of line; [it's] crooked.

In the Reserved Service, Jorge's superiors first assigned him to a torture squad; he was given preparation for this service by watching six torture sessions. But Jorge "challenged it," telling his superior, "I didn't think they needed all of that." Jorge's superior warned . . . [him] to keep [his] opinions to [him]self," but Jorge retorted that "instead of torturing the person, just kill him outright, [to] keep on torturing isn't for me." With that, Jorge was transferred to a murder team, his superior fearing that "some day [Jorge would] kill all . . . who we are torturing." His superior assumed that because Jorge "still had to overcome [his] own tortures, . . . some day [he'd] take on the pain of the victims and end up killing them" just to put them out of their misery.

Once in a DOI/CODI murder team—on loan from the Militarized Police Reserved Service—Jorge breathed a sigh of relief: "At last I can quit seeing . . . stupid things" like torture. Quickly promoted to the highest level within the murder squad, Jorge knew that he was good at murder.

But he found this work "dangerous" and "exhausting": "It was hard to get away from work. . . . We'd frequently go on a mission that'd take . . . even weeks or . . . months. We were literally . . . away from contact with people." Moreover, during a murder operation,

It was as if everybody was carrying a liter of nitroglycerine and there wasn't any way to get rid of it: It was total tension. No one could speak, nobody joked, . . . there was no relaxation. . . . Anything . . . could represent a risk. I didn't have any friends back then . . . nobody could say they had friends [in the group]—no one. Anybody who said that was [considered] . . . soft.[7]

Comparing his work to that of the torturers, Jorge describes murder as morally and professionally preferable: "It was much easier to kill because the torturer had to have a commitment to his victim. The killer had no commitment to his victim." Thus, for Jorge, murder was more humane than torture. For example, on a mission in the Amazon region near the Venezuelan border, his DOI/CODI team, in a helicopter, arrested a group of foreigners and threw them on board. Some members of the team began torturing the prisoners: "There were women [being] raped." Jorge "felt badly . . . [and] even had to kill one of [the women] because they were torturing [her] . . . too much—she was screaming." Jorge is proud that he killed this victim to save her from more torture and so that she was not thrown alive out of the helicopter: "The rest were alive when they were thrown out."

After almost 5 years of being what Jorge himself labels a "murderer for the state," Jorge began to ask, "What am I going to do with my life if I only know how [to kill]? I wanted to be myself a little . . . , to know, to think, to have all of the emotions that humans have and I never had a chance to have."

Today, in prison for committing a murder for which Jorge says he was "framed," Jorge argues that he has spent almost his entire life within government bureaucracy:

I gave [the government] almost my entire life and I've never had anything. I've never known civilian life since I was put in FUNABEM [as a child]—the army, the Militarized Police, and now I'm in jail. I don't know what it's like to put a labor registration card in my pocket and work and have a profession.

Jorge, an institutional functionary, is unlike Marcio, João, and Fernando; Jorge was a subordinate within police hierarchy. He was a "murder functionary" in a "Taylorized system": Lists of victims were passed first by nameless public safety officials—judges, the Secretary of Public Security—to nameless senior Military Police officers, who then passed them on to his team during a weekly planning meeting. Usually hooded and working at night to ensure anonymity, Jorge's team rounded up the "subversives" whose names appeared on the list. The victims had been depersonalized—mere "projects" to be eliminated from a list.

Jorge did not need the excuse that when he murdered he was "just following orders," because no one person had ordered him to kill. Jorge was just one of several police in a hierarchy carrying out a task that had been divided into so many distinct segments that no one actor was fully responsible for any particular outcome. This is a classic example of what Arendt (1964) calls "rule by nobody," "one of the cruelest and most tyrannical versions" of rule (p. 40) that regulates the behavior of the modern bureaucratic institutional functionary.

Bureaucratizing Masculinity

The lone-wolf police, unlike the institutionalized police functionaries, shared several characteristics stereotypically associated with hegemonic Western patriarchal masculinity. They placed a premium on interpersonal (rather than structural) control, on individual responsibility and autonomy, on demanding respect, and on demonstrations of force to maintain others' deference and keep deviants in line. Yet there was diversity even within this modal lone-wolf masculinity. Julio and Sergio, who especially revealed these qualities, appeared to be controlling, aggressive, silent, emotionally frozen, and socially alienated from others. But Isadoro, the quintessential example of traditional Brazilian masculinity, reported that he sought connections with poor communities, liked spending time "passeando,"—hanging out, talking with people for hours. Using favors to create interpersonal connections and obligations, he prided himself on his ability to help others solve their problems. Isadoro openly communicated his feelings and used violence only where his personal or masculine "honor" was violated. Of course, like the other lone-wolf cops, Isadoro's masculinity was not subordinated to an internal security bureaucracy. They all stood at least partially outside bureaucracy and even social class, though not without their own hierarchies of interpersonal dominance and deference.

In marked contrast, the masculinities of the institutional functionaries were muted—they were absorbed by the internal security bureaucracy: "The demands of authority [were] paramount; the thoughts and feelings of individuals disregarded" (Skovholt, Moore, & Haritos-Fatouros, n.d., p. 7). The Brazilian military state of 1964 through 1985 assumed that only emotionally and organizationally controlled police could successfully repress subversion. Therefore, the institutional functionary was favored over the "nonprofessional," emotional, and "irrational" lone-wolf policeman. Of course, the latter considered such institutional functionaries a perversion of policing and even of "real" masculinity.

It could be argued, following Liddle (1996), that the shift from the hegemony of one to the other of these two masculinities follows and reflects changes in the structural demands of Brazil's modernizing state. The lone-wolf cops, numerically dominant before the installation of Brazil's National Security State (post-1969), characterized a less "modern" period, when policing was decentralized and policemen used their own charisma in working for charismatic local and state officials (see Fernandes, 1979; Holloway, 1993; Huggins, in press-b). This "old-style" policeman was his own boss within the limits set by the politicos for whom he worked. An example is Sergio: Selected by the governor to head his state's DOPS political police organization, Sergio assumed a position that gave him great autonomy, as long as he upheld the governor's political interests. Sergio quit police service in 1969, just when Brazil's national security state had emerged full-blown.

After 1964, as Brazil's authoritarian state moved toward this "bureaucratic-authoritarian" form (Huggins, in press-b; O'Donnell, 1988), the ideologies of technocratic professionalism linked to national security encouraged the development of a more "professional" police. They were to give allegiance only to an impersonal internal security organization subordinated to Brazil's authoritarian military state. Accordingly, the lone-wolf police were treated with disdain; they were distrusted, marginalized, and even punished by Brazil's militarized police system. Their mode of policing was considered unacceptable and even dangerous to a regime that believed Brazil's internal war could only be won by a unified, obedient, centrally controlled internal security force that subordinated individual identity to the organization. Where modernity was taken to mean efficiency and specialization, the system had to subordinate lone-wolf police, with their traditional and charismatic masculinities, in order to shape a new technocratic, legal-rational internal security bureaucrat.

This meant replacing traditional Brazilian cops and their old-style masculinities with relatively faceless social control technocrats without personal identity. These were given management of Brazil's social control system, their impersonal mode was defined as "good" policing (see Huggins, in press-b). In fact, these new functionaries were mere cogs in the administrative machinery," to use Arendt's (1964, p. 289) characterization of bureaucratic functionaries. As Jorge explained, it didn't take a "change of identity [to commit murder]; I don't think we even had an identity." In other words, it was not that the institutional functionaries were so cold-blooded that they easily could think the unthinkable, they did not think at all (from Arendt, 1970, p. 6).

It therefore seems ironic that with the gradual replacement of the national security state by Brazil's post-1985 redemocratization, lone-wolf police have reemerged in an important role within Brazil's social control system—they murder "criminals" and street children and massacre civilians in reputed "drug zones." The now institutionally privatized lone-wolf police—in symbiosis with the formally professionalized "public" police—occupy a legal and political space neither fully public (i.e., state) nor fully private (see Huggins, in press-a; Shearing, 1996, pp. 285-286). Lone-wolf policing has been transformed from a charismatic quality of the actor to a position within a police organization into which a variety of masculinities can be recruited and shaped. The most dramatic example of the functional symbiosis between institutional functionaries and lone-wolf police is the modern "death squads." Made up primarily of institutionally privatized lone-wolf police under the indirect or clandestine control of the social control system's institutional functionaries, this is clearly a different arrangement from when hired thugs were the personal "militia" of powerful *politicos*. Today, as an institutionally reattached secret arm of the formal police system, "lone-wolf" masculinities carry out the state's dirty work from a liminal status that falls somewhere between being on-duty and off-duty—doing what the democratizing state cannot formally do while it still claims to be democratic. The relative invisibility of institutionalized lone-wolf death squads makes them a perfect supplement and shield for the failed policing of Brazil's redemocratizing but still authoritarian state. Thus, the reformers' assumption that lone-wolf police just need to be "professionalized" to eliminate death squad violence, leaves Brazil's police system still violent and Brazil's fledgling democracy navigating a treacherous course between the Scylla of vindictive but unofficial lone-wolf police death squads, and the

Charybdis of institutional functionaries' impersonal but controlled violence.

Notes

1. The authors wish to thank Lee Bowker for pointing to the masculinities embedded in Brazilian torturers' and killers' discourse and for inviting us to contribute to this important volume. We also wish to thank Philip Zimbardo for being our consultant to the larger study of torturers. William Shelton carefully transcribed and translated the interviews. Erika Migliaccio helped assemble the bibliography; Ilyssa Kaufman provided an undergraduate student analysis of the chapter. Malcolm Willison gave invaluable insights and manuscript-edited the chapter. Carolyn Micklas did the typing.

2. Because Brazil's Military Police is no longer subordinated to the military itself, this organization will be referred to in this study as the Militarized Police.

3. DOI/CODI is short for Destacamento de Operacões/Centro de Operacões de Defeza Interna (Information Operations Detachment/Center for Internal Defense Operations).

4. Bill Shelton, a trained translator, transcribed and translated the interviews.

5. With the granting of amnesty to all former "subversives," internal security forces were also "amnestied" for their crimes. Most of the more important Brazilian states have an organization for considering a policeman's amnesty petition.

6. Julio gave Martha Huggins three pictures of a man who had been tortured to death on the "Parrot's Perch," explaining that he had taken the pictures while torture was taking place.

7. Several of the interviewees (e.g., Sergio, Jorge) manifest symptoms of burnout from their violent careers, a subject that we have examined in *Being "Hung Out to Dry": Case Studies of Torturers and Killers in Authoritarian Brazil* (Haritos-Fatouros & Huggins, 1997).

PART TWO

MEN VICTIMIZING
WOMEN AND CHILDREN

4

Doing Violence to Women

Research Synthesis on the Victimization of Women

NEIL WEBSDALE
MEDA CHESNEY-LIND

At the World Conference on Women, held recently in Beijing and Huairou, China, women from across the world shared their political and cultural experiences. Many topics surfaced, including women's poverty, education, health, and access to decision making; the media and women; and women's role in shaping the environment. Amid all these issues and more, violence against women was of central and critical importance as an experience that transcended both national and cultural boundaries. As Rita Maran (1996) observes, "Violence against women constituted a top priority in both Huairou and Beijing. As an issue, it garnered the greatest consensus and served, coincidentally, as a unifying element" (p. 354). One of the major platforms for action to emerge out of the meetings was the "prevention and elimination of violence against women and girls" (p. 354).

The World Conference on Women served as yet one more vehicle for reemphasizing the international and epidemic proportions of violence against women. This violence cannot be explained away as a deviant phenomenon that lies outside of the otherwise "harmonious" relationships between men and women. Rather, violence against women is endemic to the social condition of women, across both time and cultures. To write of the victimization of women, then, is to enter the lives of different women and expose their various social conditions. Therefore we cannot document the magnitude or locus of violence against women without simultaneously mapping women's social, economic, and political disadvantage vis-à-vis men. Our conception of men's violence is broad and includes not only physical and sexual violence, its threat, or both, but also emotional abuse, economic violence, and institutional violence. As Jalna Hanmer (1996) observes, whether perpetrated by known or unknown men, this violence is "designed to control, dominate and express authority and power" (p. 8). Our comprehensive conception of violence against women recognizes that women themselves define violence much more broadly than men (see Hearn 1996, p. 27; Stanko, 1994). For example, women are more likely than men to identify emotional abuse and economic subordination as forms of violence. We identify the imprisonment of women in general, and more specifically of those who have killed their abusers, as forms of state violence against women. The incarceration of battered women resembles what Pierre Bourdieu (1993) refers to as "symbolic violence" insofar as their confinement utterly ignores the underlying power relations that women are subject to and that lead women to commit acts of resistive violence. At the same time, we note the harassment and degradation of women inmates by correctional personnel as yet another form of violence.

Our wide-ranging and fluid use of the word *violence* allows us to explore a number of forms of women's victimization. Often these forms of victimization are seen as discrete entities and are written and talked about widely in isolation from each other and the broader deployment of men's power. However, we highlight so-called social phenomena such as nonlethal and lethal battering, the mass killing of women, the sexual victimization of women by known and unknown men, the victimization of women prostitutes, sexual harassment, and the incarceration of women as continuities in the politics of gender relations.

During the past 20 years an enormous amount of multidisciplinary and interdisciplinary research has been published on violence against women. Much of this research has been stimulated by feminist concerns to publicize the hitherto marginalized personal experiences of women, particularly women's relationships with men. As Linda Gordon (1988) shows, violence such as woman battering has been elevated to the status of a "social problem" during periods when the feminist movement has been strong.

Nonlethal Violence Against Women

Men are much more likely to commit acts of violence against women than women are against men. If women do use violence, it is often in self-defense or as a preemptive strategy to prevent further brutalization or death. Dawson and Langan (1994), using data from 1987 through 1991, found that females reported more than 10 times as many incidents of male violence as males reported incidents of female violence (p. 2). Judging from available research, this gendered nature of interpersonal violence has a long history (see Fink, 1992; Gordon, 1988; Pleck, 1987; Taves, 1989; Tomes, 1978; Websdale, 1992). Both historical and contemporary research also shows that interpersonal male violence against women is as common in allegedly more tranquil rural communities as it is in urban centers (see Bachman, 1994; Websdale, 1995).

A number of studies have linked the power relationships within families to the levels and severity of intimate violence. Kalmuss and Straus (1982) found that the greater the economic dependence of a woman on a man, the more likely she was to experience acts of severe violence. Dobash and Dobash (1979) found in their interviews with 109 battered women in Scottish shelters that men resorted to battering when they perceived that their wives were not living up to the patriarchally ordained role prescriptions of the "good wife." There were three main triggers that sparked male violence: his jealousy; his perception that she fails to perform her housework or other wifely services such as preparing him a hot meal; and her challenging him about economic matters within the family such as housekeeping money. For Dobash and Dobash (1979), male violence is a cultural phenomenon that is linked to the patriarchal domination of women by men. That most men do not batter their wives should not be understood to mean that patriarchy does not exist. Rather, men have many avenues of control available to them, some coercive and some more consensual.[1]

Work by Yllo and Straus (1984) finds that levels of wife beating are highest when the family norms are the most patriarchal. Levels of wife beating are highest in states where women's status is highest, prompting the researchers to suggest that perhaps the tension between the relatively high structural position of women and the intrafamilial ascendancy of men is the trigger for more male violence.

Michael Smith (1990) employs the notion of "patriarchal ideology" to describe that system of beliefs, values, and ideas that supports men's domination of women and depicts that domination as natural. Although acknowledging that patriarchal relations vary by culture, Smith argues that most societies have some form of patriarchy. Quoting Kate Millett (1969), he notes how these different forms of patriarchy are sustained in part by ideologies that act as the "energy source" of patriarchal domination (Smith, 1990, p. 258). These ideologies cast men and women in different roles. Smith, using data from a telephone survey of 604 Toronto women, finds that men who adhere to an ideology of familial patriarchy (according to their female partners) are more likely to have assaulted their female partners at some point in their relationships. Husbands who are less well educated and in low-income or low-status jobs are more likely · to subscribe to "an ideology of familial patriarchy" (Smith, 1990, p. 268). Smith's findings are consistent with others' that point to the existence of a "patriarchal subculture" of men who are socialized into keeping their women in line, through the use of violence if necessary (see Bowker, 1983, 1985).

Lethal Violence Against Women

The fact that in the U. S. wives kill husbands nearly as often as husbands ⁊ kill wives, has led some researchers to suggest that spousal murder is a similar process for men and women (see McNelly & Mann, 1990; McNelly & Robinson-Simpson, 1987; Steinmetz, 1977-1978; Straus & Gelles, 1990). These researchers focus on the fact that in the United States, for every 100 men who kill their wives, 75 women kill their husbands. This ratio is based on statistics from the period 1976 through 1985, during which time 10,529 wives were killed by husbands and 7,888 husbands were killed by wives (see Maxfield, 1989, p. 677; Mercy & Saltzman, 1989). More recent figures show that for U.S. interspousal killings, women constituted 41% of the killers (U.S. Department of Justice, 1994, p. 1).

However, these statistics do not tell us about the reasons for the homicides and especially whether there was any history of violence in the relationship. According to Stark and Flitcraft (1996), woman battering lies at the root of the majority of spousal, intersexual, and child homicides (p. 124). Dobash and Dobash (1992) report the same, pointing out that,

When the woman dies, it is usually the final and most extreme form of violence at the hands of her male partner. When the man dies, it is rarely the final act in a relationship in which she has repeatedly beaten him. (p. 6)

Most intrafamilial homicides are what Stark and Flitcraft (1996) call "gendered homicides," insofar as the central dynamic is a "female's subordination to a male partner" (p. 124). This dynamic is not widely appreciated in either the scholarly literature on lethal violence or in popular discourses on homicide. Stark and Flitcraft note: "In contrast to the prevailing opinion that homicide is generally impulsive and unpredictable, gendered homicides have a predictable etiology, usually rooted in woman battering" (p. 124).

From their research, Stark and Flitcraft argue that at least three themes are common to gendered homicides: rising entrapment, intense conflict around gender role behavior, and a history of interactions with helping agencies. Prior to the fatality, the partner abuse culminates in a degree of "entrapment," usually characterized by physical and sexual abuse in tandem with the rigid control of women's movements, sociability, money, food, working life, and sexual activities (p. 146). It is this rising level of entrapment that is the most significant risk factor for gendered homicide.

Another important antecedent to gendered homicide is the intense conflict between partners over the respective roles in the relationship. In discussing the case of "Dila," who endured 6 years of battering before finally killing her abusive husband, Stark and Flitcraft (1996) highlight aspects of the sexual politics that for them "frame every aspect of inter sexual homicide" (p. 147). Dila's abuser "Mic" not only made Dila keep a log of all her daily activities, including her meal plans, but he also tried to regulate her contacts with other men, her control over the money she earned, her body weight, and her various housework activities.

Daly and Wilson (1988), using a theoretical model they call "evolutionary psychology," examine homicides across a wide range of cultural settings including industrial and aboriginal societies. They argue that marital violence arises out of men's attempts to control women, especially women's reproductive capacities. For these authors, spousal murder, whether committed by men or women, is rooted in "male sexual proprietariness" (p. 295).

Many domestic homicides in the United States are preceded by a trail of contacts with so-called helping agencies. Angela Browne (1987) points to the "cries for help" in domestic homicides prior to the fatal incident. Citing research in Detroit and Kansas City, Browne observes that in 85% to 90% of domestic homicides police had been called to the scene at least once (pp. 10-11). For Stark and Flitcraft (1996), the health, justice, and social service response to battering often ends up reinforcing women's entrapment, thereby increasing rather than decreasing the chances of a fatality (p. 148).

Homicide-suicide entails the killing of one or more persons followed soon after by the suicide of the perpetrator. There is no national data on the incidence of homicide-suicide. However, preliminary studies show that this form of killing constitutes a form of gendered homicide followed by suicide. It is nearly always men who kill their wives, ex-wives, lovers, and ex-lovers, sometimes in combination with the couple's children. Woman battering is a significant antecedent to the homicide-suicide episode. In tandem with Stark and Flitcraft's observations on gendered homicides, Marzuk, Tardiff, and Hirsch (1992) note, "While some murder-suicides occur shortly after the onset of 'malignant jealousy,' more often there has been a chronically chaotic relationship fraught with jealous suspicions, verbal abuse, and sub-lethal violence" (p. 3180).[2]

A Kentucky study also reveals that many homicide-suicides are preceded by a history of woman abuse. Currens (1991) notes that, "the typical perpetrator is a man married or living with a woman in a relationship marked by physical abuse" (p. 653).[3]

The murder of Glenda Greer, and the subsequent suicide of husband Shannon, in the state of Kentucky, epitomizes a number of the characteristics of murder-suicides, and indeed the violent victimization of women in general. Glenda decided to end her relationship with her abusive husband Shannon by filing for divorce. These and other similar acts of resistance by women to terminate violent relationships often enrage abusers. It is during this period of attempted separation that roughly three quarters of battered women are killed. Glenda Greer was well known in the small community of Waynesburg, Kentucky, where she had worked as the secretary at the local elementary school for 11 years. When Shannon learned of the pending divorce he went to the elementary school and shot Glenda in the face and back with a 12-gauge shotgun, killing her. Shannon then drove to a remote forest where he killed himself. On the dashboard of Shannon's car police later found the divorce papers. Across the papers Shannon had written a note saying, "there was not a divorce" ("Slain Secretary," 1990).

The Mass Killing of Women

So far we have explored women's experience of nonlethal and lethal violence at the hands of men they know. Our analysis would be incomplete without examining the profoundly gendered character of intersexual mass killing. We distinguish between two types of these albeit rare, but nevertheless often highly publicized, forms of murder. By *simultaneous mass killing* we refer to the killing of several people in one brief episode. By *serial killing* we mean the killing of a number of people in distinctive episodes, often separated by long periods of time. The intersexual variants of these forms of killing almost always involve men as perpetrators and women as corpses. The meaning of this gendered dynamic must not be underestimated, for these offenses are often underpinned by or tinged with an intense misogynism on the part of the perpetrator. Radford and Russell (1992) employ the specific term *femicide* to refer to the "misogynist killing of women by men." Many mass killings of women fall into this category.

During the early stages of deer hunting season in 1957 in rural Waushara County, Wisconsin, Edward Gein killed a number of women. One victim, Bernice Worden, was found hanging in a barn. She had been "completely dressed out like a deer with her head cut off at the shoulders" (Levin & Fox, 1990, p. 66). Her body had been gutted, and investigators felt she had been butchered elsewhere. Gein later admitted to robbing the body parts of dead women from gravesites. Apparently Gein made a belt of nipples, and crafted a hanging human head as part of an ornament collection. In a shoe box, nine vulvas were found.

In what Joanne Stato (1993) has called the "Montreal Gynocide," Marc Lepine killed 14 women on December 6, 1989, in their classroom at the engineering school at the University of Montreal. Lepine later shot himself. In a three-page statement found by police, Lepine blamed feminists for his problems. As Stato notes, this incident could not be attributed to the ravings of an isolated maniac because Lepine stated that his intent was to kill feminists (p. 132). Stato therefore links these 14 killings to misogynism in general, thereby tying them into the systemic oppression of women in patriarchal societies. In a similar vein, Jane Caputi (1993) theorizes the still unknown number of women murdered and mutilated by Christopher Wilder as "sexually political murders" (p. 6). Wilder apparently bound, raped, and systematically tortured his victims before killing them. Likening this killing to lynching, Caputi observes, "His were sexually political murders, a form of murder rooted in a system of male supremacy in the same way that lynching is based in white supremacy. Such murder is, in short, a form of patriarchal terrorism" (p. 6).

Most serial killers are men. Jenkins argues that only 10% to 15% have been women (see Jenkins, 1994, chap. 7). Women murdered by serial killers are typically relatively powerless women who work in vulnerable occupations such as prostitution. Therefore, even with serial killers and their actions we see the social condition of women playing a crucial role in placing them at risk. Although all women are at risk from male violence, it seems that acutely disadvantaged women such as prostitutes, runaways, "street women, women of color, poor women, single and elderly women, are at an elevated risk of being killed by serial killers" (see Egger, 1984, p. 348).[4] As in the case of rapists, these simultaneous mass murderers and serial killers appear, for the most part, to be ordinary men rather than deeply disturbed individuals. For a number of researchers, this normalcy is yet further evidence of the powerful connection between the structure of hetero-patriarchal relations and the murder and mutilation of women. The small number of women serial killers tend to share life experiences with those battered women who have killed their abusers. As noted, when women kill it is usually after they have suffered at the hands of their abusers. Aileen Wournros, one of the few women serial killers, suffered tremendous abuse at the hands of men throughout her life. She was convicted of killing a number of johns she claimed abused her while she was providing sexual services to them in her role as a prostitute (see Kelly, 1996, p. 41). To comprehend fully the act of killing another human being it is always necessary to look at the sociopolitical context within which that killing occurs. The actions of Wournros cannot, we contend, be equated to the murderous actions of male serial killers, because male serial killers are backed by a social power, to the likes of which the Aileen Wournros's of this world do not have access.

Sexual Victimization

Known Men as Perpetrators

The traditional image of the rapist is that of the strange and mentally disturbed man who preys impulsively upon unknown women. However, a plethora of studies attest to the fact that rapists are more often known to their victims (Finkelhor & Yllo, 1985; Russell, 1990), are not psychiatrically disturbed (Smart & Smart, 1978), and more often than not plan their attacks (Amir, 1971). Indeed, it is within the confines of heterosexual relationships in general that the majority of rape and sexual assault occurs. Although Russell (1990) found that 55% of rapes reported to the police were committed by strangers, her random sample survey of 930 women in San Francisco revealed that only 6% of the total number of 2,588 rapes or attempted rapes were committed by strangers. Out of these 2,588 incidents, 38% were committed by husbands or ex-husbands and 13% by lovers or ex-lovers (see Russell, 1990, p. 67, table 5-3).[5] Other surveys also point to the high percentage of raped women who know their abusers. For example, surveys of college age students on 32 college campuses found that 84% of rape victims knew their attackers (see Warshaw, 1988). If the rapist is known by the victim, then there is a greater likelihood of a repeat offense. In the Russell survey, between 70% and 80% of the victims of wife rape reported being raped more than once. This high figure is borne out by the research of Finkelhor and Yllo (1985) using a sample of 323 women in Boston. These authors found that half the victims of wife rape had experienced sexual assault on more than 20 occasions (p. 23). Although a number of authors have noted that roughly 30% to 60% of intimate violence against women involves sexual abuse (Walker, 1979, p. 112), and that battered women are twice as likely to experience multiple marital rapes (Finkelhor & Yllo, 1985, pp. 23-24), some authors stress that the rape of women by intimates is not always accompanied by battering (Russell, 1990, pp. 100-101). In their survey of Boston women, Finkelhor and Yllo (1985) found that marital rape "occurred in relationships in which there was little or no other violence; in relationships where there was little verbal or psychological abuse" (p. 37).

Finkelhor and Yllo (1985) distinguish between forced sex and rape. They argue that in cases where wives submit to husbands' sexual advances because they feel it is their duty as wives to submit, they experience forced sex but not rape. They comment:

A woman whose husband tells her he is going to humiliate her publicly if she won't perform some sexual act, for instance, may be making a more fearsome and devastating threat than a man who threatens only to push himself on his wife. We would be prepared to call this kind of coercion forced sex, but not rape. (pp. 89-90)

Finkelhor and Yllo's concern about expanding the definition of rape to include nonconsensual sexual intercourse is that it will end up "diluting" the meaning of the word *rape* (p. 86).

The suggestion that rape sometimes occurs without violence, or the threat of violence, draws attention to those instances of coerced sexual intercourse that occur, for example, in workplaces where pressure is used by men that does not amount to threats of violence or outright violence (see Box, 1983, pp. 122-127). Similarly, when such "nonviolent" rape occurs between couples in heterosexual relationships, it alerts us to the fact that sexual relations do not have to be violent to be nonconsensual. For Box, and a number of feminist authors, the definition of rape warrants expansion to all those cases where a woman's overt genuine consent is absent (see Box, 1983, p. 125). In a similar vein, Catherine MacKinnon (1987) reminds us that seeing rape only as a form of violence is limited:

> Calling rape violence, not sex, thus evades . . . the issue of who controls women's sexuality and the dominance/submission dynamic that has defined it. When sex is violent, women may have lost control over what is done to us, but absence of force does not ensure the presence of that control. (p. 144)

Unknown Men as Perpetrators

The rape of women by strangers has been so enmeshed in the ideology of the individual "predator" who lurks and pounces, that it is easy to lose sight of the mass rape of women in much broader contexts of mass violence such as war and ethnic cleansing. The commission of sexual atrocities against women for the purposes of furthering genocidal regimes is well documented. Nenadic (1996) draws attention to a number of studies showing the use of sexual atrocities by the Nazis against Jewish women in the extermination camps (see Lengyel, 1947; Perl, 1948; and Rittner & Roth, 1993, all cited by Nenadic, 1996, p. 459). For example, Jewish women who were pregnant upon entering the extermination camps were targeted for immediate gassing (Nenadic, 1996, p. 459). In a similar vein, Susan Brownmiller (1976) observes that approximately 200,000 to 400,000 Bengali women were raped by Pakistani soldiers during the 9-month conflict between the Bengalis and Pakistanis in 1971 (pp. 78-86). Of these raped women, roughly 25,000 became pregnant and, as a consequence, became virtual outcasts in Bengali society. Some Bengalis speculated that this mass rape represented an official policy on the part of the Pakistani government to create a new race or to dilute Bengali nationalism.

As Brownmiller (1976) notes, the sexual victimization and related killing of women during war has a long history (chap. 3). During medieval times, when foot soldiers were poorly and irregularly paid by their leaders, the promise of women's bodies was often held up as one of the perks of successful conquest. In many instances, sexual conquest went hand in hand with military conquest, with the former being both an incentive for the latter and a badge of military success. Brownmiller (1976) puts it as follows:

> Down through the ages, triumph over women by rape became a way to measure victory, part of a soldier's proof of masculinity and success, a tangible reward for services rendered. . . . Booty and beauty General Andrew Jackson supposedly named it in New Orleans during the War of 1812. He was commenting, naturally, on the English attitude. (pp. 35-36)

At this time of writing, women in Serb-occupied Bosnia-Hercegovina and Croatia endure sexual atrocities and systematic extermination. As Nenadic (1996) reports, the use of sexual atrocities as a means of genocide is currently being undertaken by Serbian fascists as a way of cleansing society of non-Serbs. Nenadic locates women and girls at the center of the ethnic cleansing and identifies rape and other sexual atrocities as central technologies in the purification process. She comments that, "Rape is an efficient and economical tool of genocide" (p. 457). According to Nenadic, the systematic sexual atrocities directed at Moslem women goes far beyond that experienced by Jewish women in Nazi extermination camps (p. 459). She observes,

> The sexual atrocities during the Shoah did not occur with the same breadth and frequency as in this genocide, in which almost every survivor reports being a witness to, or a victim of, sexual atrocities and in which almost every woman who entered one of a variety of Serbian concentration camps or a rape/death camp was a victim of sexual atrocities whether or not she, herself, lived to tell about it. Moreover, Nazi policy against Jews did not conceptualize rape for forced impregnation and forced childbirth as a method of genocide as does Serbian genocidal policy. (p. 459)

The sexual mutilation and murder of Moslem women in Serb-occupied Bosnia-Hercegovina and Croatia includes the slicing off of women's breasts and the ripping out of their wombs. In Odzak, the bodies of 600 women were found butchered and laying on the street. According to Omerdic (1992), "The dead women were naked, propped up on fence spikes" (cited in Nenadic, 1996, p. 458, footnote 7). Ian Geoghegan (1996), reporting for the *Guardian Weekly* from the War Crimes Tribunal in the Hague, recalls how a drunken Serb soldier shot dead a young man after ordering him to rape his dead mother, who had been killed by the same soldier moments before (p. 5). The Serb soldier apparently forced the mother to strip off her upper clothing. He then shot her in the back of the head. One Moslem survivor of the Bosnian prison camp, Suljeman Besic, told the tribunal how he was taken to a complex that housed women and girls. There he was shown blood-spattered bodies of two girls in their early teens lying by an outside toilet. Other inmates of the Bosnian camp told Besic that groups of Serb soldiers had arrived during the night to select girls they liked. Elderly women who tried to prevent this selection were killed.

While the rape, mutilation, and killing of women during war serve to remind us of the utility of women to men in battle, the entire discourse on the victimization of women "during war" leaves us with a silence that is itself one of great mantras of patriarchy. By this "silence" we refer to the "gender war" seemingly hidden by the glory of men fighting each other with all the destructive power their respective military regimes can muster. To talk and write of the brutalization and sexual mutilation of women during war risks understating that such wartime victimization is, in fact, part of one of the longest wars ever fought, rather than an incidental, albeit horrendous, sideshow in the particular and localized war being fought by men against men. As Foucault (1981) so eloquently reminds us, the arena of sexuality is saturated with power and replete with its own weaponry, tactics, propaganda, victims, and resistive strategies. It has been our argument that everyday gender relations constitute a type of battlefield or war zone. In military conflicts between nations, not all of the citizenry have to be employed in the military to ensure the military and political might of one nation over another. Likewise in the gender war, which takes place at numerous levels, not all men have to use lethal and sublethal violence against women to enjoy the fruits of patriarchy.

The Victimization of Prostitutes

Within the broader power relations of what Hester, Kelly, and Radford (1996) call "hetero-patriarchy," women occupy a range of subordinate positions. When women become wives, partners, and mothers, patriarchal discourse extends to them the role of decent/respectable womanhood. Patriarchal ideology deems that decent/respectable women who "choose" marriage and maternity live out their biological destiny as both the physical and emotional compliments of their husbands, and the producers of children.

The maintenance of images of "ideal" womanhood depends in part upon the construction of "evil" women, or women who, for whatever reason, eschew the "trappings" of marriage and family. Prostitutes constitute one such group of women who adopt a lifestyle where they sell their sexual skills for money. As we shall demonstrate, prostitutes experience tremendous levels of violence, rape, and sexual assault at the hands of men. However, few of these experiences have permeated the research literature on violence and rape. In documenting these levels of victimization, Miller and Schwartz (1995) argue that people often see prostitutes as unrapeable; incapable of being harmed, and "deserving of" being raped. Nanette Davis (1990) cites studies that reveal high levels of victimization reported by prostitutes (Barry, 1981; Edwards, 1984; James & Meyerding, 1978; Hatty, 1989; Hunter, 1989; Millman, 1980). These prostitutes were raped, physically and sexually assaulted, and murdered. Erbe (1984) concluded that more than 70% of the prostitutes in her survey had been the victims of sexual assault. Davis (1990) argues that, "prostitution is an extension of a culture that devalues women and provides unconditional sexual access so that some women are available for purposes of sexual abuse and exploitation" (p. 3).

Violence is first and foremost a reason that many young women "decide" to engage in prostitution. Escaping from homes characterized by high levels of sexual and physical abuse, girls often engage in "survival sex" while on the streets as runaways. Research on teenage prostitutes consistently finds that they are more likely than their male counterparts to have been sexually abused, and they are more likely to use prostitution to survive on the streets (see Chesney-Lind & Shelden, 1992, for a summary of this research).

But why do young women stay in sex work? The answer is linked to the nature of women's work in patriarchal economies, where, contrary to what one might expect, prostitution might be seen as an "outgrowth" of certain types of women's jobs. James (1976), in her work on prostitution in Seattle, cites two studies that connect the employment in "occupations . . . that adhere most closely to the traditional female service role, often emphasizing physical appearance as well as service," to the entrance of women into prostitution (p. 188). Employers often require women employees in service jobs to "flirt with customers and 'be sexy,' " which frequently results in the women finding that the men they must serve at their jobs already consider them to be "no better than a prostitute" (James, 1976, p. 188).

In Hawaii, women were recruited directly out of what might be called bar-related female professions into prostitution. Interviews with women in prison who had a history of prostitution revealed that half were working off and on in these entertainment or bar-related jobs while they were involved in sex work—indicating that these occupations, in themselves, serve as "adjuncts rather than alternatives to female criminal activity" (Chesney-Lind & Rodriguez, 1983, p. 55). Interviews with women prostitutes in both Milwaukee and Hawaii link their decision to prostitute to their survival needs. Women's comments indicated that the most common reason they started working as prostitutes was financial. Prostitution, it is often observed, does not provide women with "easy" money, but it is "fast" money. In the words of one former prostitute, however, "fast money doesn't last" (Kelly Hill, personal communication with Chesney-Lind, April 11, 1996).

Due to the degradation and violence that is so much a part of the street prostitute's life, drug use and addiction often becomes a problem for women involved in prostitution, even for those who were not involved in prostitution to support their drug habits. Chesney-Lind and Rodriguez (1983) found that the need to buy drugs was a factor in women's involvement in theft, burglary, and robbery, for which they were also more likely to be incarcerated than for prostitution. In the interviews with these women, it was obvious that, for most, their entry into prostitution predated their heavy drug use. However, drug dependency, perhaps developed as part of life "in the fast lane," quickly made their exit from the profession unlikely and quite probably encouraged them to seek even more money through burglary and theft (Chesney-Lind & Rodriguez, 1983, p. 57).

What is life like for women engaged in prostitution? Ethnographic fieldwork conducted in the neighborhoods of Chicago (Ouellet, Wiebel, Jimenez, & Johnson, 1993), Harlem (Bourgois & Dunlap, 1993), and New York (Maher & Curtis, 1992; Williams, 1992), as well as interviews with young women in Miami (Inciardi, Lockwood, & Pottieger, 1993), Harlem (Fullilove, Lown, & Fullilove, 1992), and San Francisco (Schwarcz et al., 1992), clearly document the links between a woman's "choice" to engage in prostitution and poverty and racism that surround her as she grows up. The role played by drugs, particularly crack cocaine, in modern prostitution is also important to explore because it clearly facilitates continued sexual and physical violence against women in economically devastated neighborhoods. Finally, the link between the victimization of prostitutes and other forms of women's crime, particularly offenses that sound violent (like robbery), must be briefly explored to challenge racist and sexist notions that women, particularly women of color, are somehow more "violent" today (Baskin, Sommers, & Fagan, 1993).

Three studies of street girls and women conducted in Miami during the years 1985 through 1991 (Inciardi et al., 1993) document the dramatic expansion of the role of crack cocaine in these women's lives. About half (49%) of the women reported "current" use of cocaine in the late 1970s compared to 73% in the early 1980s (Inciardi et al., 1993, p. 113). Bourgois and Dunlap (1993) caution the reader against demonizing such increases, noting that crack cocaine is simply the "latest medium through which the already desperate are expressing publicly their suffering and hopelessness" (p. 98). Research on the impact of different drugs (alcohol, marijuana, and crystal methamphetamine) among Hawaii's women underscores the need to study the situation of people in poverty, not particular drugs (however horrific) (Joe, 1996).

The extensiveness of the violence in girls' and women's lives is dramatically underscored in interviews with women crack users in Harlem, most of whom were African American. This research focused on the lives of 14 women crack users and documented that "trauma was a common occurrence in their lives," which, in turn, propelled the women into drug use (Fullilove et al., 1992, p. 277). These women's lives are full of the chaos and abuse common in neighborhoods of extreme poverty. They are also distressed and depressed at their inability to "maintain culturally defined gender roles" (specifically, functioning as mothers) because of their drug use. Finally, these women are further victimized by the "male-oriented drug culture," which has developed a bizarre and exploitative form of prostitution around women's addiction to crack cocaine.

Specifically, these neighborhoods have seen the development of a "barter system in which sex—rather than money—can be exchanged for drugs." This system feeds on the particular nature of crack usage where the drug is consumed in periodic binges and where "pursuit and use of the drug outweigh other concerns" (Fullilove et al., 1992, p. 276). This pattern of drug use has created the "crack 'ho' "—a prostitute who will trade sex for extremely small amounts of money or drugs—often, but not always, in crack houses generally run by men. Crack addiction, in short, has facilitated the development of a form of prostitution that "may involve participation in bizarre sexual practices for very small amounts of money" and the subsequent "degradation of women within crack culture" (Fullilove et al., 1992, p. 276).

An example of the sort of desperation seen in these neighborhoods is supplied by another Harlem researcher (Bourgois), who reported being stopped by a "high school girl" who grabbed him by the arms in a housing project stairwell, "sobbing hysterically" and begging him, "Please! Please! Let me suck you off for two dollars—I'll swallow it. Please! Please! I promise!" (Bourgois & Dunlap, 1993, p. 102). Likewise, Inciardi

and his associates (1993) observe that women have become the special victims of crack cocaine, and they provide harrowing stories of sex-for-drug exchanges in crack houses. Here, according to the authors, vulnerable and victimized girls and young women trade sex for extremely small amounts of crack (sometimes as little as $3 worth) and, in the process, expose themselves to the risk of AIDS.

These ethnographies leave no doubt that the crack scene has affected street prostitution, long a mainstay in women's survival in marginalized communities. In a study of the impact of crack in three Chicago neighborhoods, it was noted that although "street-level prostitution has probably always had rate cutters" (Ouellet et al., 1993, p. 88), the arrival of crack and the construction of the "crack 'ho' " has created a desperate form of prostitution involving instances of extreme degradation that had previously been seen only in extremely impoverished countries like the Philippines and Thailand (Enloe, 1989; Studervant & Stoltzfus, 1992).

Most women involved in prostitution, even those involved in crack-related prostitution, view their activities as "work" and feel that this work is more ethical and safer than either stealing or drug dealing (Bourgois & Dunlap, 1993, p. 104). According to this perspective, because the crack epidemic has virtually destroyed the economic viability of street prostitution in some neighborhoods, some women might even prefer to go to these houses to get their drugs directly, rather than to risk the dangers of the streets and violence from johns who are even less well known to them than the men in the crack houses.

Not all women addicted to crack choose this path, particularly when times get hard. For this reason, crack has also changed the nature of street prostitution in neighborhoods where it is present. Maher and Curtis's (1992) work on women involved in street-level sex markets in New York, as an example, notes that the introduction of crack cocaine "increased the number of women working the strolls and had a significant impact on the kind of work they did, the remuneration they received and the interactions that occurred in and around street-level sex markets" (p. 21). Maher and Curtis found that women involved in prostitution were also involved in other forms of crime, like shoplifting, stealing from their families, and, occasionally, robbing johns, as a way of surviving on the streets—not because they were seeking some sort of "equality" with male offenders.

In essence, increased competition among women involved in prostitution, plus the deflation in the value of their work, has created a more hostile environment among New York streetwalkers, as well as an increased willingness to rip off johns (see also Ouellet et al., 1993). To understand this, it is important to convey the enormity of the violence that women in sex work are routinely exposed to at the hands of johns. Maher and Curtis (1992) provide many such examples. One women they talked to told them,

> I got shot twice since I bin here . . . was a car pulled up, two guys in it, they was like "C'mon gon on a date." I wouldn't go with that so they came back arund and shot me . . . in the leg and up here. (p. 23)

Here's another:

> I got punched in the mouth not too long ago they [two dates] ripped me off—they wanted their money back after we finished—threw me off the van naked—then hit me with a blackjack 'caus I jumped back on to the van because I wanted to get my clothes. It was freezing outside so I jumped back onto the van to try and get my clothes and he smacked me with a blackjack on my eye. (p. 244)

In fact, some "robbery" becomes much more understandable, when seen up close as it is in this work. Take Candy's story:

> I robbed a guy up here not too long ago—5 o'clock Sunday morning . . . a real cheek gonna tell me $5 for a blow job and that pisses me off—arguing wit them. I don't argue no more—jus get in the car sucker, he open his pants and do like this and I do like this, put my hand, money first. He give me the money I say, "See ya, hate to be ya, next time motherfucker it cost you $5 to get me to come to the window" (Maher & Curtis, 1992, p. 246)

Prostitution is often called the "oldest profession," which is a sad but telling comment about the stability of girls' and women's work—legal and illegal. Many have argued that it is a "victimless" crime because the customers and the prostitute are knowing and willing participants. This section, however, has certainly provided evidence that the phenomenon can set the stage for violence against women, and certainly the prostitute herself sees little of the true profits of her labor. Finally, in part because she sees so little of the money due her, she is tempted to use the role of prostitute to rip off violent and callous johns (Kelly Hill, personal communication with Chesney-Lind, April 11, 1996).

Finally, discussing prostitution and women's violence responsibly is impossible without recognizing the gendered nature of the lives and work of the prostitutes themselves. As we have seen, women involved in drug use, prostitution, and other forms of women's crime, have experienced victimization directly related to their gender in the form of incest, sexual abuse, and rape. Finally, contrary to notions that their "nontraditional" violent offenses—like robbery—signal a change in their orientation toward women's place in male society, their lives demonstrate, if anything, the tragic ways in which gender in marginalized communities works to create and legitimate horrific violence against women labeled as prostitutes.

The Victimization of Imprisoned Women

The number of women imprisoned in the United States tripled during the 1980s, and the 1990s have seen the continued escalation in the number of women behind bars. Even in states like New York that imprison large numbers of women, the number of women in prison jumped sixfold (Craig, 1996b). As a result, on any given day, more than 100,000[6] women are locked up in American jails and prisons[7] (Bureau of Justice Statistics, 1995a, 1995b).

The rate of women's imprisonment is also at a historic high. The rate of women's imprisonment grew from a low of 6 per 100,000 in 1925, to 45 per 100,000 in 1994 (Bureau of Justice Statistics 1995b, p. 6). Taken together, these figures signal a major and largely undiscussed policy change in society's response to women's crime, one that has occurred with virtually no public discussion.

So, as the number of people imprisoned in the United States climbs, our nation has achieved the dubious honor of having the second highest incarceration rate in the world—following the newly formed Russian nation (Mauer, 1994). Who are these women in prison and are they so profoundly dangerous that vast sums must be expended to incarcerate them?

The most recent research on the characteristics of women doing time in state prisons across the country underscores the salience of themes identified earlier in this chapter—particularly the role of sexual and physical violence in the lives of women who come into the criminal justice system. It also argues forcefully for a national discussion of the situation of women in our jails and prisons.

Snell and Morton (1994) surveyed a random sample of women and men ($N = 13,986$) in prisons around the country during 1991 for the Bureau of Justice Statistics. For the first time, a government study asked questions about women's *and* men's experiences of sexual and physical violence as children.

They found, when they asked these questions, that women in prisons have far higher rates of physical and sexual abuse than their male counterparts. Forty-three percent of the women surveyed "reported they had been abused at least once" before their current admission to prison; the comparable figure for men was 12.2% (Snell & Morton, 1994, p. 5). For about a third of all women in prison (31.7%), the abuse started when they were girls, but it continued as they became adults. A key gender difference emerges here. A number of young men who are in prison (10.7%) also report abuse as boys, but this does not continue to adulthood. One in four women reported that their abuse started as adults compared to only 3% of male offenders. Fully 33.5% of the women surveyed reported physical abuse, and a slightly higher number (33.9%) had been sexually abused either as girls or young women, compared to relatively small percentages of men (10% of boys and 5.3% of adult men in prison).

This research also queried women on their relationship with those who abused them. Predictably, both women and men report that parents and relatives contributed to the abuse they suffered as children, but women prisoners are far more likely than their male counterparts to say that domestic violence was a theme in their adult abuse; fully half of the women said they had been abused by a spouse/ex-spouse compared to only 3% of male inmates.

A look at the offenses for which women are incarcerated quickly puts to rest the notion of hyperviolent, nontraditional women criminals. "Nearly half of all women in prison are currently serving a sentence for a non-violent offense and have been convicted in the past of only non-violent offenses" (Snell & Morton, 1994, p. 1). In fact, the number of women in prison for violent offenses, as a proportion of all women offenders, has fallen steadily over the past decades while the number of women in prison soared. In 1979, about half of the women in state prisons were incarcerated for violent crimes (Bureau of Justice Statistics, 1988). By 1986, the number had fallen to 40.7%, and in 1991 it was at 32.2% (Snell & Morton, 1994, p. 3). Essentially, one out of three women in U.S. prisons is there for a violent crime, compared to about one out of every two male prisoners.

Snell and Morton also probed the gendered nature of women's violence that resulted in their imprisonment. They noted that women prisoners were far more likely to kill an intimate or relative (50% compared to 16.3%), whereas men were more likely to kill strangers (50.5% compared to 35.1%). Two New York studies provide further information on the relationship between abuse and women's violence. Examining women committed to the state's prisons for homicide offenses in 1986, the researchers found that 49% of these women had been the victims of abuse at some point in their lives and 59% of the women who killed someone close to them were being abused at the time of the offense. For more than half the women committed for homicide, this was their first and only offense (Huling, 1991, p. 3).

A more recent interview study of 215 women incarcerated in New York prisons for homicide revealed that of the women who killed sexual intimates (one fifth of the total number), two thirds reported that the victims struck them prior to the homicide (Hall, Bronstein, Crimmins, Spunt, & Langley, 1996). Of the women who killed their children (about another fifth of the total group), extremely high levels of physical and sexual abuse as children were noted; 65% of that group of women had suffered physical abuse (an average of 12 or more incidents) and well over half (57%) had suffered sexual abuse (an average of nine or more incidents). The women who killed their children "drew direct connections between their own upbringing and their lack of coping skills," one mother saying,

I was so stressed out and depressed . . . everytime I picked up the baby and she started crying and I said she must hate me . . . I was convinced this child hated me. . . . It was my mother and me all over again. (Hall et al., 1996, p. 7)

Again, though, most women who are increasingly filling U.S. prisons are property or drug offenders. Given the past history of women in prison, it should come as no surprise that drug use, possession, and trafficking[8] are now major themes in women's imprisonment. In 1979, only 10.5% of women in state prisons were serving time for drug offenses. By 1986, the proportion had increased to 12%; but in 1991, nearly a third (32.8%) of all women in state prisons were doing time for drug offenses (Bureau of Justice Statistics, 1988, p. 3; Snell & Morton, 1994, p. 3). Changes in sentencing practices, particularly mandatory sentences for drug and other offenses, often driven by public perceptions that such laws will put "drug king pins" in prison, go a long way in explaining the surge in women's imprisonment.

Thus, with virtually no public discussion or debate, thousands of women offenders are being swept into a system that has a long history of alternatively ignoring and abusing women inmates (see Rafter, 1990). The sexual abuse of women is a particular problem. In 1996, the international organization Human Rights Watch noted that, "in women's prisons across the United States, ill-trained male officers guard female prisoners with little appropriate guidance or oversight regarding sexual misconduct" (Craig, 1996a, p. 1A). Sexual abuse of women inmates at the hands of male guards is as old as women's imprisonment (Beddoe, 1979). Nonetheless, with the soaring increases in women under lock and key in the United States, the sexual victimization of women in U.S. prisons is a problem of growing seriousness. Women prisoners in California, Georgia, Hawaii, Ohio, Louisiana, Michigan, Tennessee, New York, and New Mexico have brought this matter to public attention despite considerable risk to themselves (Craig, 1996a; Curriden, 1993; Lopez, 1993; Meyer, 1992; Sewenely, 1993; Stein, 1996; Watson, 1992). The assumption is increasingly that prisons, here in the United States and elsewhere, are rife with this problem.

Details of these scandals yield the predicable charges and counter-charges, but the storyline remains essentially unchanged; women in prisons, guarded by large numbers of men, are vulnerable. As one advocate for women in prison has noted, "We put [women] into an environment where they're controlled by men and men are willing to put their hands on them whenever they want to" (Craig, 1996a, p. A1). The story that prompted this observation dealt with one of a series of sexual assaults reported by a young woman in a New York Prison:

> Correctional officer Selbourne Reid, 27, came into the cell of a 21-year-old inmate at the maximum security prison in Westchester County. The inmate, at first asleep was startled to find him in her cell. . . . On this night, Reid forced the woman to perform oral sex on him, according to the Westchester County district attorney's office. After he left, she spit the semen into a small bottle in her room. She told prison authorities about the attack, and gave them the semen for DNA analysis. (Craig, 1996a, pp. 1A, 6A)

Other such accounts appear with distressing regularity, and even more disturbing is the fact that so few of the cases, unlike the one reported above, actually go to trial or result in the perpetrators' being found guilty. Institutional subcultures in women's prisons, which encourage correctional workers to "cover" for each other, coupled with inadequate protection accorded women who file complaints, make it unlikely that many women inmates will be able to show the courage of the young woman in New York. Indeed, according to a memo filed by an attorney in the Civil

Rights Division of the U.S. Department of Justice, the Division found "a pattern of sexual abuse by both male and female guards" in Michigan's women's prisons (Patrick, 1995).

Sexual abuse of women in jail is also a serious concern. A judge reviewing the situation of women in Washington, D.C., jails noted that "the evidence revealed a level of sexual harassment which is so malicious that it violates contemporary standards of decency" (Stein, 1996, p. 24). If this is true, why do so few of these cases make it to court? Sadly, some of this involves the histories of women in prison, many of whom have engaged in prostitution, which allow the defendants to access the misogynist defense that it is impossible to rape a prostitute. Beyond this, the public stereotype of women in prison as "bad girls" means that any victim must first battle this perception before her own case can be fairly heard. Finally, what little progress has been made is severely threatened by recent legislation that has drastically curtailed the ability of prisoners and advocates to sue about prison conditions (Stein, 1996, p. 24)—changes again likely motivated by public perceptions of prisoners as violent males.

Other routine correctional practices such as strip searches (sometimes involving body cavity searches) have also produced problems. In New York prisons, as a response to complaints by male inmates that strip searches were often accompanied by beatings, video monitors (usually mounted on the wall) were installed in areas where searches occurred. When the women's prison (Albion Correctional Center) also began to tape the women's strip searches, though, fixed cameras were replaced by handheld cameras (Craig, 1995, p. 1A).

Fifteen women prisoners incarcerated at Albion filed complaints based on their experiences with strip searches. Specifically, they said that doors to the search area were occasionally kept open, that male guards were sometimes seen outside the doors watching the searches, and that unlike the male videos that surveyed the whole room where the searches occurred, according to the women's lawyer, "these videotapes were solely focused on the woman. That amplified the pornographic effect of it" (Craig, 1996a, p. 1A). Said one woman who was searched while men were "right outside a door and could see the whole incident, 'I knew they was watching . . . I was so humiliated . . . I felt like I was on display. I felt like a piece of meat' " (Craig, 1996a, p. A6). Advocates for the women also stressed the traumatic effect of such searches given the histories of sexual abuse and assault that many women bring with them to prison.

Beyond this, the women inmates suspected that prison officials were viewing the tapes, and eventually filed complaints to stop routine videotaping of women prisoners. In addition to receiving over $60,000 in damages, the women were able to change the policy of routine videotaping of women's searches. As a result of their complaints, "a female inmate would be filmed only if officers believed she would resist the search" (Craig, 1996a, p. A6). Presently, very few searches of women inmates are being videotaped in New York, but the possibility of abuse is present in virtually all prisons.

Even without videotaping and other possible abuses, strip searches have quite different meanings for women and men. As an example, a key point made by the Albion women was that given the high levels of previous sexual abuse among women inmates, such searches had the possibility of being extremely traumatic. In fact, similar concerns have also surfaced in a Task Force Report to the Massachusetts Department of Health about the use of "restraint and seclusion" among psychiatric patients who have histories of sexual abuse (Carmen et al., 1996).

It also appears that women in prison are "overpoliced" and overcontrolled in other ways. As an example, McClellan (1994) examined disciplinary practices at male and female prisons in Texas. Utilizing Texas Department of Corrections records, McClellan constructed two samples of inmates (271 males and 245 females) and followed them for a 1-year period (1989). She documented that although most men in her sample (63.5%) had no citation or only one citation for a rule violation, only 17.1% of the women in her sample had such records. Women prisoners were much more likely to receive numerous citations, and for different sorts of offenses then men. Most commonly, women were cited for "violating posted rules" while males were cited most frequently for "refusing to work" (McClellan, 1994, p. 77). Finally, women were more likely than men to receive the most severe sanctions, including solitary confinement (McClellan, 1994, p. 82).

Her review of the details of women's infractions subsumed under the category "violation of posted rules" includes such offenses as "excessive artwork ('too many family photographs on display'), failing to eat all the food on their plates, and for talking while waiting in the pill line" (McClellan, 1994, p. 85). Possession of contraband could include such things as an extra bra or pillowcase, peppermint sticks, or a properly borrowed comb or hat. Finally, "trafficking" and "trading," included instances of sharing shampoo in a shower and lighting another inmate's cigarette (McClellan, 1994, p. 85).

The author concludes by observing that there exist "two distinct institutional forms of surveillance and control operating at the male and female facilities . . . this policy not only imposes extreme constraints on adult women but also costs the people of the State of Texas a great deal of money" (McClellan, 1994, p. 87). Research like this provides clear evidence that women in prison are overpoliced and overcontrolled in institutional settings—a finding earlier researchers have noted as well (see Burkhart, 1973; Mann, 1984).

What is clear from all these accounts is that women in modern prisons may be subjected to what might be called the "worst of both worlds." If McClellan's findings can be extended to other states, women in modern prisons continue to be overpoliced and overcontrolled (a feature of the separate spheres legacy of women's imprisonment). At the same time, they are also the recipients of a form of equity with a vengeance that results in abuses that are likely unparalleled in male institutions (sexual exploitation at the hands of guards and degrading strip searches). Beyond this, correctional leaders are, in some cases, implementing grossly inappropriate and clearly male-modeled interventions such as chain gangs and even boot camps to deal with women's offending (Kim, 1996; MacKenzie, Elis, Simpson, & Skroban, 1994). Proclaiming his department "an equal opportunity incarcerator," an Arizona sheriff has started a chain gang for women "now locked up with three or four others in dank, cramped disciplinary cells" (Kim, 1996, p. 1A). To escape these conditions, the women can "volunteer" for the 15-woman chain gang. Defending his controversial move, the sheriff commented, "If women can fight for their country, and bless them for that, if they can walk a beat, if they can protect the people and arrest violators of the law, then they should have no problem with picking up trash in 120-degrees" (Kim, 1996, p. 1A). In the few TV and print media stories on women in chain gangs, women are reported as having mixed reasons for "participating." On balance, it seems that women's willingness to participate stems largely from the conditions of the disciplinary cells rather than any great desire to venture into the great outdoors.

The enormous and rapid increase in women's imprisonment has clearly exposed tens of thousands of women, many of whom have extensive histories of abuse, to further abuse at the hands of a system designed with male offenders in mind and staffed by poorly trained correctional officers. The silence about women's victimization, particularly the violence in the lives of economically marginalized women of color, means that they are forced to survive in ways that bring them into the criminal justice system. Once there, they are further punished by a system whose very structure facilitates further abuse.

Toward a Diverse and Inclusive Understanding
of Doing Violence to Women

We began by highlighting the worldwide nature of violence against women and framing that violence as part the structure of hetero-patriarchy. It is not our argument that hetero-patriarchy takes the same form in all cultures. Rather, we have tried to show how men use violence against women in different cultural settings and social situations. Nevertheless, male violence against women is both a reflection of their sociopolitical domination over women, and, at the same time, yet another way of establishing control, maintaining it, or both. To make sense of male violence against women, then, is to grasp the limited social, political, and economic opportunities available to women. Women do not enjoy or invite male violence. They are not responsible for that violence and they are not susceptible to it because of certain psychological frailties. Rather, the constellation of disadvantaged situations women live out expose them to violence at the hands of men.

The structure of hetero-patriarchy results in women being controlled in a number of ways. Not all men have to commit violence against women to enjoy the fruits of social superiority. Women's employment opportunities are more limited than those of men; they perform more hidden, undervalued, and unpaid labor; and they are culturally channeled by the ideology of pornography, being depicted as the objects of male desire, rather than human subjects in their own right.[9] Violence is but one mechanism in the arsenal of patriarchal control mechanisms. It is a powerful mechanism, however, and as we have shown in our discussion of lethal violence, it is a chilling mechanism of last resort.

We have argued for a diverse and inclusive understanding of men's violence against women. It is crucial to frame the lethal and nonlethal violence against women by men they know alongside the killing and brutalization of women by men who are strangers. The murder of Glenda Greer with a 12-gauge shotgun by her soon-to-be-divorced husband, Shannon, is part of a mosaic of murder that includes the loss of the 14 women in the Montreal Gynocide and the serial killing of prostitutes. Likewise, rape within marriage is conceptually continuous with the much less common rape by predatory strangers and the very common sexual harassment of women in the workplace. The fact that rape is most common between those in intimate relationships tells us something about "intimacy" under patriarchy. Various forms of violence against women coalesce in the mass murder and rape of women in Serb-occupied Bosnia-

Hercegovina and Croatia. Rather than understanding this mass rape and murder as simply a "by-product" of war, we emphasize that these atrocities are part of a worldwide war against women. Though not all men are front-line soldiers in this war, all men do occupy a different political territory than women.

Due to the tendency to fragment the literature on violence against women, some victims of male violence have received more attention than others. Feminists and others successfully confronted the myth that women are only at threat from predatory men they do not know. As noted, we now have a much better sense of the interpersonal victimization of women. However, violence against certain groups of women has not received due attention. In our "inclusive" approach we report the victimization of sex workers and argue for the recognition of the continuities between their victimization and the brutalization of other women. Sex workers, like married women prior to the passage of marital rape laws, are indeed "rapeable." If we do not include women such as sex workers, we run the risk of ignoring violence against some of the most profoundly victimized women in the patriarchal regime.

Our fluid and diverse analysis of violence against women, and our framing of that violence as just one weapon in the patriarchal arsenal, might appear to present patriarchy, to borrow the Weberian phrase, as an "iron cage." This is not our intent. As we also pointed out, women sometimes resort to violence themselves. Our discussion of the incarceration of women and the abuse women inmates endure shows yet another face of violence against women. The patriarchal state has a long history of not taking violence against women seriously when passing laws on divorce, child custody, and marital rape. We argue strongly that the state, and often its individual male personnel, actively revictimize women in prison. If ever there was an "iron cage" of patriarchy, the women's prison is it. Incarcerating women for killing their spouses who abused them for years is to reproduce the oppressive patriarchal dynamic from whence these women came. The miserable conditions of women in prison and the harassment and abuse they endure there, is, for us, in many ways the ultimate victimization because it punishes many women for their resistance and courage in the face of grave desperation.

Notes

1. See, for example, Edgell (1980) for an analysis of decision making in middle-class families and the way in which husbands make most of the "important" decisions with only minor input from wives. No important decisions were made by wives alone.

2. Marzuk refers to the research of Allen (1983), Berman (1979), and Dorpat (1966) to support his argument.

3. Studies cited in support of a prior history of domestic violence include Rosenbaum (1990) and West (1967).

4. As Jane Caputi (1993) points out, there are a couple of notable exceptions to the argument that serial killers generally victimize the most disadvantaged women. Both Ted Bundy and David Berkowitz (Son of Sam) "chose victims on the basis of their correspondence to a pornographic, objectifying, and racist ideal" (p. 19).

5. Russell's analysis of "completed rape" yields a higher proportion of strangers among the ranks of rapists. Twelve percent of all completed rapes were reportedly committed by strangers, 23% were committed by husbands and ex-husbands, 17% by acquaintances, and 15% by lovers or ex-lovers (see Russell, 1990, p. 65, table 5-1).

6. According to federal statistics, during 1994, 64,403 women were held in state and federal correctional facilities, and the "average daily population" of U.S. jails included 48,894 adult women.

7. This figure is up from 35,400 in 1984 (Maguire & Pastore, 1994, pp. 591, 600).

8. Although drug trafficking sounds serious, often women who serve as drug mules are coerced or threatened into such roles by abusive boyfriends or husbands. In some instances, women from impoverished, Third World countries are forced by threats to their families into carrying drugs (Huling, 1996).

9. For a good discussion of the nature of patriarchy, see the work of realist feminist Sylvia Walby (1990, 1992).

5

Ladykillers

Similarities and Divergences
of Masculinities in Gang Rape and Wife Battery

CHRIS O'SULLIVAN

A neighbor in Queens described Fitzroy Morris, a 30-year-old employee of Mama's Mini Mart:

> He would get dressed up Friday nights and get excited to go to clubs and meet girls. He liked to go out and try to pick up ladies. He couldn't pick them up. He would go to clubs and try to seduce them. (Cooper, 1996, p. B3)

This would-be ladykiller was arrested on New Years Day, 1997. Two young women he had accompanied to a hip-hop club earlier in the week had been reported missing. The 23-year-old woman was dead and her 21-year-old friend was near death when they were found inside the closed mini-mart. The woman who survived the bludgeoning was wearing his jacket; the woman who died from the hammer attack was naked. Brooklyn police were also seeking him for raping his ex-wife in July.

Women, as are men, are most likely to be assaulted and raped by men. In fact, men kill other men more often than they kill women, but the disturbing reality for women is that the assault often includes sexual abuse and that the greatest risk of violence comes from their intimate partners: husbands and ex-husbands, lovers, boyfriends, and fathers of their children; their own fathers, brothers, uncles, and stepfathers; their mentors, pals, dates, and acquaintances. Obviously, masculinity is related to violence and has a special relationship to violence against women. But do different forms of violence against women relate to masculinity in different ways?

Gang Rape and Masculinity; Domestic Violence and Masculinity: Separate Spheres of Research and Intervention

For 8 years, I studied campus gang rapes. This research began with a long trial of seven Michigan State men charged with raping a young female student in 1984 (they were acquitted). It continued with the 1989 trial of five Kentucky State football players charged with raping an older female student (they were acquitted). Reactions of many students and not a few faculty and administrators were notably victim-blaming and perpetrator-exonerating.[1] There was little on gang rape in the library except outdated Freudian studies that discussed the victims' wish fulfillment— Peggy Sanday's (1992) Fraternity Gang Rape, would not be out for years. Informal surveys of classes revealed that gang rape was a significant phenomenon in students' lives, with its own lexicon ("trains" and "Amtrak" and more). More intensive research revealed a dominant "fraternal culture" on campus, centered in men's residences (fraternity houses and athletic residences), which was the source of this form of woman abuse.

In 1993, when I presented the resulting theory of gang rape to clinicians in a workshop at a family violence clinic, we stunned each other: The fulfillment of the exigencies of masculinity through gang rape clearly differed from the expression of masculinity through wife beating. The prescription for preventing group sexual abuse was the opposite of the prescription for preventing battering. On the one hand, there are the perils of "male bonding," the dangers that cohesive groups of young men pose to young women. Forming a close, respectful, committed relationship with one woman seems to liberate a gang rapist from the exigencies of his fraternal group. In contrast, batterers, according to the family violence therapists, are obsessively attached to one woman whom they expect to meet all their needs, and they have trouble relating openly to other men. The prescription for batterers was to break them loose from exclusive dependency on their partners and from social isolation by developing friendships with other men; hence the group treatment format that is nearly universally adopted with batterers. The goal for batterers was to foster male group cohesiveness, and the goal for potential gang rapists was to discourage it.

This chapter will explore the apparent difference between gang rape and wife beating and attempt to answer the following questions. Are gang rapists and wife beaters the same men? If not, are they different personalities responding to a singular "masculinity"—the same socialization processes, patriarchal values, and social tolerance for male violence? Or do these forms of abuse spring from different "masculinities"? Even though both seem to be expressions of male superiority and patriarchy, isn't there a significant difference between men who abuse women they "love" and men who abuse women they hardly know? Or is the fundamental difference not the relationship with the victims, but their relationships with other men?

A first step to answering these questions is to delineate the roles of male socialization and patriarchal conceptions of sex, gender, and power as they relate to each behavior.

Gang Rape and Fraternal Culture

The *structural element* of the gang-raping fraternal culture is a high-prestige, exclusively male group (O'Sullivan, 1991, 1993). Usually, they share a space—a residence hall, apartment, hotel room, or even a workplace—that provides a private group territory for sexual exploitation of women who venture onto their turf. The activity that brings them together is tied to their male identity; one can belong to the group only if one is biologically male. Compared to their reference group, they are the elite. Groups that have these structural characteristics and among whom I have documented gang rapes[2] are the following: athletic teams; fraternities, especially wealthier or more prestigious ones; rock groups, and other male groups "on the road" together; street gangs (see Hunter Thompson, 1971); police officers; and soldiers (e.g., Lang, 1969). Membership in these groups is difficult to achieve (it frequently involves hazing, as well as particular attributes, such as skill, money, or brutality) and the group is successful, or enjoys status in the community. It is the athletes on national championship teams, the members of exclusive fraternities, conquering soldiers or occupying forces, and powerful street gangs that are most likely to gang rape.

The *ideological elements* of gang rape are

- a view of women as "other," essentially different beings, who threaten the cohesiveness of the male group;

- the designation of men who are tender, protective, or respectful of women as "sissies" or "pussywhipped"[3];
- a sense of entitlement due to the group's prestige that condones lawlessness, akin to groupthink (Janis, 1982)[4];
- a traditional conceptualization of sex roles and sexuality, under which women are supposed to be sexual gatekeepers who do not enjoy sex, and women who do not conform to these notions are fair game for exploitation (the virgin/whore dichotomy)[5];
- sex as dirty and demeaning, especially to the person on the bottom,[6] and
- homophobia and a need to establish masculinity through sex with women but without intimacy with women.[7]

Some of the *socialization factors* that foster gang rape, including both childhood socialization and socialization to the group (i.e., induction and indoctrination practices), are

- boys' friendships are centered on group activities rather than sharing intimacies in pairs;
- there is competition and cooperation among the group members;
- in particular, there is competition over "outrageous" behavior, such as risky and/or antisocial acts, to establish a valued identity (fearless and fearsome) within the group[8];
- hazing is common although not universal; it is advocated by group members as giving them real loyalty to the group and fostering their "rebirth" with a new identity and acceptance as a brother[9];
- cultural practices of misogyny, such as songs and jokes glorifying sexual violence[10];
- sharing in each other's heterosexuality, the bachelor party motif of one sexually available woman (but nonperson) and many men. Mechanisms include "mandatory" reporting of sexual experiences to the group (e.g., in Little League [Fine, 1987], fraternities [Scott Straus, 1996[11]], and locker rooms [Curry, 1991]); "voyeuring"—watching other men have sex;[12] and videotaping sexual liaisons ("Two Guilty in Video-Rape," 1992), usually without the victim's knowledge[13]

These practices serve to enhance the value of membership in the group, increase commitment, and keep women outside. The shared heterosexuality and the misogynist "humor" protect the group against "loss" of a member to a woman. As Scott Straus (1996) describes it, the process of transformation from pledge to brother, "becoming men," lay in "demonstrating heterosexual prowess, hatred for women, and loyalty to the fraternity. This was a foolproof recipe for raping women" (p. 26). From a Dartmouth fraternity to the streets of a Southern African American neighborhood, the message is the same: "The old-heads said there was no place for love in a *real* man's life. The pursuit of women was a macho game. The object was to 'get the pussy' without giving love. . . . If he fell for a babe, developed feelings for her, he lost" (McCall, 1994, p. 40).

Wife Beaters

The characteristics of batterers are described by Ellen Pence and Michael Paymar (1993), who developed the prevailing curriculum ("the Duluth model") in consultation with some of the early experts in the field, Barbara Hart, Susan Schechter, and Michael Adams. The premise of this model is that battering is an outgrowth of patriarchy, based in batterers' belief in male supremacy as the natural order.

The batterer's violence is a means of power and control, but it is only one of a constellation of methods men use to maintain dominance over their wives. Other methods include economic abuse (taking her money or not allowing her to earn money; giving her an allowance; making her account for every penny she spends);[14] emotional abuse (humiliating and verbally abusing her); threats and coercion (threatening suicide, making her engage in illegal activities, sexual coercion); social isolation (controlling whom she sees and talks to, where she goes, limiting her contact with her family); intimidation (destroying her property, hitting walls instead of her, giving her looks that threaten violence); and "using male privilege" (defining roles, making major decisions, treating her like a servant). To the outside world, they may present a face of the model family, hiding the violence. Some battered women say that the psychological abuse is more incapacitating than the physical violence; they are trapped and demoralized. Three women's stories from a focus group I conducted with current and former members of a support group for residents of domestic violence shelters represent a range of experiences:

One young woman had literally been a captive. When her husband found out that she was applying to college, he locked her in the house for 3 weeks, without a key or telephone. She finally left him after another confrontation in which he broke her arm. She declared that she was determined to separate from him permanently but still had to struggle against impulses to return to him. For example, when he threatened suicide, she was tempted to try to save him.

Another woman had left her husband a year before. During her marriage, she held a full-time job but her husband frequently abused her—psychologically and physically, in ways that didn't show—for her "imperfections." They were both very active in a church, and she sought help from their minister. Her husband was a pillar of the community, though: active, upstanding, and decent. She maintained that he was crazy, but she was the one who appeared crazy. The minister and the congregation supported her husband. After 9 years of calling a domestic violence hot line, she finally left him and the church.

A third woman sought shelter with her three children after her husband came in at 4 a.m., drunk with a bunch of drunk friends, and ordered her to get up and cook them dinner. She refused and he beat her. The other men supported him. She was planning to return to her husband, though. The main reason was that her teenage daughter was very unhappy at the shelter and she didn't know where else to go. Her husband promised that he would do all the cooking and housework if she would come home.

The following are common characteristics of batterers, distilled from quantitative research, primarily Saunders, Lynch, Grayson, and Linz (1987), who developed the Attitudes Toward Wife-Beating Scale that discriminated between batterers and college students, and my own (O'Sullivan, 1996, which used the scale), as well as my observations and interactions with batterers:

- "excessive" jealousy, which makes them suspicious of their wives and any possible interactions with other men[15];
- victim-blaming and denial of their violence; they believe that *they* are the real victims and have no sense of agency about the violence they inflict[16];
- a belief that sexual infidelity in men is acceptable, even necessary, but must be punished in women, and that their wives must be sexually available to them at all times;
- a belief that women, especially their wives, are incompetent and infantile, as well as manipulative and deceitful;
- a belief that they are entitled to respect as men, and that disrespect for their "manhood" must be punished[17];
- the belief that they are entitled to "discipline" or retaliate physically against their wives who violate their "rules" or disappoint their expectations;
- a belief that they might have an anger problem and sometimes "lose control"

In the first national survey on family violence of a representative sample of married couples, Straus, Gelles, and Steinmetz (1981) found a strong correlation between violence and nondemocratic decision making. "Wife-beating is much more common in homes where power is concentrated in the hands of the husband. The least amount of battering occurs in democratic households" (pp. 192-193). Having children increases the likelihood of battering, and men are particularly likely to beat their wives when they are pregnant. Straus et al. (1981) attribute battering during pregnancy to the woman's sexual unavailability due to mistaken beliefs that sex is unsafe, to the fear of responsibility, and to the loss of the woman's sole attention, but comments that men make when they batter their pregnant wives (accusations that they are fat and disgusting) suggest that they are angered by their partner's temporary failure to meet their "need" to have a shapely, "desirable" wife.

The national survey of married couples also found socioeconomic correlates of domestic violence: Stress was correlated with battering only in families with incomes of $20,000 or less. Violence was more common if the husband was unemployed or employed part-time. The relationship between violence and education had a bimodal distribution: The most violent men had completed high school; the least violent men had either dropped out of grammar school or completed college. Bowker (1983) suggested that men with low incomes have difficulty maintaining dominance in the family and are therefore more likely to resort to violence to establish control that they cannot exert through money and concomitant resources.

Yllo conducted a study looking at patriarchal norms or beliefs, actual inequality in the family, and women's status in the state. She found a correlation between patriarchal beliefs and wife-battery, but, unlike Straus et al.'s (1981) national survey, she did not find a correlation between actual structural inequality in the family and battery (Yllo & Straus, 1984). The relationship between support for male dominance in the family and battery was strongest in states in which women had the highest status; apparently, there is more conflict when patriarchal norms for dominance in the family are strong but women enjoy more power in society.

To test the patriarchal hypothesis and the links with social class, Michael Smith (1990) conducted a random telephone survey in Toronto, assessing (a) severity of wife beating; (b) husband's support for male dominance in marriage and for violence against women who violate norms (obedience, loyalty, respect, dependency, sexual access, sexual fidelity); and (c) socioeconomic variables. Both patriarchal beliefs and approval of violence were strongly, and independently, associated with wife beating. Low-income men in low-status jobs were more likely to subscribe to patriarchal beliefs and to beat their wives. This finding is consistent with Bowker's theory of a "patriarchal subculture" of lower-income men who share and reinforce a belief in the necessity of keeping women in line to maintain male dominance.

Convergence and Divergence Between Gang Rapists and Wife Beaters

Similarities between gang rapists and batterers include general beliefs in male supremacy, hostility toward women, and different standards for sexual behavior in men and women. A salient difference is that batterers appear to be tightly bound to one woman while gang rapists avoid such connections. But all the themes come together around *football*.

Football as the Common Ground

Football players are particularly prone to gang rape on campus (a quarter of the 48 cases of gang rape by college students from 1983 to 1993 that I was able to document were committed by football players; this is highly disproportionate to their numbers on campus); to solo rape (Hofmann, 1986a, 1986b); and to assaults on women and men. Jeffrey Benedict (1996), who is writing a book on criminality and the NCAA, cites a 1994 study of 10 Division 1 schools with "powerhouse" football and basketball teams that found that basketball and football players were responsible for 19% of the sexual assaults and 35% of the "acts of domestic violence" although they constituted only 3% of the male student body. There is also indirect evidence that football *fans,* too, are particularly prone to assault their wives and girlfriends in the aftermath of games (White, Katz, & Scarborough, 1992). On closer examination, however, the patterns of and explanations for these violent behaviors are somewhat different.

The general assaultiveness of football players—their propensity for violence against other men, girlfriends, acquaintances, and property—is usually attributed to the rewards they receive for violence on the field and the training they get to be "animals," insensitive to their own and others' pain (Sabo, 1989).

Some football players are generally criminal, however, robbing and dealing drugs, owning guns, as well as assaulting and raping. The Sooners, the Heisman Trophy and Bowl-winning football team of the University of Oklahoma, are illustrative. In one month, February 1989, police made three trips to the athletic dorm where the Sooners reigned: first, a player was arrested for shooting and wounding a teammate in the dorm; 8 days later, three players were arrested for gang-raping a young woman visiting the dorm on a blind date; 5 days later, a starting quarterback was arrested for selling cocaine. The previous week, the cocaine-dealing quarterback had lectured to elementary school students about the evils of drugs; during the summer, he had been charged with petty larceny and assault and battery. One of the gang rapists was the subject of a rape complaint 3 years before. Subsequently, he was dismissed from the team for stealing from his teammates, but he was later reinstated when they needed a tight end. Another of the alleged gang rapists had had a previous gang-rape charge filed against him. The third was arrested for drug trafficking while out on bond. Players reported that a group of men having sex with one woman was a common event in the athletic dorm (Telender & Sullivan, 1989;[18] Clay, 1991)

Criminality in some football players is often explained in ways that covertly refer to class and race differences among young men recruited to play for colleges because of their athletic prowess and the student body in general: that they are alienated from and lack understanding of the middle-class campus milieu, that they grew up in fatherless homes (Benedict, 1996), and grew up poor and without love.[19] In addition, data showing the higher rape rate of athletes are often contested as resulting from racism and the high visibility of star athletes.[20] More to the point is the fact that boys who grow up with a great deal of exposure to violence— at home, on the streets, in school—are more likely to be violent as adults, including beating their wives (Fagan, Stewart, & Hansen, 1983). A poor child is more likely to witness violence than a middle-class child and, because of racism, children of color are disproportionately likely to grow up in poverty.

As wife beaters and solitary rapists, college and professional football players may belong to the category of "generally violent" or "antisocial" batterers (Holtzworth-Munroe & Stuart, 1994; Saunders, 1992). There is a growing belief among domestic violence researchers that there are different *types* of batterers, with different psychological and social profiles and different patterns of violence (see Gondolf, 1988). Minimally, there is a distinction between "family-only" (Saunders, 1992) or "typical" (Holtzworth-Munroe & Stuart, 1994) abusers and "generally violent" (Fagan et al., 1983; Saunders, 1992) men.

A limitation in the utility of the distinction between family-only and generally violent batterers is that the lack of gender consciousness in regard to men has obscured potentially important differentiations between the types. Specifically, when researchers present data on wife abusers who are "generally violent," they do not draw a distinction between violence against men outside the family and violence against women outside the family. In fact, in the cluster analysis Saunders (1992) performed to substantiate a typology, men who abused people outside the family so frequently also abused their parents and siblings that these three items (assaults on strangers, parents, and siblings) were collapsed and termed "general violence." Consequently, violence toward a member of the family of origin is collapsed into general violence rather than family violence. No distinction was made between assaults on fathers versus mothers, or brothers versus sisters. Given the chauvinism that affects analysis and language, when gender isn't specified, it usually means "male" (O'Sullivan & Heinz, 1991). Thus, it is probably safe to assume that "generally violent" means violent against *men* inside and outside the family, analogously to the masculine generic.

It is also not clear whether "family-only" batterers abuse their children as well as their wives (Saunders didn't ask about child abuse when collecting the data). Therefore, with further refinement and clarification, it may turn out that "family-only" batterers abuse only women with whom they are intimate *or* only their female partners and their children; and "generally violent" batterers may abuse women and men in their families, as well as women and men who are acquaintances or strangers. Without this information, it is difficult to categorize Fitzroy Morris, who battered only women he knew, though not necessarily in his "family." Perhaps he wasn't "generally violent" because he didn't abuse men.

In any case, generally violent batterers are especially likely to have been exposed to violence in childhood, whether through experiencing child abuse or witnessing violence against their mothers (Fagan et al., 1993; Saunders, 1992).

Some football players may then be categorized as "generally violent," committing violence against wives and girlfriends, raping women acquaintances, and gang-raping women, but also violently assaulting other men. They are socialized to violence, many through childhood exposure to violence, as well as through the training for violence in their sport. The sports milieu is also classically antifeminine. Stories abound of locker room misogyny, such as coaches putting sanitary napkins in players' lockers to get them to play harder, and the fact that the ultimate insult is that they are playing like women (see Miedzian, 1992; Nelson, 1994).

While their general violence may be a contributing factor to gang rape participation by football players, the common feature of campus gang rapists is membership in a high-prestige male group, not necessarily one that plays a violent sport: 35% of the 48 campus gang rapes in my data set were committed by fraternity men. Men who play nonviolent team sports are also likely to gang rape—especially if the team is national championship material: 15% were committed by basketball players, and others were committed by lacrosse, baseball, and hockey teammates.

Gang rapes by men who participate in *individual* violent sports are rare. Interestingly, in looking for cases of gang rape by wrestlers and boxers, I found instead cases of wrestlers sexually assaulting other men, including a postmatch rape of a defeated opponent, a sort of triumph of dominance, and two cases of group sexual abuse of weak teammates (Jaeger, 1992; "Town Split," 1992). Among boxers, I found examples of individual rape, nonsexual abuse of women, and nonsexual violence against men. There was one case of a brutal group sexual and physical assault of a woman by a boxer and his entourage. (Only the postmatch rape was by a college athlete; the group assaults on wrestling teammates were by high school students; and the boxer who participated in a gang rape led by a member of his entourage was a successful professional.)

Therefore, although football players are especially likely to engage in gang rape, solo rape, or woman abuse, and although there may be similar contributing factors to these three forms of violence against women, the primary explanation for the influence of masculinity on gang rape extends beyond the violent sport, encompassing other men. Just as the "typical batterer" is not generally violent (Holtzworth-Munroe & Stuart, 1994), so the "typical gang rapist" is not generally violent (note that "typical" does not necessarily mean statistically most prevalent: Most batterers who are arrested or whose victims seek services are "generally violent" [Fagan et al. 1983]. However, that sampling is biased because generally violent batterers inflict more severe injuries on their wives than family-only batterers [Saunders, 1992], and their victims are therefore more likely to report them and seek services.)

Fans present an interesting case, as revealed by an epidemiological study by White, Katz, and Scarborough (1994). Emergency room admissions for injuries due to severe violence (gunshot wounds, stabbings, and assaults) in Northern Virginia increased for women following a Washington Redskin's *victory,* and increased for men following a *loss.* This pattern suggests that the masculinity fostering violence against women is different from the motivations for violence against men As with gang rape, it appears that woman abuse by fans is part of a glorying in male superiority, entitlement, and dominance, but violence against men is more compensatory for damaged masculinity.

Essential Differences Between Gang Rape and Wife Beating

Gang rape and wife beating are both forms of woman abuse. What is the essential difference—that one is (ostensibly) sexual and the other not? That one is a group activity and the other solitary, hence one is a public performance of masculinity and the other a private one? Or that the gang rapist's target for abuse is an acquaintance (not wife-, or even date-, material) while the batterer targets an intimate partner? All the above?

1. *Are gang rape and wife beating essentially different forms of male violence against women because gang rape is sexual abuse and wife beating isn't?*
The distinction between wife beating and sexual abuse is specious in that batterers often engage in sexual abuse of their wives, including rape and humiliation (see McCloskey, Figueredo, & Koss, 1995; they also note that daughters of battered women are particularly at risk of sexual abuse by their fathers or stepfathers, and suggest that this abuse is motivated by the desire to harm the mother). At the initial meeting of a batterers group, I heard a skilled facilitator deal with the men's resistance. Although all the men in this group had been mandated to the group by criminal court, they vociferously denied having committed any act of violence the facilitator brought up, including sexual assault and coercion. Then he asked if they had ever had sex with their wives, over her objections, with the door open so that the children could hear. Suddenly, there was silence, then mumbling rationalizations.

If wife abuse is often sexual, conversely, gang rape is often asexual, or at least not erotic. It is the use of sexuality to conquer, show off, and bond, but the men often don't ejaculate and often use objects to penetrate the woman (because they aren't sexually aroused, and because of the added humiliation).[21] Thus, gang rapists and wife beaters have in common the use of sex to demean women. They have a preference for sexual activities that the women find painful or humiliating, or that seem so to the men. Anal intercourse, for example, is frequently recounted by victims of both forms of abuse. Underlying this similarity may be the view that "getting over" on women sexually is a particularly "masculine" act of interpersonal dominance. A common ground of batterers and gang rapists is that hostility toward women is conceived of as an attribute of masculinity. Machismo is attributed to a brutal sort of heterosexuality, and disinterest in sexual aggression is regarded as evidence of homosexuality. When Jackson Katz spoke at Bucknell University as the "Feminist Fullback" against rape, he was indirectly questioned about his sexual orientation by one of the resentful athletes required to attend his lecture. The assumption behind this frequently offered attribution for his opposition to rape seems to be that anyone who likes women wants to rape them, or that a man who opposes rape must not love women. Apparently, real (heterosexual) men rape, or want to. For batterers, hostility toward women is not so specifically sexual; it is more generalized although it may be expressed sexually. Saunders (1992) reports that batterers do not score high on the "Burt scales," which include a measure of adversarial sexual attitudes, but campus rapists do (Burt, 1991).

2. *Is the essential difference between gang rape and wife beating that one is a male group activity and the other is solitary?—that one is public, the other private?*

This question harks back to the issue raised by the family violence therapists—that batterers are socially isolated and overly dependent on their wives for emotional connection, social needs, and self-esteem. Their relationships with other men are relatively reserved and limited. Like authoritarian personalities, they are disdainful and rigid toward those beneath them in the social hierarchy (women and children) but defer to those they see as having more power. Dependency on women can be ameliorated by connecting with other men more comfortably. Gang-rapists are virtually the opposite: they are overly dependent on other men for social, emotional, and self-esteem needs. Their relationships with women are distant and fearful.[22] In fact, some men participate in gang rapes to please the instigator. Groth (1979) suggested that gang rapists are emotionally dependent on the leader.

The treatment providers' goal of breaking down the social isolation of batterers from other men is qualified. Batterers group facilitators are usually aware that they tread a fine line between helping the men to develop healthy relationships with other men versus providing the opportunity for batterers to coalesce around their common "persecution."[23] The intent of the group treatment is that friendships in the group can take pressure off the marital relationship, call the batterer to honesty, and support efforts to change. Creating a cohesive group, however, can also provide support to each batterer for his abusiveness, victim blaming, denial, and self-perception of victimization. Batterers intervention programs can backfire if the wrong sort of male "bonding" occurs.[24] This may explain Harrell's (1991) surprising finding that men who completed a program were more likely than men who did not attend a batterers group to recidivate. Furthermore, this contrast is qualified by the heterogeneity of batterers. Not all batterers are socially isolated. Rather, some receive support from other men for beating their wives. According to Smith (1990) and to Bowker (1983), this may be particularly true of working-class batterers, who share traditional patriarchal conceptions of family roles, and a greater acceptance of violence, than more educated men. In the three stories from the battered women's support group recounted above, one of the husbands beat his wife in front of his friends and received support for it, but the other two husbands (both businessmen) hid their violence, which would have socially stigmatized them.

It seems, then, that some batterers may be like gang rapists in that they believe in male superiority and receive social support from other men for abusing their wives, while other batterers present a different face to other men, in part trying to impress them with their perfect (nonviolent) families. For the latter, battering is private. Group sexual abuse, though, is always public, and it is not only among working-class men with patriarchal norms that it is socially acceptable. Pi Kappa Alpha, an elite Southern fraternity, is associated with more gang rapes in my data set than any other brotherhood. The fraternity advisor summoned to the Florida State Chapter after a gang rape protested to a reporter in disbelief that they could be guilty, "Pikes are a cut above most students on this campus. They have more money. They are better dressed. They drive better cars" (Hull, 1988, p. 6F). One of the frightening aspects of the gang rape mentality is that some men who have it also have real social power. Not atypically, fraternity men at the University of Florida accused of a gang rape went on to become lawyers and doctors (the victim dropped out). The abuse may be public—it is at least shared without shame among the men—but the patriarchal values are not detected by society or the rapists themselves, who point to their nonexploitative relationships with "good" women as evidence of their respect for women. Gang rape (perceived as consensual, or noncriminal by the perpetrators) may be a more socially acceptable enactment of misogyny among the middle-class and "outlaw" elements of society, and battering a more socially acceptable performance of misogyny among the working class.

3. *Is the essential difference that gang rape is committed against a stranger, acquaintance, or friend, and domestic violence is committed against a partner?* This question could be rephrased: "Do gang rapists also physically abuse their girlfriends and wives? And do wife beaters also attack acquaintances and strangers?" The answer to these two questions is that it depends on the type: generally violent wife beaters also attack acquaintances and strangers; generally violent gang rapists also batter wives and girlfriends. But family-only and even "emotionally volatile" batterers usually do not attack strangers and acquaintances, and the "typical" gang rapist does not attack a wife or girlfriend.

In my data set, there were *no* cases of gang rapes against a girlfriend or wife of one of the rapists. Of the 48 campus cases that I documented, the relationship of the perpetrators to the victim was not determined in 11 cases (the information I had in these cases was simply that the victim was visiting the men's living quarters in 3 cases; in 1 case the victim was Asian and the men were taking part in an "ethnic sex challenge" of their fraternity; in 2 cases, the woman was merely identified as a fellow college student; and in 1 case she was a high school student). The remaining 37 cases broke down as follows:

Met at Party (32%). This was the largest single category. The woman was usually a first-year student (17 or 18 years old), and it was usually a fraternity party.

Picked Up and Brought Home to "Party" (19%). These included a 14-year-old picked up in a park and taken back to an apartment by college football players; an 18-year-old local college student picked up and taken to a motel room by college basketball players after an away game (they won the game); a 34-year-old woman who went back to an athletic dorm to continue drinking after the bars closed and was later found by police running down a street without a coat in frigid weather; and a 19-year-old working-class woman who was driving in a small town with her thirtyish aunt when they were hailed down by some college men and invited to a party.

Acquaintances (16%). In these cases, the students knew each other from around campus but there was no particular relationship (romantic or friendship) between the victim and any of the men. It seemed likely that these victims were "hanging out" in the hope of developing a romantic relationship with a particular man in the group. *Dormmates (13%).* In two cases, these were temporary dormmates in summer programs for high school students in college readiness programs. *Friends (8%).* These cases included two "Little Sisters" of fraternities, and a woman who was a friend and drinking buddy of her rapists.

In a few cases, the woman had a closer relationship to one of the men in the group. One woman who was raped at a fraternity party was the girlfriend of a brother, but he did not participate in the rape and helped her report it. In two cases, the victim had previously dated one of the men casually but no longer had a relationship with him.

Four cases don't exactly fit into any of these categories. In one, the victim, 19, was the blind date of a football player; the date was set up by a 17-year-old friend of the victim who knew the players sharing a suite in the athletic dorm. The victim had a long telephone conversation with the man before agreeing to the date. In another case, the victim, a fellow student, was doing a striptease in a freshman male dorm. (When the DA learned what she had been doing before she was assaulted, he decided it wasn't rape and dropped the case.) In the third case, a prostitute picked up on a street and driven to an isolated location charged the men with rape. She said they offered her a ride to meet her friends. The men's attorney said she was filing rape charges only because she didn't get paid; however, she was also kicked and punched while lying on the ground. She told the men she had AIDS; they thought she was "trying to get out of it," but at the trial it was revealed that she was HIV positive (these men were friends and football teammates from high school; two were currently in college and aspiring to be police officers and one was in the Marines. They were convicted and served jail sentences). In the fourth anomalous but revealing case, a gay couple was walking in an alley behind fraternity row, holding hands, when men in one house gathered at a window and yelled epithets at them. One of the gay men fled but the other yelled back insults. The fraternity men chased and caught him, brought him into the house, and sodomized him.

In none of the campus cases, nor in the 25 cases of high school and middle school gang rape cases I have documented, nor the 15 cases of adult groups of men gang raping, was the victim a girlfriend or wife of any of the participants. Such a group violation of the "property" of one of the men would not be brotherly, and it would not accrue masculinity credits to the man associated with her—unless he didn't want her exclusively and "gave" her away. When I surveyed my students in a sex roles class about their knowledge of "trains" or gang rape, one man who had been the resident advisor in a dorm when a notorious "gang bang" by seven football players occurred several years earlier said it wasn't rape because her boyfriend "gave her away," and therefore the men had "consent."

Gang rapes of women who have established friendships with the perpetrators do occur, but they are less common than rapes of women who are only acquaintances. That these women friends could be the target of the men's violent misogyny comes as a surprise to the victims. In the University of Pennsylvania case, Meg Davis said that she knew that the seven football players she socialized with at parties sexually abused other women but she felt immune. One night when she was drinking with them at a fraternity party, she passed out, and they raped her orally, anally, and vaginally. "I never thought it would happen to me," she said afterwards. Similarly, the Little Sister in a gang rape at Stetson University believed there was a difference between the way her Big Brothers in the fraternity treated "loose" or outsider women, and the way they would treat her. Along with other Little Sisters, she celebrated the men's birthdays, hosted their parties, cleaned, decorated, and gave them gifts. At a fraternity party, she had a drinking contest with the girlfriend of a brother as the men cheered them on. Later, she passed out on the dance floor. When she came to and found one of her brothers on top of her and another man standing by, she asked, "How can you do this to me? I've done so much for them." Her friend answered, "You're a beautiful girl and we were all drunk." When she reported it to school authorities, some of the men admitted having sex with her but said "she was willing." When she filed a criminal complaint, the men denied having intercourse but admitted that they poked her, slapped her, poured shampoo over her, and laughed at her while she lay naked in a drunken stupor. In these cases, the victims thought that they were protected by a special relationship with sexually abusive men, but because it was a generalized relationship, rather than a relationship with one man, there was no protection. Their heavy drinking also changed their categorization from respectable to rapable (one of the Stetson perpetrators can be heard saying on an audiotape of the internal hearing, "It's almost like when she starts to drink she becomes a different person").

Thus, there appears to be a clear and important distinction between gang rape and domestic violence in that gang rape is committed against a woman who is *not* connected to an individual man in the group, while partner abuse is committed against a woman closely connected to the perpetrator. This difference, of course, is related to the fact that one is a group activity and the other a solitary activity. (Presumably, if other men abused a wife-beater's wife, he would feel compelled to protect her from them.) In fact, Farr's (1988) research on "Good Ol' Boys Sociability Groups" (GOBS) suggests that middle-class men in the fraternal culture may have egalitarian relationships with their girlfriends and wives at the same time that they have exploitative and potentially abusive relationships *as a group* with one outsider woman who represents sexuality. The men whom Farr describes, who maintain the fraternal bond from college into adulthood on golfing trips, boys' nights out, and so on, may actually take pride in having a wife who is educated, accomplished, and independent enough to allow them their freedom. At the same time, they enjoy retreating into the male world of their college days. In that setting their wives are unwelcome, but a woman of lower social status, a "fun" woman (usually younger), serves as a foil to their bonding around sexism and heterosexuality. Farr (1988) observed that "fun and trouble" is a theme of male group socialization, and an activity that fits that description is fooling around with a "bad woman," defined as any woman who is not the wife or girlfriend of a group member (p. 271).

In parallel, family-only and emotionally volatile batterers are not generally sexually abusive and seem to reserve their violence for women with whom they are in close relationships (Saunders, 1992). Their sexual abuse of their wives and girlfriends serves their need to control the woman who is supposed to meet their expectations. As noted earlier, research on batterers' attitudes and beliefs suggests that sexual abuse stems from the belief that the partner should always be sexually available and that she should be punished if she "withholds" sex. Sexual abuse is also used to humiliate and intimidate the partner, to keep her in a subordinate and fearfully obedient posture. As Claire Walsh put it, gang rapists divide women into two categories; they will gang rape only a whore and enter into a relationship only with a respectable woman, more of an equal than the abusable but untouchable victims. But the batterer "sleeps with the whore; the whore is the woman he lives with."[25]

4. *Are there other differences between the victims of gang rape and domestic violence?*

It appears to be frequently the case that gang rape victims were previously sexually abused or physically abused in childhood. A prospective study of college rape victims (Gidycz, Coble, Latham, & Layman,

1993) found that college women who had been sexually assaulted before they started college were over 3 times more likely to be raped in the course of a single college quarter than women who had not been previously assaulted. Initial results of a study of college gang rape victims by Claire Walsh indicate that gang rape victims are also likely to have a distinctive history of abuse. Walsh is conducting a study parallel to mine of gang rape but with a focus on victims rather than perpetrators. She is encountering difficulties isolating the psychological effects of gang rape because in most, though not all, cases, the women had been previously victimized by incest and by battering relationships in high school. An important factor in their revictimization in gang rape is that they were traumatized by the prior abuse and, as a result, they tend to "dissociate" when in a sexually threatening situation (which the victims describe in testimony as "going into shock," to explain why they didn't move, didn't run away, became passive as they were attacked). Walsh's results are consistent with analysis of the 40 gang rape cases in Koss, Gidycz, and Wisniewski's (1987) national survey: Half the gang rape victims had been sexually abused by family members when they were younger than 14. (The fact that the national college survey turned up only 40 gang rape victims may be attributed in part to the fact that most gang rape victims leave college after the incident. Of the 18 cases in my data set in which the victim was a student at the same college and the information is available [in 12 cases it isn't], 14 dropped out and 4 remained in college. Of the 4 who stayed, 1 flunked out because she stopped taking tests; Meg Davis said she was determined not to let the men drive her from school but it took her 5 years to graduate; another sued the university, saying that the administration and campus police tried to force her to drop out.)

In many cases in my data set the victim was alcoholic, a typical outcome of childhood sexual abuse (see Wilsnack & Beckman, 1984). Further-more, it is common now for college students to drink very heavily, even though they are underage and it is illegal. Most drinking takes place in the men's residences. Students report that first-year students are espe-cially likely to "go a little wild" as they start college, then settle down. This probably accounts for the fact that the mean age of campus gang rape victims is 18. The state of intoxication of the victim is clear in 22 of the 48 campus gang rapes in my data set: in 10, the woman was in and out of consciousness; in 8 she was seriously drunk but not unconscious (e.g., one woman was too drunk to walk to her dorm so she was carried to a man's room by six men who then assaulted her); and she was sober in 4 cases. In the cases in which the woman was sober, there was evidence of a history of child abuse (as well as in some of the cases in which the woman was drunk).

In the Florida State case, the ringleader met the victim at an off-campus drinking club and invited her back to his fraternity for a "party." Although in her first year, she was well known because her punk style stood out on the conservative campus. She had been thrown out of her Little Sisters organization for promiscuity and for not having the right look. She had also been arrested for disorderly conduct on a Tallahassee street. Excited to be invited to the "classiest" fraternity on campus, she ran back to her dorm and downed a tumbler of tequila. At the fraternity house, her host gave her a bottle of wine, which she finished. He carried her unconscious to the communal shower room and summoned three other men. His best friend left his own date waiting downstairs in the hall to join in the assault. After sexually assaulting her, the four classy men wrote fraternity slogans and "hatchet gash" on her thighs, dumped her in the entry hall of another fraternity, and called 911. At the hospital, her blood alcohol level was found to be potentially lethal and semen from several different men was found in her vagina. A few weeks later, she moved to another state and entered a residential alcohol treatment program.

Such vulnerable women are targeted by gang rapists, much as Vachss (1993) describes the way molesters choose their targets: vulnerable, isolated teenagers whom juries will not find sympathetic. The men may pick them because they know they will drink to the point of unconsciousness, because they have a reputation for promiscuity, or both. The men may also target them because they know that they are naive, gullible, and eager for acceptance. In Martin and Hummer's (1989) study of fraternal culture and rape following the Florida State gang rape, a man described the purpose of a traditional party held at his fraternity, the Bowery Ball: "The entire idea behind this is sex. Both men and women come to the party wearing little or nothing. . . . They just get schnockered [drunk] and, in most cases, they also get laid" (p. 469). The researchers asked him which women would come to such a party. He acknowledged that many women who usually socialize with the men won't attend this party. The ones who come are, "The girls . . . who are looking for a good time, *girls who don't know* what it is, things like that" (p. 469, emphasis added). Another man said that girlfriends aren't allowed to come to such "socials" so that the men can have sex with other women.

Unfortunately, among students, in courts, in the popular media, and even in research reports, such victim vulnerabilities are used to exonerate the men and blame the victim. The phrase "alcohol was involved" is frequently used but the phrase is not specific as to who was how drunk and what role is being attributed to alcohol; instead, the phrase serves as a catch-all for excusing criminal behavior and justifying a failure to analyze the intentions of the perpetrators and the social dynamics of gang rape. The fact that many victims of gang rape are drunk does not imply that the remedy for gang rape is for college women to control their drinking. There is an important distinction between *avoidance* and *prevention*. Men determined to engage in group sex will find victims, whether they exploit other vulnerabilities than intoxication, become more coercive, or cast a wider net for naive women—and girls. Gang rapists are organized, unlike batterers. Gang rape often involves forethought, strategic planning and preparation, and coordination. It has become increasingly common for men to slip drugs into drinks to lay the way for gang rape, just as they used to spike the punch with "Everclear," as happened in a 1985 case at Pi Kappa Alpha at San Diego State University. In the one gang rape trial in which the victim's childhood sexual abuse was introduced to explain her passive response to the group sexual assault (she wasn't drunk), the defense turned it around and instead argued that the childhood victimization led her to consent to or even elicit sexual abuse (Hampton Institute, Virginia). The men were acquitted. This outcome discouraged the next gang rape victim at this college from reporting.

Battered women, despite widespread beliefs to the contrary, do not have common characteristics. Repeated research efforts to identify these characteristics came up empty (e.g., Follingstad, Laughlin, Polek, Rutledge, & Hause, 1991; Hotaling & Sugarman, 1990). The psychological profile of a battered woman is a result, not a precedent, of the battering, researchers have concluded. The way in which a victim's psychology and prior experiences with violence relate to revictimization is that who she is and what has happened to her, and, equally important, her resources, influence her *response* to violence (Follingstad et al., 1991). Whether that response is effective in preventing her revictimization by the same batterer depends both on the strategy (passively waiting for it to get better is usually ineffective, and fighting back tends to escalate violence [Bowker, 1986a; Feld & Straus, 1990]), and on the batterer's characteristics (threats of divorce are sufficient to stop the violence by some men but have no impact on others; employed men with a stake in the system are more often deterred by arrest than unemployed men; some men increase their violence if a woman leaves). Nor is there evidence to support the common belief that battered women repeatedly "choose" batterers for partners, due to exposure to domestic violence in childhood (Jaffe, 1996).

A Final Similarity: Social Constructions

Despite the differences in motivations and behaviors, society's view of the social phenomena—but even more so of the victims—bear striking similarities. To begin with, the category of behaviors to which gang rape and "domestic violence" are usually assigned is "violence against women," rather than "male violence." Leaving men out of the picture enhances the tendency to focus on the woman's role in her own traumatic victimization. Over and over, in regard to both battered women and gang rape victims, the same question is asked: *"Why didn't she leave?"* when the prior and more important question is, *"Why did he do it?"* Often, we don't even get to that question because we are debating why she didn't leave.

As Ann Jones (1994, pp. 132-136) reports, this question is asked even when the woman *did* leave. WCBS covered the trial of a woman who murdered her battering husband. The field reporter's background story made it clear that the woman had left her husband but could not afford a divorce. Two years after she left him, she was living in her own home with an order of protection when he broke in, raped her at knifepoint in front of her children, threatened to kill her, and she killed him. All of this was discussed in the taped interview with her attorney and with Jones—how she had tried 10 times to have him arrested but failed, how he came after her. Yet in the wrap-up, the anchor, Jim Jensen, asked the field reporter in the studio why she "murder[ed] her husband instead of just walking away." Clearly, this phrasing makes the victim culpable. Even more remarkable to Jones is that the field reporter, despite the documentation that the woman had not only walked away but tried everything to keep her husband away, answered the anchor's question by explaining why the woman *hadn't* walked away . . . helplessness, psychological dependency. A woman network producer didn't get the point of Jones's complaint about the anchor's question, saying that men don't understand women's fear. When Jones pointed out that the woman had already left the man, the producer asked, "Then how did she get raped?"

I have seen gang rape victims try to field similar befuddling questions: "Why didn't you leave before they had sex with you?" "Why didn't I leave before they raped me? Before they locked the door and told me I couldn't leave? At what point should I have left before they wouldn't let me leave?"

The assumption in all these constructions seems to be that women could avoid being victimized if they really wanted to, if they wanted to take responsibility for their behavior and not put themselves in harm's way.

' We do not seem to have advanced as far as we think beyond the days when we believed rape was impossible because it would be like putting a straw into a moving bottle.

A second area of denial in social constructions of male violence against women is the resistance to connections between cultural expressions of misogyny or celebrations of violent masculinity and rape or wife abuse. A brouhaha erupted when Fairness and Accuracy in Reporting put on a public service announcement about domestic violence during the Super Bowl. The clamor, the outrage, the denial, proceeded in typical fashion. First, the original claim, based on a study in Los Angeles County, was misrepresented in press reports and debates, then this inflated description of the claim was denounced and refuted.

There is a similar pattern of misrepresentation, then refutation of the incorrectly reported overblown statement regarding the influence of the media on sexual violence against women and children. The mainstream media and politicians are perfectly willing to accept that television and film depictions of violence might have a negative influence on social behavior, especially on children. Violence in rap music, especially against the police, is taken very seriously as advocacy of hostility and the killing of cops. When a movie depicts teenagers lying down on a highway on a drunken dare, and there is a rash of college students lying down on highways and getting run over, the movie is denounced; if a movie depicts a subway token booth being torched, and there is a rash of token takers incinerated, the connection is made. Yet if anyone notes that sexual violence and hostility toward women can be learned and encouraged by media depictions and songs, the connection is suddenly denied. The immediate cry if one even mentions the connection between violence against women and media is "censorship," even if one simply reports empirical research without making any recommendation.

A *New York Times* editorial (unsigned) once decried attempts to connect violent pornography and violence against women: the association between pornography and sex crimes "has no basis in science or psychology," is "unproven and highly speculative," and "millions of Americans who never commit crimes of any kind," just like "sex criminals," enjoy pornography ("A Damaging Remedy," 1992). On the same day, just below the unsigned editorial, was a signed editorial (called "Editor's Notebook") that decried media violence and connected it to growing violence in our society (Camper, 1992). Camper wrote, "the glamorizing of violence on television and in movies . . . contributes to increasing violence" among teenagers (not *boys*); she recommended moderating portrayals of violence and sex. Apparently science has been able to demonstrate a connection between media violence and "teen" violence, but not between media depictions of sexual violence and male violence. Claire Walsh maintains that one reason campus gang rape continues to occur is that the conditions under which it occurs and the strategies of gang rapists are not publicized. This week (typically?), news media broke the "news" that four high school boys were arrested *a month ago* for raping a 14-year-old girl who was "partying" with them in an upper-class New Jersey suburb. The DA defended the lack of publicity on the grounds that it was an "isolated incident" and no one else was in danger.

Conclusions

Gang rapists and wife beaters share some patriarchal beliefs about women; for example, double standards in sexuality. The typical gang rapist and the typical wife beater also differ, however. A man who is willing to participate in sexual abuse of an acquaintance along with his buddies may have a supportive and egalitarian relationship with a wife or girlfriend. Batterers, on the other hand, may have respectful relationships with women acquaintances but coercive and demeaning relationships with their wives or girlfriends.

Part of this difference stems from the fact that gang rape is a performance put on for other men, proving one's masculinity through heterosexual dominance and exploitation of a woman. Studies of Little League baseball players and of college athletes have found that team cohesiveness relies heavily on sexual objectification of women (Fine, 1987; Messner, 1992b). Gang rape is "about" the relationship among the men doing it rather than their relationship to the woman they are abusing. It is also "fun." It is a way of cooperating and competing with male friends through a shared risky and risqué, socially sanctioned (in the sense that it's something to brag about among men, although not something to write home to mother about), behavior. Battering, while in some cases a show put on for other men to demonstrate dominance in the family, is more often a private exercise of power with an emotional component. Wife beating is not fun for the batterer, although he may claim it is cathartic. It is more instrumental than expressive, with the goal of regulating the relationship between the man and his wife.

While gang rape and wife beating both stem from patriarchy and sexism, in terms of Michael Smith's (1990) domains of patriarchy, gang rape pertains to dominance in society and battery to dominance in the family. Wife beaters may have a more 1950s or traditional sense of masculinity, in which the man is the head of the family and is the responsible decision maker, wage earner, and disciplinarian. The gang rapist may be egalitarian at home and prefer to have a wife who is accomplished and not so submissive. Gang rape expresses and serves male dominance in society by enhancing loyalty among the men. Battering more often operates from a deficit position when men feel a loss of control in the family, a failure to share in male dominance in society, or both. Gang rapists may try to *avoid* close relationships with women, preferring to relate to men, while wife batterers seek close relationships with women.

> Whenever one of the fellas acted like he was down for a heartfelt, monogamous relationship, the old-heads made him feel that he should be ashamed of himself. ". . . you fallin' in love! You weak! You pussywhipped!" (McCall, 1994, p. 40)

Yet for both gang rapists and batterers, being "controlled" by a woman is emasculating and infuriating. Batterers, too, are trying not to be "whipped."

Notes

1. It is very difficult to keep the focus on men's behavior when discussing "violence against women." The distinction I am making here is that sometimes what we call "victim blaming" is just that, but sometimes it is actually "perpetrator exoneration." For example, in regard to the Kentucky State case, a friend of mine on the faculty protested, "But they are so young!", as though men of 18 or 19 aren't really capable of or shouldn't be criminally charged for rape. This denial of the perpetrators' responsibility for their behavior is different from the victim-blaming sentiments that students initially voiced, "She didn't have any bruises," (but she did) and, "I heard she does this all the time."

2. It was a constant issue in this research whether or not to define a case in which a group of men had sex with one woman as "rape," particularly since the men universally claimed that the woman consented. Following legal standards would leave most cases undecided. If the woman claimed she was raped and there was no strong evidence to the contrary, or if she was unconscious or exploited by men who had authority and control over her, I considered it an appropriate case for study. My focus was on the men's behavior and their motivation for collectively having sex with one woman, so the legal definition was not pertinent.

3. One man in my study was ostracized by his fraternity brothers because he found a woman friend unconscious and naked in the hall of the fraternity house and kept her in his room overnight; his brothers were angry at him because he didn't "share." An athletic

director who was trying to design a program to discourage the students from abusing women admitted that he had learned to stand up to racism but still didn't have the guts to stand up to sexism.

4. Autobiographies of star athletes usually provide ample examples. Nigel Clay, a football player for Oklahoma, wrote an op-ed from the cell where he was serving a sentence for a gang rape charge. He said that he had been lulled into the sense he was above the law because of the athletes' freedom from penalties for their behavior and the corrupting influence of money and things thrown at them "for nothing." It started with his recruitment from a Los Angeles high school, when he received a gift of money from an alumnus, the use of a Mercedes, and suitcases full of new clothes. He got carried away, too, with the ease of finding women because there were "a lot of . . . sluts" who would consent to crudely advertised one-night stands "just to have sex with a football player" (Clay, 1991, p. 8c).

5. Sometimes gang rapists misread the cues as to the appropriate category for a woman they encounter. A woman who was gang raped at the University of Oklahoma athletic dorm was taken for a "loose woman" because she wore a short tight skirt that the men and their friends kept referring to at the trial; in fact, she was a virgin. I also hypothesize that a reason that the St. John's University lacrosse players who shared a house called "Trump Plaza" were finally caught and forced to stand trial for their allegedly frequent group sexual attacks on women visitors is that there was mutual cultural misunderstanding. The 21-year-old black woman that the white ringleader invited in after a Rifle Club meeting was not American; she was a recent immigrant from the Caribbean who had had a strict upbringing, had not been allowed to date, and had rarely tasted alcohol. His racism misled him; her naïveté misled her about a trash-talking white college man.

6. The men's incredulity that a woman would consent to have "sleazy" sex with them illustrates that the men assume that the way they treat women sexually is demeaning and not pleasurable for the women. An excerpt from an essay by a Rutgers student in Moffat's (1989) sexuality class, unedited for grammatical errors, shows this reaction: "The thing that baffles me is that girls know what's going on at fraternity houses but still insist on returning. What could be the reason for this type of person unless they enjoy it as much as the guy who is doing it. Don't laugh it may have happened to your sister once" (p. 205). An ex-fraternity man I interviewed blamed women for allowing "the system" of abusive sexuality at the fraternity to survive. He was bothered that women allowed themselves to be passed around, or came back to see a man when they knew he was seeing other women. He said he was looking for a woman like himself, who "just doesn't care," but he thought that if he found one, there would have to be something wrong with her so he would reject her.

7. Nathan McCall (1994) provides perhaps the most honest firsthand account of a gang rape. Earlier in the book, he described his socialization by the older boys on the street and in school. He learned that sex is viewed as a sport in which men win and women lose, and that confers masculinity on the boy: "Nutbrain said, 'Why you wanna bruise your hands on some hardhead when you can be somewhere fucking? . . . That's the only sweating I'm gonna do.' . . . Nutbrain commanded *big* respect on the block by virtue of his status as an established lover, a silver-tongued player who conquered women for sport" (p. 39).

8. A college student who knew the Glen Ridge, New Jersey, gang rapists compared the boys' sodomizing their retarded friend with a bat to a time in his childhood when he

was challenged by his peers to jump a barricade on his bike; he knew he wouldn't make it but he did it anyway to maintain his standing among his peers. He broke his leg. My ex-fraternity informant established his identity within the fraternity by eating his brothers' vomit, and he described with admiration a brother who could knock over a stack of cans or bottles with his penis.

9. A student described his team initiation as a rookie athlete: The rookies were locked in a dark basement, told to strip and drink a keg of beer in a half hour; then called out one at a time. When his turn came, he was taken into another room where the older players stood around a Ping-Pong table, also naked. They doused him with beer and asked for his name, hometown, and name of his last sexual partner. He was hoisted onto to the table and crawled its length while beer was poured over his naked body. When he reached the end of the table, they put a beer keg tap into his mouth and he drank until he vomited into a "strategically placed barrel." Then they lifted him down, shook his hand, and welcomed him to the team! He said he never experienced such closeness, such pride; it was "beneficial." He believed he would not have survived the rigors and demanding schedule of varsity sports without this experience.

10. A fraternity song to the tune of "The Candyman" has the lyrics, "Who can take a chain saw, shove it up your hole, mix it all together, make taco casserole?" and a rugby song to the same tune, "Who can take a baby, spread its tiny thighs, fuck it up the ass 'til the blood squirts out its eyes?" The source of the fraternity lyrics is the UCLA Phi Psi fraternity songbook, but the songs are shared across fraternities. Another song bemoans the fate of Lupe, an 8-year-old Mexican whore who died "sucking [fill in the name of your fraternity here] cock." The source of the rugby song is a student's study of a rugby club for a course on group processes.

11. Scott Straus's (1996) fraternity induction included describing his first or most exciting sexual experience (with a woman). Weekly house meetings involved reporting sexual adventures: "sex for any one brother was for the communal consumption of the brotherhood" (p. 27).

12. A number of interviews I conducted brought out "voyeuring" or "ledging"—standing on a ledge and watching through a window—as have newspaper reports of alleged gang rapes. Moffat (1989) quotes a student's paper in a sexuality course at Rutgers: "When my friends pick up chicks . . . everyone else runs to the window to look at somebody else 'domineer' a girl and I tell you what you get almost the same satisfaction. . . . By the same token, I enjoy conquering girls and having people watch" (p. 205). Note also that the two verbs he uses for sexual congress are "domineer" and "conquer."

13. A woman sued her boyfriend because, unbeknownst to her, he videotaped their copulation with the assistance of two friends. She learned of the tape after he showed it to his fraternity brothers at the University of Texas and sued him for invasion of privacy. The law firm that defended him was fined for playing the tape in the presence of 16 firm employees while they celebrated the outcome of the trial with champagne (Margolick, 1990).

14. One battered woman I know is required by her husband, who has a much larger income, to pay for the mortgage, the food, and the children's medical expenses because the home and children are a woman's responsibility. Like a batterer discussed in Pence and Paymar (1993), one motive for controlling her money (and keeping her strapped) is to prevent her from leaving the marriage.

15. The research subcommittee of a New York City committee studying the impact of welfare "reform" on battered women on which I served found that job-training programs

for women are having security problems and program attrition because the women's partners show up at the training site, certain that the women are dressing up and going out for a rendezvous with another man.

16. I overheard one man describe to his fellow perpetrators during a break in a batterers program session how his wife went flying across the room, horizontally, like a witch, and got hurt when she hit the wall—the wall injured her, not he; he didn't say how she became airborne. Ann Jones (1994) presents many such examples in which it seems the woman inflicted the injuries on herself or objects became animate, but Jones's examples are from police and medical reports, rather than the men who inflicted the injuries.

17. These beliefs are not distinct from views acceptable to the conservative mainstream. For example, the Promise Keepers, a religious program of social salvation of men that has been filling stadiums with men eager to hear the message of responsibility, gives the following advice in their publication, "Promises of a Promise Keeper," according to Laura Flanders (1997): "The first thing you do is sit down with your wife and say something like this: 'Honey, I've made a terrible mistake. I've given you my role. I gave up leading this family, and I forced you to take my place.' " The advice continued, "I'm not suggesting that you ask for your role back, I'm urging you to take it back. If you ask for it, your wife is likely to [refuse]" (p. 8). Flanders also reports that a videotape of a rally shows a woman "on a massive video screen" saying, "We ask you to forgive us for not showing you the respect that you deserve." This approach, not surprisingly, has alarmed some battered women's advocates.

18. Charles Thompson, the quarterback who was arrested for selling cocaine, said in his autobiography that earlier that year, a football player, naked and holding condoms, walked up and down the hall knocking on doors and inviting his teammates to join in sex with a woman in his room. Fifteen men lined up outside the door. Two men held her down on the bed. When she became hysterical, they stopped (Telender & Sullivan, 1989).

19. When I "debated" Richard Lapchick, founder/director for the Center for the Study of Sports at Northeastern and son of the famed St. John's basketball coach, on the *Today Show* (June 19, 1990), he disputed my evidence that there was a link between masculinity and gang rape that implicated football players by arguing that many football players gang rape because they grew up poor and weren't loved by their parents. The implication that poor people don't love their children is questionable.

20. Benedict's editorial on criminal athletes on campus sparked a letter from Professor Earl Smith (1997): "Although the majority of student athletes who get into trouble are male and play football or basketball, the majority of abusers are not athletes but 'regular students.' The high profile nature of intercollegiate sports makes these students answer publicly for their behavior." This argument suffers from the base-rate fallacy.

21. In a case at Florida State University, one man who penetrated the victim with a "pump type toothpaste dispenser" said he couldn't get an erection. (He pleaded guilty.) In a case at Bloomsburg University, one man said he used a hairbrush because he was concerned about cleanliness, since other men had gone before him; and a participant in a gang rape at a McGill fraternity used a paintbrush handle for similar reasons and because "she wanted it." In the infamous Glen Ridge, New Jersey, case, in which high school baseball players assaulted a mildly retarded classmate, objects were used (sports equipment, in fact), except one man had oral sex with her. Of the four men tried, the jury acquitted only the man who had oral intercourse, apparently because it was the only normative sex act.

22. As anthropologist Moffat (1989), who studied campus life, wrote, "if you wanted to be surrounded by other men who also thought that sex with sleazy sluts was the way to prove your manhood, then the fraternities, or some of them . . . were the places for you. In them . . . you could escape the . . . more egalitarian contemporary gender relations of the coed dorm. . . . Once again, as in the good old days [of boyhood], only other men needed to be your friends. Women were once more at a safe distance."

23. The source of this observation is a national telephone survey of batterers programs that I conducted, results of which will be published in the National Institute of Justice Issues and Practices report, *Batterers Intervention Programs, A Criminal Justice Approach*, Kerry Healey, PI.

24. One victim interviewed for a batterers program evaluation said that her husband brought back from a meeting the notion that it's legal to kill your wife in the Caribbean, and suggested they move there; in more successful cases, though, the men report that they learned the most from their fellow batterers and it was that support that kept them in the program (O'Sullivan, 1996).

25. Claire Walsh, personal communication. Walsh is the director of Campus and Community Consultation in St. Petersburg, Florida. She was a pioneer in the design of campus rape education and prevention programs at the University of Florida. In her private practice, she counsels and provides expert testimony for domestic violence victims.

6

The Coaching Abuse of Teenage Girls

A Betrayal of Innocence and Trust

LEE H. BOWKER

Girls and young women have been excluded or only minimally included in school athletic team play throughout American history. The rising tide of female athletic participation was given a boost by Title IX, the federal requirement for gender equity in education. This raised the status and eventually the salaries of girls' and women's team coaches, which had the effect of making coaching women a desirable job for men. The result at the collegiate level has been a drop in the proportion of women coaching women's teams ("The Last Laugh," 1994a, 1994b). For some men, this presents an opportunity for abusiveness that was not previously available to them.

Traditionally a male preserve and integral to the development of many varieties of masculine role behavior (Messner & Sabo, 1990), organized athletics did not easily yield to demands for equality of opportunity (Birrell & Cole, 1994; Cohen, 1993). Many barriers remain to women who seek experiences in organized athletics, including sexual harassment, abuse, homophobia, and a masculine sports ethic that is inconsistent with many women's values and girls' developmental needs (Lenskyj, 1990). Sports language expresses these values and is closely allied with the language of the wartime battlefield (Jansen & Sabo, 1994) and the "sportspeak" of sexual relations (Segrave, 1994).

The wonderful humanistic description of the coach's role by Sullivan and Wilson (1993) may be fairly taken as an ideal type that is approached by few coaches, male or female. At the other end of the continuum of coaching quality is the behavior described by Donna Lopiano, writing from her position as executive director at the University of Texas. Sexual harassment or even sexual assault by male coaches of female student-athletes is a significant problem in school and open amateur sports settings throughout the country that often goes unreported ("Homophobia," 1994).

Or as Helen Lenskyj (1992) puts it, "there is evidence that the coach's authority, and even psychologically manipulative or abusive behavior, is rarely, if ever, challenged by these women" (p. 2).

Bavolek (1994) defines child abuse in sports as any adult behavior "which results in the direct or indirect physical and\or emotional harm to children" (p. 12). Anderson (1994) sees it as creating "a hostile, destructive environment that erodes self-esteem, confidence and trust" (p. 4). She understands that these immediate negative effects are heightened by the loss of the benefits of sports participation in the future, for many victims of coaching abuse have their careers cut short by the traumatic aspects of the experience.

There are no national estimates of the incidence or prevalence of the coaching abuse of schoolgirls. However, Anderson (1994) cites an unpublished survey of youth sports participants in Minnesota that may be very close to the national rates of abuse. This survey was carried out by the Minnesota Amateur Sports Commission in 1993. The commission found the 45% of the participants had suffered verbal abuse; 18% had been hit, kicked, or slapped; 21% had been persuaded to play while injured; 8% had been pressured to try to harm players on the opposing team; 8% had been called names with sexual connotations; and 3% reported having been pressured into sex or sexual touching. These percentages combine male and female respondents, so the figures for schoolgirls may be either higher or lower than these samplewide statistics. In any case, if the national figures are similar to the Minnesota results, one might describe coaching abuse as an epidemic.

I am indebted to Maria Burton Nelson (1994) for her brilliant chapter on coaching abuse in *The Stronger Women Get, the More Men Love Football.* She experienced coaching abuse herself between the ages of 14 and 16 and has researched unpublished materials on the subject, bringing unknown data into print in her chapter. Nelson understands the fantasy world of sexually abusive coaches, as well as the nuances of power relations between male coaches and female athletes. She explains how the power differential and the coach's attentions to a desired player often produce the player's crush on him, which eases the seductive sequence. What happens as the relationship develops is best described with Nelson's words.

> If the coach has learned to respect women . . . his admiration of her young beauty will remain private, irrelevant to the task of coaching. If, on the other hand, he believes he has a right to women as playthings, as sex enhancers, he will interpret the fondness and excitement between them as irresistible sexual attraction or romantic love. He will rationalize that she is a consenting adult, or at least mature for her age. (p. 161)

Methodology

Survey forms were mailed to all female coaches of American college women's basketball teams, with a request that the forms be distributed to team members who expressed interest in participating in the project. A few additional forms were passed on to non-team members through friendship links. Sending questionnaires via coaches was unlikely to elicit many responses because so many of the young women who were abused in high school or earlier did not continue their sports participation in college. This methodology was employed because it was a cost-efficient way to test ideas derived from my personal observations of abusive coaches.

Supportive comments were received from a few female women's coaches and critical comments were received from one female and several male women's coaches. The supportive comments contained an awareness of the seriousness of the problem and appreciation that somebody finally was investigating the problem. Some recounted victimizing experiences that players had shared with them over the years. The critical comments contained expressions of distaste because it was felt that I was being unfair to men. This is because I used masculine pronouns in referring to abusive coaches when I gave six examples of abuse in the instructions for the respondents. I explained this by stating "In all of these examples, the coaches are men, since my experience is that a very high percentage of the abusers of female athletes are men." I provide this information here so readers can judge for themselves if I was being unfair, or merely accurate. Nelson (1994) provides copious evidence for the accuracy of my statement.

One assistant coach summarized the critical response without any attempt to recast his opinion in more politically correct terminology. He said he had a hard time believing that there was any gender difference in the incidence of the coaching abuse of girls. Then came the reference to abusiveness by lesbian coaches—"Certain stereotypes which have come to exist, and [are] thankfully ceasing to exist, about women coaches were created for a reason." While rejecting my approach as hopelessly biased, this coach had his own idea of what I should be doing. He was concerned that "being married will soon be a qualification of getting a job" and recommended that I provide "tips to competent coaches on what they can do to protect themselves from having wild accusations made at them." That was when I realized he assumed I was a man-hating woman instead of a man who is concerned about reducing the damage caused to girls and young women by abusive coaches.

As an exploratory study with a small, nonrepresentative sample, the research reported here cannot address questions about the prevalence of coaching abuse nationally or in any other population. My personal experience is that approximately 1 male coach in 10 is abusive, whereas poor taste is the worst behavior I have seen in a female coach. I have no idea whether this is better or worse than the national average. The gender difference in abusiveness found in this research, both as to relative numbers and as to the content of the abuse, also cannot be generalized beyond the study's respondents. The purpose of the study is to explore uncharted territory and to develop enough insight into the varieties of coaching abuse to be able to make good decisions for structuring larger studies in the future.

Results

Twenty-five usable questionnaires were received from self-identified victims of coaching abuse, residing in 15 states from all regions of the United States. The respondents ranged in age from 18 to 38, with most of them being 18, 19, or 20 years old. They first began to experience coaching abuse at an early age, 1 before puberty, 14 in early adolescence (ages 13-15), 8 in pre-adulthood (ages 16-17), and only 2 as an adult (ages 20-21). The abuse lasted between 1 and 84 months with peaks at 3, 24, and 36 months. The mean length of coaching abuse was 21.9 months.

The 25 abuse victims identified 29 perpetrators, which indicates that revictimization is rare in this group of respondents. In some cases, revictimization was not technically possible because the team members left organized sports until they went to college. Six of the perpetrators (21%) were female, 23 (79%) were male. The distribution of types of abuse differed considerably by gender of perpetrator. The abuse was scored separately on three dimensions: verbal, physical, and sexual. A given perpetrator could have carried out one, two, or all three forms of abuse against a victim. Four of the female coaches (67%) committed verbal abuse, three (50%) physical abuse, and one (17%) sexual abuse. The pattern for male perpetrators was quite different. Sexual abuse was the most common form reported (13 perpetrators, 57%), followed by verbal abuse (12 perpetrators, 52%) and physical abuse (4 perpetrators, 17%).

Following the statistical analysis, the incidents were qualitatively analyzed according to the apparent severity of the incidents. Incident descriptions did not differ by gender of perpetrator, so I have collapsed male- and female-perpetrated incidents for the qualitative phase of the analysis. The best fit of the complex data to a linear classification scheme eventually was determined to be two 5-point scales on coaching abuse, one sexual and the other nonsexual. Each scale begins with moderate verbal abuse and increases in severity until physical or sexual abuse is introduced at Level 4. The five levels of nonsexual coaching abuse are summarized below.

Level 1: Coach says negative things to player that are not necessary to the coaching process. These negativities are sufficiently destructive that they damage player's self-image.

Level 2: Same as Level 1, except that coach not only damages player directly, but also goes beyond this by saying destructive things about player to one or more others who are important to player (teammates, parents, etc.).

Level 3: Coach physically threatens and psychologically terrifies player without making physical contact. Throwing objects near player, mistreating equipment, violent cursing, and promising to assault player are examples of Level 3 coaching abuse, nonsexual type.

Level 4: Coach initiates aggressive physical contact against player without hitting or thoroughly beating up (assaulting) player. Examples include pushing, tripping, shaking, knocking player against walls or furniture.

Level 5: Coach hits player with fist or very forcefully with open hand, or with a foreign object (including weapons). Coach may use multiple blows thoroughly to beat up (assault) player, or even go farther and permanently disable or kill player.

For some years, my main area of sociological practice has been assessing the ways in which violence is used to dominate women in intimate relationships and testifying in court on behalf of battered women who have killed their batterers in self-defense or have been forced by their batterers to commit a crime (duress) for which these innocent women are being harassed and prosecuted by the district attorney's office. What strikes me about the five levels of nonsexual coaching abuse is how closely they parallel the continuum from verbal and psychological abuse to escalating overt physical abuse in battering relationships. I see nonsexual coaching abuse to be one of the varieties of masculine role performance that is an expression of the same hypermasculinity that Hans Toch (Chapter 9, this volume) finds to be so highly concentrated in correctional institutions and Tracy Kramer (Chapter 11, this volume) labels as toxic in Vietnam combat war veterans who are suffering from post-traumatic stress syndrome.

Sexual coaching abuse differs from nonsexual abuse in that physical contact occurs at Level 1, but the contact is so carefully orchestrated by the all-powerful coach that it appears to be incidental. I have talked with young women who know they are uncomfortable with their coach's touches, but they can't figure out why. Sometimes they think the fault is with themselves rather than the coach. I define the five levels of sexual coaching abuse as follows.

Level 1: Coach makes sexual insinuations about player, gives player some special treatment, and makes player uncomfortable through seemingly incidental physical contact. Coach simultaneously discriminates against players who are not defined as attractive and desirable.

Level 2: This is an extension of Level 1, in which the special treatment escalates and the sexual insinuations intensify. The physical contact no longer seems to be incidental, but is suspicious. Coach extends control over player beyond what is necessary to the coaching process, such as by demanding the wearing of inappropriately revealing clothing.

Level 3: Coach directly propositions player for sex but no overt sex occurs. Coach openly gawks at and comments about sexual aspects of player's body. Coach may attempt to blackmail player sexually, as by trading sex for playing time.

Level 4: Coach touches player sexually, or induces player to touch coach sexually, constituting foreplay and sexual assault. If present, threats and blackmail intensify.

Level 5: Coach completes one or more sex acts with player, constituting statutory rape. If present, threats and blackmail are maximized.

Though the nonsexual coaching abuse scale reminds me of woman battering, the sexual coaching abuse scale reminds me of the grooming activities of a pedophile. The sexually abusing coach starts with the most innocuous of activities and gradually escalates over time, never going any farther than appears to be safe. For some coaches I have known, this means that they fantasize a lot and verbalize to trusted friends who have a similar sexual interest in young girls, but their actual treatment of players never rises above Level 1. Nobody would doubt the damage caused by coaches who engage in sexual abuse at Levels 3 through 5. Few would argue about Level 2. How damaging is Level 1?

I suspect that many readers might dismiss Level 1 as no more than good experience with the hard knocks of life. Permit me to explain why this is not the case, and why Level 1 sexual coaching abuse often is devastating to the victims. To begin with, there is the time factor. An incident of Level 4 sexual coaching abuse might last but a few minutes, while Level 1 is often a long-term affair, lasting a year or more. Then there is the importance of team membership to a girl's self-image, friendship networks, and status among both boys and girls in the school. These factors bind an abused player to the coach so she generally will take a great deal of abuse at Levels 1 and 2, and sometimes at higher levels, before quitting the team, reporting the coach to the superintendent, or telling her parents. A final consideration for the better athletes is the possibility of obtaining a scholarship to attend a more expensive college than they could afford, which requires a great deal of playing time and the coach's recommendation in addition to considerable physical talent on the part of the player.

Level 1 sexual coaching abuse isn't just sexual harassment. It also results in favoritism for those who fit the coach's construct of desirability and discrimination for those who do not. At the very least, discrimination can damage a player's self-image; at the worst, it can spoil her plans for college athletic participation and even prevent her from attending college at all. Here are some examples of Level 1 sexual coaching abuse in action.

1. Coach allows the team to learn only plays that lead to shots by the favored player or players, who otherwise would not justify such an unbalanced offense.
2. Rather than risking harming a relationship with a desired player, the coach directs needed criticism to her via a second player, pretending that the second player made the error instead of the desired player.
3. Coach gives special gifts and attention to the desired player, paving the way for her career success so long as she is receptive to his manipulations.
4. Coach tries to create situations in which he is alone with a desired player, such as in a back room at the gymnasium to talk about the player's problems or with an invitation to his house to watch game films.
5. Coach praises the desired player endlessly and inappropriately while being excessively critical of one or more undesired players who become scapegoats. During games, this can take the form of constantly yelling criticisms at the scapegoats for everything that goes wrong on the court or field of play. One function of this behavior is that the desired player or players can clearly see what could happen if they were to fall from favor and that the team members who are neither desired nor scapegoats realize that their own precarious positions could deteriorate overnight should they dare to complain about the coach's favoritism.
6. When the coach goes too far or too fast and a desired player rebels, her fall from grace can be alarmingly quick. Her playing time can decrease, plays can be redesigned to lead to shots by other team members, and the coach might meet with her parents to tell them that he is having doubts about her potential for an athletic scholarship in college.

The crucial point to grasp is that the sexually abusive coach, even at Level 1, creates a total environment in which desired players, scapegoats, and all the others who are in between are manipulated to stimulate the coach's sexual fantasies. The players do not have enough life experience to understand what is happening to them. At Level 1, the sexual coaching abuse is subject to so many alternative interpretations that it is very difficult for parents and school administrators to identify it and correct the problem before any more damage is done. Detection at Level 1 is also thwarted because the scapegoats usually suffer more damage then the desired player or players. As the abuse level escalates, the desired player or players suffer increasing damage, soon outstripping any negative effects experienced by the scapegoats.

It should also be noted that many coaches have so high a degree of control over their players, particularly those players they target for abuse, that they do not need threats or blackmail to compel sexual favors and maintain secrecy. The huge power differential between coaches and players is sufficient to produce adoration and hero worship from many players. When sexualized, this turns into an adolescent infatuation, or "crush." Players experiencing this intensity of positive feelings toward a coach are extremely vulnerable to sexual abuse.

A particularly revealing example of the secondary effects of sexual coaching abuse comes from the collegiate level. A newly hired debate coach turned out to have a sexual interest in the younger male college students on his team, which initially was concealed by his heterosexual marriage. When the debate season started, the coach favored several male students to whom he was attracted and kept all the female students at arm's length. They did not receive much of the debate training and debate competition experience that was lavished on male team members in general, and the desired young men in particular. The situation was bought to my attention by a young man who had fallen out of favor because of his lack of sexual responsiveness. He had managed to implicate the coach by seducing him into discussing "the kind of boys he liked" while the young man recorded the coach on a small machine the young man had hidden in his bag. I used the tape to secure the coach's immediate resignation. In this case, the young men currently favored did not complain and refused to cooperate in the investigation. They were having a great time, with alcohol and other drugs supplied to them at no charge and with a great deal of success in their debating efforts. The women and the young man who no longer was desired were the only ones who defined themselves as having been victimized.

Returning to the two scales of coaching abuse, I would like to conclude the presentation of the results with examples of each level of abuse taken from the words of the respondents. These vignettes add a necessary human dimension to the rather bloodless descriptions of the abuse levels that I have described above. Here are real-life examples for the five levels in the nonsexual coaching abuse scale. The names of the coaches have been removed, and the identities of the players have been obscured.

Level 1: Least Severe

Coach used to tell me things like I [was] "sorry" and would never amount to anything. I thought Coach told me these things to make me a better player, and want to improve, but it just . . . lowered my self-esteem.

Level 2

Everything I did in practice was wrong, even if other people did the same thing and were praised for it. Coach told my parents that I had no talent and that basically I was terrible at [my sport].

Level 3

This coach was not abusive sexually towards me. Coach abused the team verbally, emotionally and physically. If we did not perform to coach's standards, coach would curse at all the players, throw things at or near us, and make us do 'punishment' drills or sprints. . . . I am in the military, and boot camp was easier than coach's practices. I suspected that coach was having a sexual relationship with one of my friends who was only 14 or 15 at the time . . . my suspicions were never confirmed. But years later coach was caught with a 16-year-old in a hotel room . . . coach was a teacher at [her] high school.

Level 4

Coach really mistreated almost all the players; one girl, coach picked up by the collar and pushed her against the locker . . . coach never made us feel like a part of the team, no matter how well we played. . . . We didn't fight back [because] we wanted to be on the team.

Level 5: Most Severe

Coach yelled at me furiously, sometimes shaking [me] and spitting . . . coach would pop me (open-handed) in the face, and tell me to "get with it." Coach hit me during an away game because I wasn't paying attention in the huddle. Coach hit me so hard she knocked me off balance, bruised my eye and face, and busted my lip on the inside and out.

Forgive me for using a female coaching abuse example for the highest level of nonsexual abuse. I did so to demonstrate that men do not have a monopoly on violence and also for a more elusive reason. In my experience, violence and other forms of exploitation are strongly associated with some, but not all, varieties of masculinities. These varieties are socially shared roles, not biological entities. They are predominantly occupied by heterosexual men, but also can be occupied by gay men, lesbians, and heterosexual women. If we array masculinities on a continuum from hypomasculinity to hypermasulinity, those complexes of roles in the most hyper quarter of the continuum are the ones with which violence is most closely associated. My conclusion is that the woman who engaged in serious violence against one of her team members was playing a hypermasculine role, that is, living a hypermasculine lifestyle. With this in mind, the female coach in the Level 5 example does not break the rule, she is the exception that proves the rule.

When reading the sexual abuse vignettes that follow, notice the multiplicity of techniques used by the coaches to envelop their targets. Also notice how difficult it would be to prove abusive intent at Level 1, or even at Level 2. Who would administrators believe if the player in Level 3 reported the coach's proposition? With no witnesses, how many girls would report it?

Level 1: Least Severe

Coach favored players by their looks or their legs. Coach would call us "Honey," and pinch our cheeks and pat our butts. Coach took me into the office and turned off the lights "as a joke," as if coach was going to do something physical with me. The "special treatment" got worse; coach would offer me rides and would try to buddy-up to me by talking and being overly nice to me. Coach said something to me at the end of the season, apparently after the administration had confronted coach. Coach said, "I would never want to hurt you; you're a vessel of beauty and kindness." Coach tried to make me feel stupid for telling someone what coach had done.

Level 2

Coach misused coach's power and authority to degrade all the girls on the team. Coach outstepped coach's boundaries, requiring weigh-ins on a regular basis. Also, coach required us to lift weights in tank tops and short shorts and/or Spandex. Coach was always in the girl's locker room, and hugged and kissed the girls on the team, apparently to comfort after a game lost, etc. . . . Coach told my sister that he put her on the team because she looked like an old girlfriend of coach's. Coach sent her flowers and a stuffed animal on her birthday. . . . Coach required rub-downs after hard practices. Coach demonstrated on someone, and we had to rub each other's calves.

Level 3

When I was a sophomore in high school, coach told me that I couldn't get any playing time unless coach could have sex with my mom. Coach would watch us run, and look at our breasts when coach talked to us, and looked up our shorts when we stretched. We had to wear Spandex to stop that. Coach threatened to kick me off the team. The worst thing was when it was coach's birthday; coach took me after practice to see the new uniforms and asked me when I or my mom was going to jump out of the cake and have sex with coach.

Level 4

My coach and our team were coming back from a meet and coach started feeling my leg and playing with my hair. Coach thought I was asleep, but coach woke me up, but I was scared to move . . . at first, I wasn't sure it would last. But after it continued, I felt scared . . . coach told me what coach was doing was wrong, and I shouldn't tell anyone because coach could lose his job and spouse. Coach was touching me, rubbing against me, and making me feel coach's genitals. This kept on and on. I wish I would have told the school board now. I'm afraid coach is doing the same thing to other girls.

Level 5: Most Severe

After befriending me in practice, the coach would invite me to coach's house. Being new in town, I appreciated the attention. After about a month, coach kissed me, and this led to sex (I was a virgin before this) and emotional abuse. Coach was very manipulative, telling me it was OK and it all meant that coach cared for me. Coach's treatment of me as a player and as a student, I feel, worsened. Coach would expect more of me than others, and I was penalized more. It seemed I could never do enough to please coach. It was a game of coach's—keep me dependent upon coach for praise and approval by never quite giving it 100 percent. Coach pressured me with a threat of suicide if I left coach.

Controlling Coaching Abuse

We have become acquainted with the varieties of the sexual and nonsexual coaching abuse of schoolgirls. While we cannot say anything about the incidence or prevalence of coaching abuse nationally, we can be sure that coaching abuse does exist and that reducing the incidence and prevalence of abuse by screening male coaches carefully and arranging early retirement for existing abusive coaches is a worthy goal.

Looking at the vignettes and the descriptions on the two continua of coaching abuse, it is evident that schoolgirl coaching abuse is located at the intersection of sexual harassment, physical and emotional child abuse, and pedophilia. It has many of the characteristics of each crime, and multiple damaging effects on its victims. Because of the historical dominance of hypermasculinity in school sports, which borders on totalitarianism in many school districts, most of the evidence of coaching abuse is dismissed as the coach's prerogative. There are no specific laws dealing with coaching abuse the way there are for sexual harassment, pedophilia (under child sexual abuse), and the child abuse laws that are enforced by child protective services agencies as well as police departments. There are no administrative codes requiring heightened supervision of coaches because of the vulnerability of their charges, or specifying ways of screening new coaches, or regulating the behavior of coaches and the content of their contacts with players.

Parents, school administrators, and concerned citizens need to be provided with educational materials on proper coaching behavior and its perversions. This probably is the only way to begin to reduce coaching abuse in our nation's schools. Once coaching abuse can be identified more easily, it will be possible to defend childhood team members more effectively. At present, there is no research-based publication on coaching abuse available. It is hoped that the preliminary research reported in this chapter will lead to a larger study that will provide a solid empirical grounding for such a publication. In the meantime, there are two sources of assistance in print of which I am aware: The Child Centered Coaching program produced by Family Nurturing Center in Park City, Utah, and *Keeping Youth Sports Safe and Fun,* a pamphlet published in Saint Paul by the Minnesota Amateur Sports Commission and the Minnesota Children's Trust Fund.

Child Centered Coaching: Instructors Training Manual (Bavolek, 1994) is one of six publications that, together with two videotapes, constitute an entire program on child centered coaching. Although this program does not focus specifically on coaching abuse, it includes an awareness that coaching abuse exists, conceptional definitions that are useful, and a code of ethics for coaches. One-line general examples are given of verbal abuse, physical abuse, emotional abuse, and sexual abuse. There are no detailed descriptions of coaching abuse in action or ways of identifying abusive coaches. The major contribution of the program to lowering coaching abuse is that by bringing parents intimately into the process with coaches, it provides an enhanced form of social control over coaching abuse that is bound to have a positive effect on the experiences that players have with their coaches.

A much more detailed treatment of coaching abuse is contained in *Keeping Youth Sports Safe and Fun,* by Cordelia Anderson (1994). She sensitively differentiates between girls and boys in school sports, showing that girls are more vulnerable and face additional barriers to successful team play beyond those met by boys. Anderson recognizes emotional, physical, and sexual abuse, as well as sexual harassment. She introduces the innovative concept of philosophical abuse, which occurs when hyper-masculine ideology overcomes good sports philosophy. "Winning isn't everything, it's the only thing," is an example of philosophical abuse, as is pressuring an injured team member to continue playing and condoning or encouraging deliberate attempts to injure players on opposing teams. There is a good section differentiating healthy touching (respectful, public, nurturing) from sexualized touching, and separate sections for coaches, parents, and team members on avoiding abuse. The following passage from *Keeping Youth Sports Safe and Fun* is an appropriate closing for this chapter.

> Hitting children on the back of the head, kicking them, throwing equipment at them or shaking them are indications the person is out of control of both their behavior and feelings. These behaviors are not disciplinary. They are abusive. A one-time incident may be serous enough to warrant an intervention. A pattern . . . requires intervention. (Anderson, 1994, p. 7)

PART THREE

MEN VICTIMIZING MEN

7

Men Victimizing Men

The Case of Lynching, 1865-1900

JAMES W. MESSERSCHMIDT

In the 1924 edition of *Criminology,* Edwin Sutherland (pp. 239-249) devoted 10 pages to the crime of lynching (the unlawful assault and/or killing of an accused person by mob action). Sutherland (p. 239) was concerned especially with the fact that lynching, although occasionally employed during slavery, became a systematic event in the South between 1865 and 1900. Sutherland (pp. 242-243) offered two insightful and significant reasons for instantaneous white-mob violence. The first, and to Sutherland (p. 242) the "underlying" reason, is "race prejudice or a feeling of white superiority." In particular, when African Americans were "emancipated" from their subordinate slave position, "great antagonism" by whites took the form of lynching (p. 242). Yet according to Sutherland (p. 243), lynching occurred for a second reason: as "compensation for the sex habits of white men in relation to negro women" (p. 243). Recognizing the widespread rape of African American women by white men, Sutherland (p. 243) continues: "The white woman must be shown to be infinitely different from the negro woman and lynching of the negro rapist is one way of doing this."

Through his seeming ability to transcend the intellectual climate of his time, Sutherland points to the importance of inequality in what today we call race relations (e.g., maintenance of white supremacy) and gender relations (e.g., sexuality, and its relation to masculinity and femininity). Clearly, Sutherland perceived the theoretical importance of race, gender, and sexuality to a proper understanding of lynching.[1] Although it is not surprising that Sutherland recognized the importance of "race prejudice," it is significant—and possibly surprising to many—that he underscores the "sex habits of white men" and their relation to African American and white women as well as the alleged "negro rapist." Yet this is as far as his thoughts reached and demonstrates the limitations one would expect from prefeminist work. The social and historical context in which Sutherland wrote embodied a relative absence of sociological/criminological theorizing on gender, sexuality, and crime.

Nevertheless, Sutherland was clearly on to something. Although specifying the importance of the "sex habits of white men" and their relation to the "negro rapist" to understanding the phenomenon of lynching, no investigation of the relationship among gender, sexuality, and lynching has emerged in criminology. Indeed, the topic is ignored altogether in recent sociological/criminological accounts.[2]

In what follows, I take seriously Sutherland's assertion and argue that a complete understanding of lynching is possible only through a comprehension of the interrelation among race, masculinity, and sexuality. As argued below, during Reconstruction and its immediate aftermath, lynching was a response to the perceived erosion of white male dominance and was an attempt to recreate what white-supremacist men imagined to be a lost status of unchallenged white masculine supremacy. Disguised in chivalric intimations—that is, as retribution for the alleged rape of a white woman by an African American man—lynching enforced white supremacy as well as gender hierarchies between men and women and among men. Before developing this argument further, let me outline the theoretical approach.

Structured Action Theory[3]

Historical and social conditions shape the character and definition of sex, race, and class categories. Each category and its meaning are given concrete expression by the specific social relations and historical context in which they are embedded. Moreover, in specific social situations we consistently engage in sex, race, and class attribution—identifying and categorizing people by appropriate sex, race, and class categories while simultaneously categorizing ourselves to others (West & Fenstermaker, 1995).

Nevertheless, as West and Fenstermaker (1995) argue, "doing" gender, race, and class entails considerably more than the "social emblems" of specific categories. Rather, gender, race, and class involves situated social and interactional accomplishment. In other words, gender, race, and class grow out of social practices in specific settings and serve to inform such practices in reciprocal relation. So, whereas sex, race, and class categories define social identification, "doing" gender, race, and class systematically corroborates that identification through social interaction. In effect, there is a plurality of forms in which gender, race, and class are constructed: We coordinate our activities to "do" gender, race, and class in situational ways.

Crucial to conceptualization of gender, race, and class as situated accomplishment is the notion of "accountability" (West & Zimmerman, 1987). Because individuals realize that their behavior *may possibly* be held accountable to others, they configure and orchestrate their actions in relation to how these might be interpreted by others in the particular social context in which they occur. In other words, in their daily activities individuals attempt to be identified socially as, for example, "female" or "male," "African American" or "white," "working class" or "middle class." In this way, accountability "allows individuals to conduct their activities in relation to their circumstances" (West & Fenstermaker, 1993, p. 156), suggesting that gender, race, and class vary by social situation and circumstance. Within social interaction, then, we encourage and expect others to attribute particular categories to us. And, we facilitate the ongoing task of accountability by demonstrating we are male or female, African American or white, working class or middle class, through concocted behaviors that may be interpreted accordingly. Consequently, we do gender, race, and class differently—depending upon the social situation and the social circumstances we encounter. The particular meanings of gender, race, and class are defined in social interaction and, therefore, through personal practice. Doing gender, race, and class renders social action accountable in terms of normative conceptions, attitudes, and activities appropriate to one's category in the specific social situation in which one acts (West & Fenstermaker, 1993, p. 157).

In this view, therefore, gender, race, and class are accomplished systematically, not imposed on people or settled beforehand and never static or finished products. Rather, people construct gender, race, and class in specific social situations. In other words, people participate in self-regulating social action whereby they monitor their own and others' conduct.

Social Relations, Social Structures, and Structured Action

Although gender, race, and class are "made," so to speak, through the unification of self-regulated practices, these practices do not occur in a vacuum. Instead, they are influenced by the social structural constraints we experience. Social structures—defined here as regular and patterned forms of interaction over time that constrain and channel behavior in specific ways—"exist as the reproduced conduct of situated actors" (Giddens, 1976, p. 127). As Connell (1987, 1995) argues, these social structures (e.g., divisions of labor and power and sexuality) are neither external to social actors nor simply and solely constraining; on the contrary, structure is realized only through social action, and social action requires structure as its condition. Social structures are enacted by "knowledgeable" human agents (people who know what they are doing and how to do it) and agents act by putting into practice their structured knowledge (Giddens, 1984). Moreover, in certain circumstances, agents improvise or innovate in structurally shaped ways that significantly reconfigure the very structures that shaped them (Giddens, 1984). Because people do gender, race, and class in specific social situations, they reproduce and sometimes change social structures. Thus, specific forms of gender, race, and class are available, encouraged, and permitted, depending upon one's position in these social relations. Not only are there numerous ways of constructing masculinity and femininity—we must speak of masculinities and femininities—there are likewise myriad ways of constructing race and class—we must articulate, for example, differing African American identities and middle-class identities. Accordingly, gender, race, and class must be viewed as *structured action*—what people do under specific social structural constraints.

Appropriate, then, is a theory that conceptualizes how gender, race, and class relations arise within the same ongoing practices. For to understand crime by men, we must comprehend how gender, race, and class relations are part of all social existence, and not view each relation as outside the other two. As with sex, we can identify race and class categories and, therefore, the possibility of people being held accountable as a member of any or all of these categories (West & Fenstermaker, 1995). In other words, the accomplishment of gender, race, and class occurs simultaneously through social interaction and, as West and Fenstermaker (1995, p. 24) contend, the accountability of persons to these categories is the key to understanding the maintenance of existing divisions of labor and

power. In other words, gender, race, and class relations are each constituted by a variety of social structures and, therefore, structured action.
Social actors perpetuate and transform these social structures within the
same interaction; simultaneously, these structures constrain and enable
gender, race, and class social action. The result is the ongoing social
construction of gender, race, and class relations. Consequently, "doing
race" and "doing class" are similar to "doing gender" in that they render
social action accountable in terms of normative conceptions, attitudes,
and activities appropriate to one's race and class category in the specific
social situation in which one acts (West & Fenstermaker, 1995).[4]

The Salience of Gender, Race, and Class

Nevertheless, the salience of each social relation to *influencing crime*
varies by social situation. Although gender, race, and class are ubiquitous,
the significance of each relation shifts with a changing context: in one
situation, gender and race both may be important for actuating crime; in
another social setting, class, or gender, or any combination of the three
relations may be relevant. In other words, gender, race, and class are not
absolute and not equally significant in every social setting where crime
is realized. That is, accountability to gender, race, and class are not
always, in all social situations, equally critical to the social construction
of crime. As I show below, in the particular social setting of Reconstruction and its immediate aftermath (1865-1900), both race and gender (but
not social class) were highly salient to the emergence of white-male mob
violence. That is, accountability to race and gender were equally important to the social construction of this crime, but accountability to class
was not.

In this way, then, social relations of gender, race, and class variously
join each of us in a common relationship to others—we share structural
space. Consequently, common or shared blocks of knowledge evolve
through interaction in which particular gender, race, and class ideals and
activities differ in significance. Through such interaction, gender, race,
and class become institutionalized, permitting, for example, men to draw
on such existing, but previously formed, ways of thinking and acting to
construct particular race and class masculine identities for specific settings. The particular criteria of gender, race, and class identities are
embedded in the social situations and recurrent practices whereby social
relations are structured (Giddens, 1989, p. 285).

Hegemonic and Subordinated Masculinities

In any discussion of masculinities and violence, we must recognize, first, that because men are positioned differently throughout society, they share with other men the construction of masculinities peculiar to their race and class position in society. Further, we must accept that socially organized power relations among men are constructed historically on the bases of class, race, and sexual preference; that is, in specific contexts some men have greater power than other men. In other words, the capacity to exercise power is, for the most part, a reflection of one's position in social relationships and, therefore, may actually shift in relation to different axes of power and powerlessness. That is, in one situation a man may exercise power (i.e., as a patriarchal husband) while in another he may experience powerlessness (i.e., as a factory worker). Accordingly, masculinity can be understood only as a fluid, relational, and structural construct.

Connell's (1987, 1995) notion of "hegemonic masculinity" is relevant here. Hegemonic masculinity is the culturally idealized form of masculinity in a given historical setting. Hegemonic masculinity is neither transhistorical nor transcultural, but varies from society to society and changes within a particular society over time. In any specific time and place, then, hegemonic masculinity is culturally honored, glorified, and extolled at the symbolic level, such as the mass media, and is constructed in relation both to subordinated masculinities (based on race, class, and sexual preference, for example) and to women. In fact, hegemonic masculinity is the dominant form of masculinity to which other types of masculinity are subordinated, not eliminated, and it provides the primary basis for relationships among men.

Thus, hegemonic masculinity, as the culturally dominant ideal, influences but does not determine masculine behavior. Hegemonic masculinity underpins the conventions applied in the enactment and reproduction of masculinities—the lived pattern of meanings that, as they are experienced as practices, appear as reciprocally confirming. As such, hegemonic masculine discourse shapes a sense of reality for most men and is continually renewed, recreated, defended, and modified through practice. And yet, it is at times resisted, limited, altered, and challenged. As Barrie Thorne (1993) notes, "Individuals and groups develop varied forms of accommodation, reinterpretation, and resistance to ideologically hegemonic patterns" (p. 106). Consequently, hegemonic masculinity operates as discourse that is "on hand" to be actualized into practice in a range of different circumstances. It provides a conceptual framework that is materialized in the design of social structures and, therefore, in daily practices and interactions.

The concepts "hegemonic" and "subordinated" masculinities permit investigation of the different way men experience their everyday world from their particular position in society and how they relate to other men. Although men attempt to express aspects of hegemonic masculine discourse through speech, dress, physical appearance, activities, and relationships with others, these social signs of masculinity are associated with the specific context of one's actions and are self-regulated within that context. Thus, masculinity is based on a social construct that reflects unique circumstances and relationships—a social construction that is renegotiated in each particular context. In other words, social actors self-regulate their behavior and make specific choices in specific contexts. As Connell (1987) points out, everyday masculine practices draw on the cultural ideals of hegemonic masculinity but do not correspond necessarily to actual masculinities as they are lived: What most men support is not necessarily what they are (p. 186). In this way, then, men construct varieties of masculinities through specific practices. By emphasizing diversity in gender constructions, we realize a more fluid and situated approach to our understanding of gender.

This perspective permits us to conceptualize masculinities and violence more realistically and completely, enables us to explore how and in what respects masculinity is constituted in certain settings at certain times, and how that construct relates to crime. The remaining sections of the chapter focus on explaining the differentiation of masculinities by observing the work and product of their construction in specific social settings and through certain practices. I examine such masculinities as they are constructed among white and African American men during slavery and Reconstruction. The definition and interpretation of the boundaries between masculinities—and thus the hierarchical separation of white men from African American men—are critical to understanding white-male mob violence in the late 19th-century South. Accordingly, the specific masculine meanings constructed through particular conceptions of race and the way in which violence as practice is related to those meanings and conceptions are analyzed thoroughly. As such, I argue that only through analysis of *racial masculinities*—in particular, the social construction of white-supremacist masculinity—can we make coherent sense of lynching and other forms of white-male mob violence at this time in U.S. history.

Although men are always doing masculinity, the significance of masculine accomplishment is socially situated and, thus, is an intermittent matter. That is, certain occasions present themselves as more intimidating for demonstrating and affirming masculinity. In such settings, sex category (and possibly race and/or class category) is particularly salient; it is, as David Morgan (1992) expresses it, "more or less explicitly put on the line" (p. 47)—a time when doing masculinity requires extra effort. Under such conditions, crime and violence may be invoked as a practice for doing masculinity and distinguishing masculinities from one another. Reconstruction and its immediate aftermath provide an excellent case study of white hegemonic masculinity being "explicitly put on the line" and the subsequent emergence of lynching and mob violence to reproduce that masculinity.

Slavery

Slavery legally bound all blacks to the "white father" and cut slaves off from all birthrights they may have enjoyed as members of a community. Male and female slaves were without social status or political and economic power; they could not own property, earn a living for themselves, or participate in public and political life. Slavery conveyed to all blacks that the fullness of humanity would never be available to them and overtly sought to reduce them to dependent, passive, childlike characters. In short, slavery produced a white-supremacist discourse and practice that declared the physical, intellectual, and moral superiority of whites over blacks.

The master-slave relation constructed a masculine power hierarchy in which the "white master" was the representative of hegemonic masculinity. Indeed, powerful hegemonic masculinity was associated with white-male supremacy, inasmuch as citizenship rights meant "manhood" rights that inhered to white males *only* (Bederman, 1995). Cultural ideology and discourse claimed that the most "advanced" races had evolved the most pronounced gender differences. White "civilized" planter woman (the mistress) represented the highest level of womanhood—delicate, spiritual, exempt from heavy labor, ensconced in and dedicated to home. White "civilized" planter man (the master) was the most manly creature ever evolved—firm of character and self-controlled, who provided for his family and steadfastly protected his woman and children from the rigors of the workaday world. Indeed, the symbols of hegemonic masculinity during slavery were whiteness; heading a heterosexual family; ownership of land, slaves, or both; literacy; and participation in political affairs. In particular, politics was extremely salient to white hegemonic masculinity in 19th-century U.S. slave society. Paula Baker (1984) explains:

> Parties and electoral politics united all white men, regardless of class or other differences, and provided entertainment, a definition of manhood, and the basis for a male ritual. Universal white manhood suffrage implied that since all [white] men shared the chance to participate in electoral politics, they possessed political equality. The right to vote was something important that [white] men held in common. (p. 628)

Participation in politics, then, was an essential practice for defining white men (hegemonic masculinity) in relation to black men (subordinate masculinity) and to all women. Indeed, political parties were fraternal organizations that bonded white men through their whiteness—participation in politics bound men to others like themselves. The notions of "womanhood" and "blackness" served as negative referents that united all white men. Politics, however, made gender and race the most significant divisions—white men saw past class differences and found common ground with other white men (Baker, 1984, p. 630). Participation in politics was an essential practice that triggered and consolidated racial and masculine identities; it was a resource for doing "white masculinity." Slavery institutionalized black men as "Other" and restricted male slaves from engaging in hegemonic masculine practices (Thorpe, 1967, p. 159). Indeed, "whiteness" was the standard against which all else was measured, white men and white masculinity were constructed in contrast to subordinate "Other" men and "Other" masculinities.

Moreover, according to scientific and popular ideology, the "savage races" had not evolved the proper gender differences that whites possessed, and this is precisely what made them savage (Russett, 1989, pp. 130-155). Indeed, slavery denoted black males and females as more alike than different—"genderless as far as the slaveholders were concerned" (Davis, 1983, p. 5). In the middle of the 19th century, seven of eight slaves (men and women alike) were field workers, both profitable labor-units for the master. Predictably, black slaves did not construct the gender differences of the white planter class. The race and gender division of labor and power in slavery caused black women not to construct themselves as the "weaker sex" or the "housewife," and not to construct black men as the "family head" and the "family provider" (p. 8). Because "woman" was synonymous with "housewife" and "man" synonymous with "provider," the practices of black slaves could not conform to hegemonic gender ideologies and, therefore, were considered gender anomalies. In other words, black male slaves were defined as less than men and black female slaves as less than women (Bederman, 1995, p. 20). This construction of racial boundaries through gender also had its sexual component. White southerners differentiated themselves from "savages" by attributing to the latter a sexual nature that was more sensual, aggressive, and beastlike than that of whites. Influenced by the Elizabethan image of "the lusty Moor," white southerners embraced the notion that blacks were "lewd, lascivious and wanton people" (D'Emilio & Freedman, 1988, p. 35). Both their gender similarity and animal-like sexuality, white-supremacist discourse declared, proved blacks were a subordinate species; therefore, it was natural that races must not mix and that whites must dominate blacks. Both scientific and popular thought supported the view that whites were civilized and rational, but that blacks were savage, irrational, and sensual (Jordan, 1968; Takaki, 1982). Indeed, it was this notion of race corporeality that defined inequality between whites and blacks and constructed what Frankenberg (1993) recently labeled an "essentialist racist discourse." Such a discourse constructs blacks as "fundamentally Other than white people; different, inferior, less civilized, less human, more animal, than whites" (p. 61). The articulation and deployment of essentialist racism as the dominant discourse for thinking about race marks the moment when race is constructed as *difference:* alleged white biological superiority justifies economic, political, and social inequalities in slavery.

Not surprisingly, social and legal regulations—such as prohibiting marriage between black men and white women—affecting interracial sexuality served to produce and cement racial identities. Slavery "heightened planter insistence on protecting white women and their family line, from the specter of interracial union" (D'Emilio & Freedman, 1988, p. 94). The commitment in slave society was protection of white female virtue and containment of white female sexuality within white, marital, reproductive relations (p. 95). In contrast to this draconian social control of white women,

> Southern white men of the planter class enjoyed extreme sexual privilege. Most southern moralists condoned white men's gratification of lust, as long as they did so discreetly with poor white or black women. Polite society condemned the public discussion of illicit sex, but men's private writings reveal a good

deal of comfort with the expression of pure sexual desire, unrelated to love or intimacy. (p. 95)

Indeed, rape of black female slaves by white masters rivaled separation of families as the most provocative event in black family life (Jones, 1986, p. 37). Slaves endured the daily pervasive fear that such assaults were possible, especially given the easy circumstances under which such rape could be committed. For example, one Louisiana master would enter the slave cabin and tell the husband "to go outside and wait 'til he do what he want to do." The black husband "had to do it and he couldn't do nothing 'bout it" (pp. 37-38). And Angela Davis (1983) points out that the practice was a weapon of domination and repression "whose covert goal was to extinguish slave women's will to resist, and in the process, demoralize their men" (pp. 23-24). Indeed, sexual abuse of slave women in the presence of slave husbands/fathers made the point that slave men were not "real men" (Genovese, 1974, p. 482).[5] Thus, greater regulation of white women's sexuality was matched by greater sexual privilege for white men and "provided white men with both a sexual outlet and a means of maintaining racial domination" (D'Emilio & Freedman, 1988, p. 94).[6]

Moreover, although denigration of interracial sexuality evoked the notion of virility—the sexually active black male as a threat to white women (Fox-Genovese, 1988, p. 291)—this clearly was overshadowed by the social control of white female sexuality noted earlier. Indeed, as Elizabeth Fox-Genovese points out: "The presumed threat of black male sexuality never provoked the wild hysteria and violence in the Old South that it did in the New" (p. 291). Thus, although approximately three hundred lynchings were recorded between 1840 and 1860, less than 10% involved blacks (the majority were white abolitionists). Black lynchings were carried out primarily in the wake of an insurrection scare—not because of sexual liaisons with white women—and, therefore, were insignificant numerically prior to Emancipation (Genovese, 1974, p. 32).

Moreover, during slavery black men could be acquitted or pardoned for raping white women (Hodes, 1991). In slave society, rape meant the rape of white women—for it was not a crime to rape black women. Consequently, when a black man raped a black woman he could be punished only by his master, not by the court system (Genovese, 1974, p. 33). Slaves accused of raping white women occasionally suffered lynching, but the vast majority were tried (Schwarz, 1988; Spindel, 1989). Indeed, during slavery, mob violence was not the norm as a response to a charge of black-on-white rape but, rather, public policy left the matter in the hands of the courts (Genovese, 1974, p. 34). Moreover, not all rape trials resulted in conviction, and appellate courts in every southern state

> threw out convictions for rape and attempted rape on every possible ground, including the purely technical. They overturned convictions because the indictments had not been drawn up properly; because the lower courts had based their convictions on possibly coerced confessions: or because the reputation of the white victim had not been admitted as evidence. (Genovese, 1974, p. 34)

This latter reason, the reputation of the *white* victim, is telling, for sexual conduct of slave men seemed to matter less to white southerners than did the sexual conduct of white women. White women who did not practice purity and chastity when unmarried and observe decorum when married were severely admonished (Fox-Genovese, 1988, pp. 235-236).[7] Indeed, the sexual reputation of the white woman was so important to the white community that even if the evidence was clear that a black-on-white rape did in fact occur, if the victim was of "bad character," the black rapist quite possibly would go free. James Hugo Johnson (1970), in his study of miscegenation in the South between 1776 and 1860, was "astonished" at the number of rape cases in which

> white citizens of the communities in which these events transpired testify for the Negro and against the white woman and declare that the case is not a matter of rape, for the woman encouraged and consented to the act of the Negro. (p. 258)

The case of Carter, a "Negro man slave" in antebellum Virginia, and Catherine Brinal, the white female victim, is an excellent example (Johnston, 1970, pp. 259-260). Carter was found guilty of the rape of Brinal and sentenced to death. Yet the judge determined that Carter was the "proper object of mercy" because community members testified that Ms. Brinal

> was a woman of the worst fame, that her character was that of the most abandoned in as much as she (being a white woman) has three mulatto children, which by her own confession were begotten by different negro men; that from report she had permitted the said Carter to have peaceable sexual intercourse with her, before the time of his forcing her.

Consequently, this view of white female sexuality and the social control of that sexuality strongly outweights the sexuality and social control of black men during slavery (Hodes, 1991, pp. 41-42).

In sum, white slave masters and black male slaves constructed unique types of racial masculinity (hegemonic vs. subordinate) during slavery by occupying distinct locations within the particular race and gender divisions of labor and power. Both male groups experienced the everyday world from their proprietary positions in slave society and, consequently, there existed patterned ways in which race and masculinity were constructed and represented. Clearly, white and black men situationally accomplished masculinity in response to their socially structured circumstances.

Moreover, the meaning of "white masculinity" hinged on the existence of a subordinated "black masculinity."[8] Indeed, the power of white men rested on the racializing and sexualizing of masculinities. In slave society, hegemonic white masculinity was the standard against which all else was measured. Juxtaposed against the inherent "purity" and "goodness" that was white masculinity, black masculinity was essentially "impure" and "evil." This is notably evident in the sexualizing of masculinities because black masculine sexuality was constructed as animalistic and bestial. Nevertheless, despite an emphasis on the evil and threatening black masculine body and sexuality, in slave society the social control of white female sexuality received greater attention by white southerners than did black masculine sexuality.

Reformulating Black Masculinity

The passage of the Thirteenth Amendment (1865) outlawed slavery; with Emancipation, former slaves became "African Americans." Through the process of Reconstruction (1865-1877), the Union attempted to restore relations with the Confederate states. Arguably the most crucial issue of Reconstruction was the political status of former black slaves as African Americans. As citizens—and, therefore, through changing practices in the community, family, economy, and politics—African Americans constructed gender in new ways that challenged white supremacy. Indeed, former slaves immediately began asserting independence from whites by forming churches, becoming politically active, strengthening family ties, and attempting to educate their children (Zinn, 1980, p. 195). In fact, emancipation was defined in terms of the ability of former slave men and women to participate fully in U.S. life. This meant not only acquiring citizenship rights as African Americans, but also living out the gender ideals hegemonic in U.S. society. In particular, for African American men, there was a euphoric desire to seize the rights and privileges of citizenship and, thereby, hegemonic masculinity.

As discussed earlier, under slavery black men were unable to construct hegemonic masculinity as economic "providers," as participants in social and political affairs, and their family authority ultimately was inferior to that of the white master. With Emancipation, however, came developments that strengthened their authority within the African American family and institutionalized the notion that men and women should inhabit separate spheres. By 1870, the majority of African Americans lived in two-parent patriarchal family households, where African Americans embraced the new "cult of domesticity," women worked primarily in household labor, and men became the public representative of the family.[9] African American former slave men now considered it a "badge of honor" for their wives to work at home, and thereby gained considerable power within the household (Foner, 1988, p. 86). To former slave men, the ability to support and protect a family was synonymous with manhood. Embracing this ideology, the Freedman's Bureau[10] appointed the husband as "head of the household," assigning to him sole power to enter into contractual labor agreements for the entire family. Moreover, the Freedman's Bureau Act of 1865 assigned the right for allotment of land only to males (women could claim land only if unmarried) (p. 87).[11] In short, the phenomenon of "separate spheres" as discourse for hegemonic masculinity provided the definitional space needed for gender practices by African Americans no longer denied the right to maintain family bonds (Wiegman, 1993).

Indeed, the Reconstruction program contemplated that the freedom of African American men included the "natural" social superiority over African American women, and served to perpetuate gender divisions common in 19th-century U.S. society (Wiegman, 1993, p. 457). Thus, only African American men served as delegates to statewide-organized constitutional conventions (held in 1867 and 1868) where they demanded equality with whites—from access to public education to the right to bear arms, serve on juries, establish newspapers, assemble peacefully, and enter all avenues of agriculture, commerce, and trade. And African American men were quite successful. Not only did they help write southern state constitutions, but by 1868, African American men could serve on juries, vote, hold political office, and rise to political leadership (in the Republican party); African American women, like their white counterparts, could not (Foner, 1988, p. 87). Indeed, by 1869, former-slave votes accounted for two African American members of the U.S. Senate and 20 congressmen: 8 from South Carolina, 4 from North Carolina, 3 from Alabama, and 1 each from the other former Confederate states (Zinn, 1980, p. 195). Moreover, the Fourteenth Amendment (ratified in 1868) declared that "all persons born or naturalized in the United States" were citizens and that,

No state shall make or enforce any law which shall abridge the privileges or immunities of citizens of the United States nor shall any State deprive any person of life, liberty, or property, without due process of law; nor deny to any person within its jurisdiction the equal protection of the laws.

Also, in the late 1860s and early 1870s, Congress enacted several laws making it a crime to deprive African Americans of their rights and requiring federal officials to enforce those rights. These laws gave African Americans the right to contract and to buy property (Zinn, 1980, p. 194).

The move, then, from slavery to citizenry resulted in African Americans attempting to take control of conditions under which they labored, to free themselves from economic and political subordination to white authority, and to carve out the greatest possible measure of economic autonomy. Many African American men refused to continue working under the direction of an overseer and hundreds refused to sign labor contracts with their former masters (Foner, 1988, p. 105). Indeed, freedmen understood that their status after the war significantly depended on their economic status (Zinn, 1980, p. 192). However, although many attempted to obtain some portion of the land they labored on, the vast majority of African American men emerged from slavery landless—entering the free labor market as competitors with whites in the wage labor pool. Although freedmen attempted to organize their economic and political lives as independently as possible, they consistently faced racist obstacles.

Nevertheless, these new masculine practices by African American men in family, political, and economic relations represented not only the reformulation of black masculinity but the simultaneous loss of white masculine power. Under Reconstruction, exclusive white male control of politics, property, and family life ceases—thus creating a threatening situation for hegemonic white masculinity—and the result is a striking and intensive transformation of particular gender-and-race divisions of labor and power (Wiegman, 1993).

"Doing" White-Supremacist Masculinity Through Lynching

Within the context of Emancipation, then, the race-and-gender social structures were altered profoundly. The African American emergence from slavery as citizens was characterized by a reformulation of gender and race divisions of labor and power and the simultaneous emergence of a new African American masculinity. In such a social setting, the definitions and practices outlining both race and masculinity were obscured and, as argued below, white-male mob violence emerged as an attempt to reestablish the old meanings and hierarchy.

White-male violence was immediate. For example, in May 1866, 46 African Americans were killed when their schools and churches were burned by a white-male mob in Memphis; in July of the same year, 34 African Americans were killed in New Orleans by a white mob (Ayers, 1984, p. 161).

In general, the violence against African Americans was conducted by assorted cabals of white males. Of course, one of the largest of these was the Ku Klux Klan (KKK), which was organized in 1865 by six young returning Confederate officers as a secret social "club" in Pulaski, Tennessee (Foner, 1988; Trelease, 1971). The activities of the organization soon embraced the harassment of freed people, and "club" branches were established throughout the South in 1868 (Trelease, 1971, p. 64).

Klan membership—as with other white-male mobs during this period—included men of all classes of white southerners, with leadership usually drawn from the more well-to-do (Dowd Hall, 1979, pp. 132, 139-140; Rable, 1984, p. 30). Of most concern to white-supremacist males was the equation of African American male social practices with manhood. Indeed, conduct deemed "manly" by white men (such as involvement in politics) came to exemplify "insolence" and "insubordination" when practiced by African American men. African American men who engaged in any practice defining a masculinity that indicated they were "acting like a white man" became appropriate subjects for white-male violence. As Rable (1984, p. 92) put it, the Klan "was especially sensitive" to African American male practices that challenged white-male power.

Although African American women and whites who supported the rights of African American men were also victims of terror, the greatest violence was reserved for African American men who engaged in such "improper" masculine practices. Accordingly, African American men who were politically active (e.g., voting Republican and/or becoming a member of the Republican Party), who displayed economic independence (e.g., owning property and/or doing well economically), or who violated face-to-face boundaries of the masculine color line (e.g., "talking back" to a white man) were the major targets of white-male violence (Joint Select Committee, 1871).[12] Moreover, these alleged "improper" masculine practices often were coupled with any conduct that could be construed as a threatening sexual overture toward white women (Hodes, 1991).

The violence directed against such masculine practices ranged from whippings, to lynching, to castration. For example, in 1869, approximately 20 KKK men raided the home of Aaron Biggerstaff—an African American man politically active in the South Carolina Republican Party—and severely whipped him. According to testimony given to the Joint Select Committee on the Condition of Affairs in the Late Insurrectionary States (1871, pt. 2, pp. 213, 584), Biggerstaff "was whipped for being too intimate with some white women" *and* "for being a leading Republican."

The case of Jourdan Ware (Joint Select Committee [Committee], 1871, pt. 6, pp. 44-45, 66-67, 74-75, 885, 920)—an African American man assaulted and later murdered by Klansmen in northwest Georgia in 1870—is another example of the emerging concern of white-supremacist men over African American masculine practices. Ware was considered "a prominent man among the colored people," and the assault to have been "on account of his politics" and "to break him up" economically. In other words, Ware was assaulted because he was "too political" and "fixed very comfortably." Moreover, in addition to his political activities and economic independence, Ware engaged in other "improper" masculine practices. For instance, Ware was considered to be "a big, mighty forward, pompous negro" who was "impudent" toward white men; "he pushed about among white men too much." Moreover, "he made an insulting remark to a white lady"; he allegedly stated: " 'How d'ye sis' . . . as the young lady passed down the road. He called her 'wife' and thrust his tongue out at her. The lady ran away very frightened." The eventual killing of Ware was justified by the Klan because "the lady was spared the mortification and shame of appearing in court in connection with a cause that the delicacy of any lady would shrink from in terror."

The case of Henry Lowther presents yet another example of white-supremacist male concern with political, economic, and sexual independence of African American men. Lowther was a 40-year-old ex-slave in Georgia who in 1870 was both a member of the Republican Party and was economically independent. Lowther was arrested for conspiracy to commit murder and, at 2 a.m. one morning, approximately 180 Klansmen came to the jail and carried Lowther off to a swamp. Lowther (Committee, 1871, pt. 6, p. 357) explained to the Joint Select Committee what happened next:

> Every man cocked his gun and looked right at me. I thought they were going to shoot me, and leave me right there. The moon was shining bright, and I could see them. I was satisfied they were going to kill me, and I did not care much then. Then they asked me whether I preferred to be altered or to be killed. I said I preferred to be altered.

After castrating him, the Klansmen left Lowther in the swamp to bleed to death. However, he made it home and survived to recount the violence to the Committee. Asked by the Committee why the Klan came to the jail for him, Lowther (Committee, 1871, pp. 359, 362) gave three reasons:

> They said that no such man as me should live there . . . I worked for my money and carried on a shop. They have been working at me ever since I have been free. I had too much money.
> They said I had taken too great a stand against them in the Republican Party.
> They said I was going to see a white lady.

Similarly, in 1870, ex-slave Bill Brigan was taken from his home by the Klan on suspicion of involvement with white women in Georgia; Brigan was "tied down on a log and they took a buggy-trace to him, and whipped one of his seeds [testicles] entirely out and the other nearly out" (Committee, 1871, pt. 6, p. 359).

How can we begin to make sense of such white-male mob violence directed primarily toward African American men exhibiting political, economic, and sexual independence? Under the social contract of Emancipation, African American male participation in the political/economic arena as competitors threatened white masculine status. The "invasion" of African American men into these critical hegemonic masculine spheres posed a very real threat to white men's monopoly over politics and jobs; one way to discourage such competition and to reestablish racial and masculine meanings and practices was to use violence to remind African American men of their subordinate "Otherness." In other words, white men secured a specific type of both "whiteness" and "maleness" by emphasizing the subordinate status of African American male competitors. The meaning of white-supremacist masculinity is defined through the collective practice of lynching. Indeed, mob violence helped white-supremacist men define who they were by directing hostility toward African American men as a symbol of what they were not. In the particular social context of emancipation, African American male accountability to race and sex categories is called into play. Politically and economically independent African American men confound the possibility of differentiating men according to race and, therefore, undermines the legitimacy of white male supremacy. Whippings, lynchings, and castrations conveyed to African American men that white men were ready to punish the slightest deviation from tolerated lines of masculinity. When African American men dared step over the lines, they were made examples of what was acceptable and of what was expected from the entire race (Harris, 1984, p. 19).

Although not all white males engaged in such violence, the unique social setting of Emancipation increased the likelihood of this particular type of violence because white-supremacist masculinity was "explicitly put on the line" (Morgan, 1992, p. 47). It was critical that mob violence be seen as communicating indignation against African American men for invading a white-male bastion and for threatening the economic and social status of white men.

Indeed, under slavery, political participation and economic independence was an ideal arena for differentiating racial masculinities; engaging in these activities demonstrated clearly that players were "white" and "real men." Thus, in the Reconstruction South, African American males engaging in the same activities diluted this masculine and race distinction: If African American men were permitted to do what "real men" (white men) did, the value of the practice to accomplishing white masculinity was effectively compromised. And, because part of "doing gender" means creating racial differences and, therefore, racial boundaries among men—by maintaining and emphasizing the subordinate status of African American men through violence—white men were attempting to restore those distinctions and, thus, to preserve the peculiarity of white masculinity. Mob violence served to solidify, strengthen, and validate white masculinity and simultaneously to exclude, disparage, and subordinate African American masculinity.

Finally, what the case illustrations reveal is a heightened and intense white-male concern with every interaction between white women and African American men, especially if it indicated even the slightest possibility of interracial sexuality. In other words, under conditions of Emancipation, attention to relationships between white women and African American men was intensified. Indeed, the African American male had joined with the white female as *the* major targets of sexual regulation. It is to this regulation that we now turn.

Race, Sexuality, and the Chivalric Phallacy

Most chroniclers of lynching say little about lynchings that occurred during Reconstruction (most examine lynching from the late 1880s onward). However, those who do, find that "the practice was widespread" (Rable, 1984, p. 98). Richard Maxwell Brown (1975, pp. 214, 323) writes that from 1868 to 1871, the Klan engaged in large-scale lynching of African American men. Indeed, he records over 400 Klan lynchings of African Americans in the South over this time: 291 in 1868, 31 in 1869, 34 in 1870, and 53 in 1871. Similarly, George C. Wright (1990, pp. 41-42) reports in his study of Kentucky that more than one third of the lynchings that occurred in that state (117 of 353) happened between 1865 and 1874, "with two years alone 1868 (with 21) and 1870 (with 36) accounting for the extremely high number of 57."

In the 1880s and 1890s, however, the number of lynchings gradually increased (but never reached the 1868 level). During these years the heyday occurred in the early 1890s, when the largest number of African American lynchings (106) occurred in 1892 (Tolnay & Beck, 1995, p. 271).

The vast majority of victims during this period (especially between 1882 and 1900) were charged with alleged sexual offenses with white women (Brundage, 1993, p. 263; Tolnay & Beck, 1995, p. 49). Indeed, as Brundage (1993) reports in his study of lynching from 1880 to 1930, "white southerners maintained that rape was the key to lynching" (p. 58), whether or not a rape actually occurred. Rape became such an elastic concept within the white community during Reconstruction and its immediate aftermath that it stretched far beyond the legal definition to include "acts as apparently innocent as a nudge" (p. 61). For example,

On November 8, 1889, a mob lynched Orion Anderson in Loudoun County, Virginia, for an alleged attempted "assault" of a fifteen-year-old white girl. In fact, the black youth, a friend of the girl, had merely donned a sack on his head and frightened her while she walked to school. (p. 61)

Perhaps more telling, the following event illustrates the intense white-supremacist male interest in sexuality between white women and African American men. When a 16-year-old white girl became pregnant by her African American male lover, the girl's father had the African American male

promptly arrested for rape even though the girl adamantly refused to accuse him. While he was being transported to the county jail, a mob seized him and hanged him. The tragic affair ended when the young girl committed suicide by taking an overdose of sleeping pills. (Brundage, 1993, p. 62)

In addition, lynchings for any such interaction suggesting interracial sexuality increasingly included sexual mutilation (Dowd Hall, 1979, 1983). As Brown (1975) shows, "the lynching of Southern blacks routinely came to be accompanied by the emasculation of males" (p. 151). Indeed, the typical lynching became a white community celebration, with men, women, and children cheering on the mutilation and hanging or burning at the stake, or both. As Raper (1969) shows, white women spectators figured prominently in the ordeal, inciting "the men to do their 'manly duty' " and "inspiring the mobs to greater brutalities" (p. 12).

The lynching process extended for several hours, during which the African American male suffered excruciating pain from torture, mutilation, and castration committed throughout the ordeal by certain white-supremacist males. The finale featured spectator-scavenging for "souvenirs" of African American body parts (Brown, 1975, pp. 217-218).

The 1899 lynching of Sam Holt in Newman, Georgia, provides another effective example (Ginzburg, 1988, pp. 11-14). Holt was charged with and detained for the alleged rape of a white woman. Soon a mob of whites gathered outside the jail, and the sheriff of the town "turned the negro over to the waiting crowd" (p. 13). Although the alleged rape victim "was not permitted to identify the negro" because "it was thought the shock would be too great for her," a procession quickly formed and the doomed marched at the head of the shouting crowd (approximately 2,000 white people) down several streets (pp. 11, 13). Eventually a tree was chosen, and Holt was tied from a branch facing the crowd. Immediately his clothes were torn from him and a heavy chain was wound around his body. The local press reported what happened next:

Before the torch was applied to the pyre, the negro was deprived of his ears, fingers and genital parts of his body. He pleaded pitifully for his life while the mutilation was going on, but stood the ordeal of the fire with surprising fortitude. Before the body was cool, it was cut into pieces, the bones were crushed into small bits, and even the tree upon which the wretch met his fate was torn up and disposed of as "souvenirs." The negro's heart was cut into several pieces, as was also his liver. (Ginzburg, 1988, p. 12)

None of the white-male lynchers attempted to disguise their appearance and there was no effort to prevent anyone from seeing who lighted the fire or mutilated and castrated the body. On the contrary, there was a festival atmosphere. Finally, on the trunk of a nearby tree was pinned a placard that read: "We Must Protect Our Southern Women."

Under Emancipation, African American male sexuality—viewed as dangerous and animal-like—grew to become an even greater threat assiduously waiting to be unleashed. By opposing this embodiment of evil, white-supremacist men affirmed their morality and virtue, and at the same time their status as white men. Lynching constructs African American men as "natural" rapists; by resolutely and "bravely" avenging the (alleged) rape of pure white womanhood, southern white men framed themselves as chivalric patriarchs, avengers, and righteous protectors (Dowd Hall, 1983, p. 335).

As demonstrated, hegemonic white-male masculinity was measured by a man's ability to control, provide for, and protect his home—especially the white woman at the center of it. Under conditions of Emancipation, interracial sexuality represented the loss of all this. Thus, when a white man acted to save "his woman" from the bestial African American male, he constructed himself as savior, father, and keeper of racial purity (Harris, 1984, p. 20). White women were resolved to be at risk and had to be protected in the name of the race. By this commitment, then, white men taught "their women" that there was nothing to fear by capturing the source of that fear, torturing it, and killing it (p. 20). In this way, white supremacist men regained patriarchal hegemonic masculine status by determining what was wrong with society, ferreting it out, and reestablishing the norm as it existed before the interruption (p. 20). Lynching-for-rape upheld white privilege and underpinned the objectified figure of white women defined as "ours" and protected by "us" from "them"

(Fraiman, 1994, p. 73). These beliefs formed what Fraiman (p. 73) calls the *white-male chivalric phallacy*—preservation of white masculine supremacy was refigured as protection of white females for white males. Over and over again, Klan members and other white supremacists told the Joint Select Committee (1871, pt. 2, pp. 364, 399, 422) that "females shall ever be special objects of our regard and protection." Using her emblem as the keeper of racial purity, white men cast themselves as protectors of civilization, thereby reaffirming not only their role as social and familial "heads," but their paternal property rights as well (Wiegman, 1993). In this view, interracial sexuality destroyed what it meant to be a man because white masculinity was inextricably tied to race: to be a man was to be a white man who had sole access to and the duty to protect white women. The lynching and castrating of African American men—founded on the protection of white women—was central to securing white-male power and identity and, therefore, reconstructing a hierarchal masculine difference between white and African American men.

Moreover, in the context of the 19th-century feminist movement, the necessity for disrupting potential bonds between white women and African American men was critical (Wiegman, 1993). The women's movement challenged hegemonic white masculinity by agitating for female access to activities traditionally reserved for men—in particular white men—from economic to political equality. For example, during Reconstruction Susan B. Anthony and Elizabeth Cady Stanton founded not only the National Woman Suffrage Association but also *The Revolution,* which became one of the best-known independent women's newspapers of its time. The motto of the weekly paper was: "Men, their rights and nothing more; women, their rights and nothing less." In addition to discussions of suffrage, *The Revolution* critically examined topics ranging from marriage to sexuality.[13]

It was also during the 1870s and 1880s that the "New Woman" appeared in U.S. society (Smith-Rosenberg, 1985, p. 26). The New Woman was single, highly educated, and economically autonomous; she eschewed marriage, fought for professional visibility, and often espoused innovative and radical economic and social reforms (p. 245). As Smith-Rosenberg shows, the New Woman "challenged existing gender relations and the distribution of power" and, therefore, "challenged men in ways her mother never did" (p. 245). Indeed, according to Michael Kimmel (1987) one white-male response to this visible and outspoken feminist movement—as well as to the New Woman—was "to push women out of the public domain and return them to the home as passive, idealized figurines" (p. 270)[14]

However, Kimmel overlooks the response of lynching and castrating African American men. Violence against alleged "black rapists" earned white men positions of superiority over white women as well as over African American men; thus lynching equated with the preservation of race via passive white femininity. The lynching scenario constructed white women as frail, vulnerable, and wholly dependent for protection on chivalric white men. In this way, lynching and the mythology of the "black rapist" reproduced race and gender hierarchies during a time when those very hierarchies were threatened by both the New Woman and the "New Man" (African American male). Protection of white women reinforced femaleness and thus the notion of "separate spheres," while simultaneously constructing racial boundaries between white and African American men (Harris, 1984, p. 19). Lynching, then, was a white-male resource for "doing difference" (West & Fenstermaker, 1995) between men and women and among men. Accordingly, lynching the mythic "black rapist" not only constructed African American men as subordinate to white men, but simultaneously perpetuated the notion of separate spheres and inequality between white men and white women.

Yet this still leaves unanswered the reason for castrating African American males in public spectacles. Arguably, the increased reliance on public castration made clear the profound white-supremacist male distress over masculine equality and similarity with African American men. As Robin Wiegman (1993) eloquently puts it,

> Within the context of white supremacy, we must understand this threat of a masculine sameness as so terrifying that only the reassertion of a gender difference can provide the necessary disavowal. It is this that lynching and castration offer in their ritualized deployment, functioning as both a refusal and a negation of the possibility of extending the privileges of patriarchy to the black man. (p. 450)

Both race and masculine differences were reproduced through the practice of lynching and castration by ultimately feminizing the African American male body. African American masculine equality and similarity was discredited symbolically through publicly displayed castrated bodies. Possible sameness with white men was compromised violently in favor of continued primacy of white masculine supremacy (Wiegman, 1993); the practice of lynching and castration provided a resource for the physical enactment of white masculine hegemony. Indeed, in phallocentric culture, the penis becomes the phallus through the embodiment of generative gendered power. Thus, for African American men, movement from slave to citizen encompassed this symbolic exchange between penis and phallus (Weigman, 1993, p. 449). As Wiegman concludes, "Castration circumvents this process of exchange, consigning the black male to the fragmented and decidedly feminized realm of the body," while simultaneously the white male retains "hegemony over the entire field of masculine entitlements" (p. 449).

Conclusion

Reconstruction created the social context for constructing an alarmist ideology about African American male sexuality and the resulting pronounced public mob violence employed by white-supremacist men. White-supremacist men bonded into lynching mobs that provided arenas for an individual to prove himself a white man among white men. During Reconstruction and its immediate aftermath, gender and race became extraordinarily salient and, thus, white-supremacist men developed strong ties with their neighbors, their acquaintances, and with those whom they perceived to be like themselves. In particular, participation in mob violence demonstrated that one was a "real white man." Within the social context of the white-male mob, this hegemonic white-supremacist masculinity is sustained by means of collective practices that subordinate African American men and, therefore, a specific African American masculinity. Indeed, the individual "style" of the white-male mob member is somewhat meaningless outside the group; it is the lynching mob that provides meaning and currency for this type of white masculinity. White-supremacist men, then, were "doing" a specific type of whiteness and masculinity simultaneously as they were "doing" lynching. The collective struggle for supremacy over African American men was a means with which to gain recognition and reward for one's white masculinity, and a means with which to solve the gender and race problems of accountability. Mob violence was a situational resource for surmounting a perceived threat by reasserting the social dominance of white men. Lynching the "bestial black rapist" reconstructed racial masculinities in hierarchical terms of essential, biological inequality. In short, these white-supremacist men gained status, reputation, and self-respect through participation in mob lynchings that symbolically—especially through the ritual of castration—disclaimed any African American male rights to citizenry.

Notes

1. Sutherland (1924, pp. 242-243) had several other reasons for lynching, which included the "exhilaration" lynching produced in an unexciting South and the "weakness" of the courts and police.

2. Though Sutherland can be excused for not developing further his ideas on gender, sexuality, and lynching, recent sociological work on the topic has no such excuse. For example, the most recent book-length manuscript on lynching—Tolnay and Beck's (1995) *A Festival of Violence*—renders gender and sexuality completely invisible.

3. The content of this section is a summary of the perspective more thoroughly spelled out in Messerschmidt (1996, 1997).

4. Unlike West and Fenstermaker (1995), in the "structured action theory" presented here, both social structure and social action are key. I agree with Howard Winant's (1995) recent criticism of West and Fenstermaker that their theory of "doing difference" misses the fact that "social structure must be understood as dynamic and reciprocal; it is not only a *product* of accreted and repeated subjective action but also *produces* subjects" (p. 504). This is consistent with my argument here and elsewhere (Messerschmidt, 1993, 1997) where I follow the important theoretical insights of Giddens (1976, 1984) and Connell (1987, 1995) that structure is realized only through social action and social action requires structure as its condition.

5. Nevertheless, slave men often attempted to protect slave women from such violence. As Jacqueline Jones (1986) shows, the literature is "replete with accounts of slave husbands who intervened at the risk of their own lives to save wives and children from violence at the hands of whites" (p. 37).

6. Anne Firor Scott (1970, pp. 54-55) argues that many white women found this sexual double standard difficult to accept, and engaged in premarital and extramarital affairs.

7. Indeed, throughout the North and South during this time period, the largest proportion of women arrested were charged with such "moral misbehavior" as adultery, fornication, and bastardy (Spindel, 1989, pp. 82-86).

8. Both slave men and free blacks recognized this purported subordinate masculinity. A central theme of the abolitionists' attack on slavery was that it robbed black men of their manhood. And male slaves who agitated for freedom demanded their "manhood rights: equating freedom and equality with manhood (Horton, 1993, pp. 83-85). Moreover, black men who enlisted in the Union Army and fought in the Civil War conceptualized the practice as marking a watershed in the construction of "true" black masculinity. As Cullen (1992) found in his examination, exhibiting "real manhood surfaces again and again as an aspiration, a concern, or a fact of life" (p. 77) for these black soldiers.

9. However, as African Americans were involved increasingly in sharecropping, it became necessary for African American women to contribute to family income. Thus, a "separate spheres" ideology was at best a temporary phenomenon (Foner, 1988, p. 86).

10. In March 1865, Congress created the Freedman's Bureau to protect the interests of African Americans in the South and to help them obtain jobs and establish African American hospitals and churches.

11. Many African American women resisted this forced patriarchal component of African American family life (Foner, 1988, p. 88).

12. In 1871, Congress appointed a joint committee to investigate violence against African Americans in the former Confederate states. Witnesses testified that throughout

the late 1860s, white-male terrorism was directed primarily against politically active and economically independent African American men who refused to defer to white supremacists and/or engaged in any conduct that indicated a possible sexual liaison with white women. This government document is one of the few primary sources on white-mob violence during Reconstruction.

13. For an informative account of the racism inherent in this "first wave" of the feminist movement, see Davis (1983, pp. 46-86).

14. In addition to this antifeminist response, Kimmel (1987, pp. 269-277) outlines two additional responses by men: a "masculinist" response that urged a greater participation by men in the rearing of boys and a "profeminist" response that embraced feminist principles as a solution to this "crisis" of masculinity.

8

Frat Boys, Bossmen, Studs, and Gentlemen

A Typology of Gang Masculinities

JOHN M. HAGEDORN

Q: Do you have a steady lady?

R #1: I was trying to make a life for her, man but she have an attitude problem. So at the present time, not really. If things begin to look up . . . but I'm not going to kiss no ass!

Q: What does your lady think about you selling dope?

R #2: She didn't like it at all, no she didn't like it. When I first started I had to keep it in the house . . . which that was a no-no, a big no-no.

Q: She try to get you to quit and stuff?

R #2: Oh yeah! She took it a couple times and poured it down the drain—put water in it. Yeah, she done that.

AUTHOR'S NOTE: This study was a product of NIDA grant DAO7128-02. The author acknowledges the helpful comments of Lavell Cox, Mary Devitt, Rita Lewis, and Jerome Wonders. Comments should be sent to Hagedorn at the UWM Urban Research Center, P.O. Box 413, Milwaukee, WI, 53201.

Q: What does your lady think about you selling dope?

R #3: That bitch don't want me selling dope. That's why I left her, homey. Fuck the bitch. I can't sell no dope, I don't want her.

These three men were all drug dealing gang members. Yet their idea of masculinity differed. One wanted a lady, but would not "kiss ass"; the second tolerated his woman dumping cocaine down the drain; the third comes closest to the media stereotype of a deviant, violent, women-hating hustler.

This chapter describes variation in conceptions of masculinity by drug dealing gang men. Gang researchers have historically emphasized variation in gangs: for example, in family background (Moore, 1991; Short & Strodtbeck, 1965), participation in violence (Fagan, 1990; Fagan & Chin, 1991), and roles in the drug game (Hagedorn, 1994). I am unaware, however, of any social science study that examines variation in how gang men conceptualize "being a man."

Similarly, the literature on masculinities has all too often typed gang men or street hustlers as one "ghetto" type, a "badass" or some other "ghetto-specific" stereotype. The "hypermasculinity" of inner-city African American and Latino males has been described by many social scientists as a component of a deviant subculture, attitudes that are quite different from the cultural outlook of middle-class white Americans (e.g., Katz, 1988; Miller, 1958). This chapter allows gang men to describe in their own words how they view their relationships with women, one aspect of their overall self-concept of what it takes to "be a man." It also questions whether these conceptions of masculinity are all that different from those found in mainstream American culture.

Gender and Gang Research

The treatment of gender in male gang research is a good example of academic benign neglect. Lorber (1994) could have been talking about gang research when she wrote,

> Talking about gender for most people is the equivalent of fish talking about water . . . gender, like culture, is a human production that depends on everyone constantly "doing gender." . . . And everyone "does gender" without thinking about it. (p. 13)

The incidence and prevalence of gang violence differ more by gender than by any other variable. Yet gender, like water for fish, is often taken for granted in gang research. For example, neither Klein's (1995) nor Spergel's (1995) recent well-received books cite the vast literature on masculinities in their examinations of gang violence. Female gangs are similarly neglected or put in the background by nearly all gang researchers (e.g., Decker & Van Winkle, 1996; but see Curry, 1995; Moore, 1991). I have to admit that my own prior work (Hagedorn, 1988) is not exempt from criticism. This neglect of gender by male gang researchers has deep criminological roots. Wolfgang and Ferracuti (1967, p. 153) explicitly dismissed the importance of gender in their classic study of violence. The National Research Council's report "Understanding and Preventing Violence" neglected even to mention gender as a "social process" that might lead to violence (Reiss, 1993).

If gender roles are dictated by biological facts, then aggression can be explained by immutable, noncultural factors (e.g., Wilson & Herrnstein, 1985, p. 116). However, if gender roles are socially constructed, as most social scientists concede, then differences in gender roles are likely to be crucial variables in understanding violence. Ann Campbell (1993) has argued that male violence does not come so much from "a subculture of violence as one of masculinity, for it is painfully clear that the bulk of its members are male" (p. 12; see also Polk, 1994). But do gang members or inner-city males have a "subculture" of masculinity, or is the way they "do gender" similar in some fundamental ways to white middle-class male Americans?

Gang Masculinities: Mainstream or Deviant?

Social scientists differ on whether inner-city male concepts of what it takes to "be a man" are deviant or not. For some, larger-than-life inner-city masculine behavior represents internalized norms of deviance. Masculinity, in the form of "toughness," is one of the seven "focal concerns" for Walter Miller's (1958) lower-class males. Similarly, Jack Katz (1988) describes the toughness of the "badass" as a specifically ghetto male trait. Miller argued that the explanation for hypermasculinity in lower-class males was the dominance of mothers in single-parent households with an inevitable "compulsive reaction-formation" by their sons. Adolescent boys rebelled from identification with their mother and formed male-only peer groups. For both Miller and Katz, lower class or street culture was their prime independent variable. They both asserted that an aggressive culture of violence was deeply internalized by ghetto males. Elijah Anderson (1990) also saw male ghetto masculinity as deviant and destructive. However, with William Julius Wilson (1987, 1996), he saw deviant norms as having been developed by ghetto residents as a reaction to structural constraints (see Wilson & Sampson, 1995). Following Shaw and McKay's (1942) concept of cultural transmission, Anderson described the pathology of ghetto hustlers who only wanted to "get over" and flaunt their masculinity to make women "so many conquests." These "new heads" have replaced the more traditional "old heads" and threaten to hand down a violent and misogynist set of values to younger boys. Anderson's work is the most prominent contemporary successor to Hannerz's (1969) view of mainstream and deviant cultural behavior.

Others have seen ghetto masculinity differently. Cazenave (1981, p. 181), in a clever turn of the tongue, saw a "tough guy" reputation as being earned not only "in ghetto streets" but also "in corporate suites." In his view, underclass male behavior differs from middle- or upper-class men's actions mainly due to the nature of the constraints and opportunities facing street corner men, not from basic differences in how to "be a man." In other words, inner-city notions of masculinity are not part of a deviant subculture, but prime examples of American male cultural beliefs acted out in poverty-level conditions (Valentine, 1968).

Franklin and Pillow (1994) point out that many black men have embraced the traditional American role of protector of womanhood, or "gentleman." They criticize white scholars for not recognizing that this mainstream notion of masculinity has been adopted widely by black men. They point out that the capacity of underclass men to actualize the role of "Black Prince Charming" is diminished by economic distress. But, they add, "the important thing to note is that a failure to act upon the ideal may not reflect a rejection of the ideal" (p. 100). For Franklin and Pillow, American culture is extremely powerful, as Merton (1938) argued long ago, and strongly influences the conceptions of masculinity by African Americans. Still other studies see strained lower-class African American males as striving to adapt to Eurocentric, not ghetto-specific, notions of masculinity (Harris, 1994, p. 81).

Cazenave (1981) writes explicitly in Merton's anomie tradition and types African American reactions as "innovative" or "conformist" to the "double bind" of proving manhood while being denied legitimate means toward that end. In other words, African American men either conform to mainstream cultural roles or innovate and create male roles compatible with a jobless life (Liebow, 1967; Oliver, 1994). This innovation is further clarified by Majors and Billson (1992, p. 12), who describe how "masks of masculinity" can be a variety of "poses" made by African American males for self-protection from the hurts of white society. The "cool pose" is a conception of masculinity that is "both a reaction to stress and a contributor to stress" (see also Parsons, 1951).

While social scientists differ on the mainstream or deviant orientation of ghetto male masculinity, feminist academics have described more fully the ways "masculinities" are socially constructed. Messerschmidt (1986, 1993), following Connell (1987), sees variation between how middle-class and lower-class white and minority males act out their notions of "hegemonic masculinity" based in patriarchy. Messner (1992b) explores how conceptions of masculinity permeate the American practice of sports. Both white and black men, Messner finds, had similar conceptions of masculinity, but they were played out differently depending on race and class (pp. 38, 52-60). Unfortunately, much of the feminist literature on African American lower-class masculinity does not explore within-group variation in the manner of Cazenave, Harris, or Franklin and Pillow. The feminist literature often leaves the impression that African American ghetto men are all hypermasculine hustlers and do not vary (but see Messerschmidt, 1997).

Methods

The data this chapter is based on were drawn from the first part of a 5-year National Institute on Drug Abuse study of male and female gangs, their drug use, and dealing. Taped interviews with 90 males and 11 females took place in 1992 and 1993. Sixty percent were African American, 37% Latino, and 3% white. Mean age was 28. All respondents were founding members of their gangs and were only interviewed if their name was confirmed as being on a roster of gang members developed by staff and other gang members. Each respondent was paid $50 for the interview. Further interviews of 73 female gang founders took place in 1995. An earlier study (Hagedorn, 1988) interviewed many of the same respondents in their teenage years.

The study followed the collaborative model developed by Joan Moore (1978), also a co-principal investigator of this study. "Community researchers," or former gang members, worked as paid staff and conducted most of the interviews with gang members with whom they grew up. Staff helped focus the research design, worked with academics to write interview questions, and were trained in interview techniques. Data were coded collaboratively by gang and academic staff, entered into a computer statistical analysis program (SPSS™) and a qualitative analysis program (Folioviews™) and analyzed. This and all other papers produced by the study were discussed by staff, and their conclusions were fed back to respondents for a validity check.

Three-hour taped interviews were conducted either by myself or a member of the respondent's original gang. I have known many of the founding gang members and their families for more than a decade. Most of the interviews were intense, genuine experiences, where the respondent shared his perspective on what has happened to his life and to the lives of his homeboys. Although this method has some drawbacks, it has the virtue of permitting the respondents to talk "back stage" about their experience, and drop the performances usually given to outsiders, including researchers (see Goffman, 1959; Hagedorn, 1996; Vigil, 1988). Included in the interview questionnaire were numerous open-ended questions about the nature and quality of the relationship the respondent had with his spouse or female companion(s).

A Typology of Gang Masculinities

The social situation of our respondents was the same—that is, they were all gang members who sold drugs. However, these African American and Latino men did not enact a single "sex role" in how they conceived of their relationships with women. Rather, they enacted four distinctly different conceptions of hegemonic masculinity: the "Frat Boy," the "Bossman," the "Stud," and the "Gentleman." These categories, in Messerschmidt's (1993) words, are "patterned ways that masculinity is represented and enacted" (p. 83).

These are ideal types, with gang men moving between categories and changing over time. This typology does not imply that some gang men might not become egalitarian partners with women, but it does suggest that between gang men and the women they are with, patriarchal relationships predominate. This would hardly surprise feminist scholars, who see patriarchal relationships as nearly universal today (e.g., Johnson, 1988). Each of these four categories can lead to violence, either against a woman, or in defense of the male's notion of respect and his manhood (see Oliver 1994; Pleck, Sonenstein, Ku, & Burbridge, 1996).

The Frat Boy: "Boys Will Be Boys"

The common wisdom about the hijinks of college fraternity boys, even serious acts of drunkenness and rape, is that "boys will be boys." There is a widely held view that these middle-class white kids are just "sowing their wild oats" and will eventually grow up. Even their girlfriends may excuse cheating and sexual escapades as being something in the "nature of men." Eventually these guys will come to their senses, many of these women think, get a decent job, get married, and settle down.

This describes the gang "frat boys" as well. But instead of a "frat house," it is the "drug house" that has lured these high school dropouts to "sow their wild oats." In our interviews, descriptions of life in the drug house were eagerly given and invariably bawdy, like this relatively tame tale of "boys being boys":

Q: What did you do in the house?

A: Just sat back and watched TV. Smoked squares. Drink booze. Maybe when one of the . . . females come into the house, some of them did a blow job in front of me. You know, that's pretty much all that I did. Watched TV, drink booze and maybe if I got horny or something, one of the high-paid bitches would come by some night and I'd get a little head or something. Other than that, that was it.

Gang "frat boys," like college fraternity brothers, normally had a steady lady and their wild life caused severe strains on their primary relationships. Many times a gang frat boy and his lady had started a family, and the frat boy would try to settle down in a legitimate job. But inability to support his family was one factor that pushed the man back into the dope game (Hagedorn, 1994). Selling dope was basically a venture of the old male peer group, and invariably brought men into contact with female dope fiends who traded sex for drugs. Selling cocaine in a drug house was like working the night shift, with the frat boy at times gone for days on end, drinking heavily and using drugs. His relationship with his steady lady consequently became stormy.

She hated it, 'cause it took me out all night and [she claimed I was] messing with other women, which I am. I mess with this girl and that girl. I don't necessarily mess with them all of the time, but I spend more time hustling than I do with females. She don't approve. She prefer I have a job.

The frat boys' women were strong advocates of their men settling down. Many of these women had rebelled against traditional gender norms and would no longer stand for such disrespectful behavior as their mens' sexual escapades (see Bourgois, 1995, p. 214). They disapproved of selling drugs because of the risky and wild lifestyle, particularly if the couple had children.

> Since I got out, she told me if I go back to jail, she'll leave me and since the baby's been born, she told me "don't even think about it." I've been thinking about it—it's always in my mind, cause it's been there for so many years—you can't just let it go. It's like—money is out there to be made. It's kinda hard, I feel sorry for myself but I'm wakening up now, cause of the baby, I've got somebody to be responsible for, so in a way, he kinda helped me out when he came into this world.

Both prison and selling drugs were constant threats to relationships, as this frat boy comments wistfully about a lost love:

Q: What did your lady think about you selling dope?

A: Well before I went to prison, before I got busted, my ex-girlfriend used to get on me because she had her daughter there. . . . And I stopped selling dope around my girlfriend's daughter because I was disrespecting my girlfriend and my daughter too. She disapproved. She tried to get me out.

Violence was also related to the frat boy lifestyle. Frat boys were eager participants in dope dating, and, by almost any definition, forcing women to perform various sex acts to get drugs is violence. Women in our homegirl study also described isolated incidents of group rape after parties at drug houses. But these stories were rare, arguably no more frequent than such incidents at college frat houses.

Domestic violence also resulted from the tensions in the gang frat boys' relationships with their spouses. Many frat boys had difficulty earning steady money in legitimate jobs, and their conception of masculinity was in part formed by this inability to fulfill the male "provider" role. Domestic violence, in this sense, could be seen, in part, as compensation for difficulties in being a steady provider for their family, just as it often is in middle-class marriages when the male is laid off (Campbell, 1993). Domestic violence also appeared to be strongly related to the gang frat boys' heavy use of alcohol and, to a lesser degree, cocaine.

Gang frat boys, like our earlier category of "homeboys" (Hagedorn, 1994), wanted basically to settle down with a family and a legitimate job.

I want a comfortable life, a decent woman, a family to come home to. I mean, everybody needs somebody to care for.

Our longitudinal data show that many gang frat boys, like their college counterparts, sowed their wild oats in their twenties. When we last interviewed them, as they neared thirty years of age, they were in the process of making peace with a wife or steady lady. While college frat boys can meet the requirements of the male provider role by getting a good job, for the gang frat boys the job picture was dismal. The temptations to return to the dope game were ever present. For gang frat boys, uncertainty of employment reinforced patriarchal notions of masculinity and undermined their relationships with women.

What gang frat boys most desired was a traditional relationship, with the man working a legitimate job and the woman working too . . . while also doing most of the cooking, child care, and housework. They intended to work out a relationship with their lady, while probably having their share of "boys' nights out" with the old gang. Does that sound deviant . . . or traditional? This category was the majority of our sample.

The Bossman: "You Do What I Say!"

We all know of men who are the *Boss* in their family. Their word is law, and their wife or woman better do what they say or, pow! smack in the kisser. They enforce a strict division of gender roles within the family, extracting unpaid menial labor from the "wife" under covert or overt threat of violence (see Rose, 1986). This is an even more traditional and patriarchal conception of the husband's and wife's relationship than that of the frat boys.

One type of gang man also was the undisputed "boss" in his family. This type had a steady lady, but she had no say about what her man did. Bossmen differed from frat boys mainly by the domineering relationship they had with their lady or wife. These bossmen were often deeply involved in the drug game, and, like Mafia stereotypes, kept the little woman home in the dark. Their replies to our question, "What does your lady think about you selling dope?" were invariant:

Well she didn't have much to say to me 'cause I wouldn't accept her opinions. Either what I said or that was it.

She never would tell me nothing cause I would never tell her nothing. I would do it if I wanted to and that was it. She didn't have much say in it.

I don't sell it, but I'm quite sure she wouldn't say a thing about it. I am the man of this house.

Bossmen held another behavior in common. They did not dope date.

Man . . . I don't dope date no bitches. Shit I never dope dated in my life.

This may sound strange, but the bossman's traditional conception of the "purity" of womanhood made dope dating taboo. Bossmen shunned the wild sex life of the frat boys. For the bossman, some women were "hos" and they very well might become the object of violent male rage. Their own woman also needed to be kept in line, perhaps so she would never become a "bitch" or "ho."

I ain't heard of nobody our age going to jail. . . . When we go to jail we go to jail for beating the damn bitch up. Or killing a bitch cause she's fucking around with somebody else.

Many bossmen held "old world" attitudes about marriage and the family, like European ethnic immigrants in the past. Many were married Latinos with "old-fashioned" ideas of the roles of "husband" and "wife." Their wives were very traditionally oriented women, who were likely to have been raised in Mexico or Puerto Rico. Jealousy ran rampant with these men and often led to domestic violence. Prison and the violence of the drug game also put severe strains on these relationships. The woman sometimes left the relationship when the man went to prison. Others ran away when they couldn't tolerate it any longer, but escape was obviously fraught with danger. Many other bossmen's wives simply endured. This category made up less than a quarter of our sample.

The Stud: "All Women Are Bitches"

We all know examples of the "macho man" who admires his maleness and is basically a misogynist. The walls in public men's rooms are filled with the private fantasies of men and boys who are stud-wannabes. Business executives of this type hire high-price prostitutes and lead the "fast life." These "masters of the universe," as Thomas Wolfe (1987) calls Wall Street high-rollers, may have tried marriage, but something was always wrong with the "bitch" or "ball and chain." They needed someone young and foxy by their side when they snapped their fingers. It was part of their mystique.

Gang studs, too, are men who never really settled down, unlike the frat boys or bossmen. Most of these gang men do not form steady relationships, and most of the ones they had, quickly broke up. Some of these men had relationships with women who participated in drug sales. Most studs, however, could not find it in themselves to commit to a steady relationship.

Q: Do you have a steady lady?

A: That's a hard question. Somewhat, yeah, and then again somewhat not. In other words, . . . I don't trust no bitches. 'stand what I'm saying? That's all that I'm saying. . . . I don't trust nobody, not even my momma to a certain point. And if she comes out feeling it's either me or her, my ass is south.

These men were more committed to their work than anything else, a trait they have in common with some men of the propertied classes. Studs, on the surface at least, had an image of themselves as being the male rogue they think every woman secretly desires. At work in the dope game, their customers were sexual prey.

Q: What do you like most about selling drugs?

A: Most I like about it is the money and the whores. We need plenty of whores, plenty of whores. We try to jock them in because if they figure they need to have some currency and they figure they want a little part of some type of dividend. But other than that, I like it. I like getting high. I like kicking and hanging out . . . like Negroes do, when we have the money. I don't like gaining weight, but I've been doin' pretty good.

For the stud, violence against women was commonplace. On the street, gangsta rap music reinforces a stereotype of the gangster who thinks "all women are hos." It is a stereotype in that it does not apply to all street hustlers, but it does describe a small minority of male gangsters. In keeping with the media images of misogynist violence by rappers, the studs' histories of arrests reflect repeated domestic violence.

One of my best friends got ten years in the penitentiary for beating a funk ass bitch. I did six and a half months in the county jail for something I didn't do about a funk ass bitch. They tried to give me twenty more fucking years. That was the major thing that really happened to me that changed my life.

Sometimes domestic violence is described as no more than a disturbing afterthought.

To be honest, I think I've been arrested twenty times. Last time was in '91 last year. Driving with no license. '91—that's it five cases of driving . . . and I beat a bitch. The battery was last summer.

The violent relationship of money, women, and power is strikingly portrayed in our transcripts by this "new jack," or amoral "do-whatever it takes," drug seller.

Q: How much power does selling drugs give you?

A: Oh it's given me a lot of power. You know, it's just a sensation of you can do anything you want. When you got money in your pocket, you can do anything you want. You can go out there and slap these bitches. You can go out here and shoot this nigger. You just get a power, you just think you are God because you have so much money you think you can do whatever you want to do. And everybody knowed what you about. They ain't going to mess with you, they know about how you making your money and they know you don't want no trouble or nothing like that. They will not mess with you, they will respect you, they'll like you because you make your money.

Now read that answer again and think of those words being spoken by Ivan Boesky, Michael Milken, or some other super-rich "master of the universe" (see Stewart, 1991). This attitude is a fundamental product of the fetishism of money that infects rich and poor alike in capitalist society. The gang stud varies only in race and class from Norman Mailer's (1964) portrait of the wife-murdering American hero, Stephen Rojack, in his classic *An American Dream*. Our data find this type represents less than a quarter of our sample.

The Gentleman: "Women Are to Be Protected"

Finally we have gentlemen, chivalrous males who worship "ladyhood" and do everything possible to protect the "fairer sex" from the hardships and insults of life. For these men, women are on a pedestal. Any insult to their woman becomes the occasion for a manly defense of their reputation. Gang men, too, can be "gentlemen," like the homeboy this respondent is referring to:

A: You know, we got in a little fist fight, you know, seemed like every six years we get into one . . . over how I treat women. He don't like that, you know, so . . . we get into it over that.

Q: So he called you on it huh?

A: Yeah, he called me out . . . it really wasn't you know, really nothing too big, you know, like I say, it be over women. . . . Like I know this female, this bitch I kick her outa my Cadillac. . . . You know, he don't like that, so [we fought].

Some of these gentlemen were reformed frat boys or studs. They had reflected on their own hostility to women, and that of their homeboys, and had become philosophical.

I'm trying my best sometimes to pivot . . . to let my folks see another direction. Because they're hindering their own intelligence by just thinking about money, drugs, and females. Like for example, first thing they do, they see a female and she's got to be a bitch. And I have a habit of "bitch." Like when I get angry at a female, like I said, old habits are hard to break. . . . So it's like something else. Really I don't want to see the young brothers go out like I'm seeing the older folks go out and [I want them to] to pay heed to advice. That's why I keep going. Cause I don't want to be disappointed to myself nor to my son.

While gentlemen may sell dope, they would never dope date, like bossmen but unlike frat boys or studs. Unlike studs, they speak of women in exalted, almost hushed tones. These "Prince Charmings," as Franklin and Pillow call them, would be quick to open a door for a woman and argue that the proper role for a lady is to be at home and taken care of by her man. Gang gentlemen saw themselves as women's protectors, but this role occasionally would lead to violence. When the sacred conception of the "female" would be violated by another male, as in the example above, a fight could quickly break out. More ominously, the failure of a woman to live up to her role as "princess" might also lead to violence against her. Gentlemen were a small minority of our sample.

Conclusion

The era of benign neglect of gender in gang research must come to an end. Gender needs to be taken seriously by gang researchers as we look at explanations for male gang violence. Our data is insufficient to unscramble the reasons why some gang members become frat boys and others studs. The source of the variation in roles is likely to be rooted in the modeling of masculine roles in the family, early school experiences, peer interactions, and varying influences of the mass media. We need more research that looks specifically at the sources of variation in conceptions of masculinity and to what degree they influence male gang violence.

This issue is important, first of all, because describing how gang men vary can show these young men as people, not as stereotypes. An important weapon of social science is to force policymakers and the public to make distinctions. Those distinctions can then be used to suggest that those in the underclass may have some things in common with the rest of us. No lasting changes in public policy will be effected unless we somehow succeed in presenting gang members to the public as different kinds of living, breathing, human beings.

But what kind of human beings are they? The reader has to judge. The picture of gang men I presented is not pretty, but is it all that different than descriptions of college frat boys, the domineering working-class husband, the corporate stud, or a patronizing old world gentleman? Were Chambliss's (1973) middle-class Saints all that different than his lower-class Roughnecks? Though some would argue that the behavior of inner-city male gang members represents a deviant concept of "hypermasculinity," I hope this chapter has at least caused the reader to question such an easy conclusion.

Can such men change? I think the answer is "yes." Our longitudinal studies show that the trajectory of the lives of male gang members is not unchanging. Some studs grew up in conventional homes and some gentlemen were the product of families who socialized them to the street (see Moore & Vigil, 1987; Torres, Hagedorn, & Giglio, 1996). Frat boys, bossmen, and studs can all become gentlemen. Gentlemen can become studs or bossmen as well. Some gang men may establish egalitarian relationships with women. Change, in my experience, is more of a constant than a question.

But the issue becomes what causes men raised on patriarchal norms of masculinity to change those ideas and behavior? On this issue, I have data from my own life as well as from the transcripts of my respondents' interviews. I suspect male readers of this chapter can find data in their own lives as well. The key issue in change for me has been my relationship with my partner, Mary Devitt. Just as the anxiety of the frat boys over the need for a stable relationship was prompted by the demands of their partners, so my changes have been prompted—and that word may be too weak—by Mary. Like Mary did with me, these strong central-city women demanded that their men change some old ideas.

What aids Mary and me in our struggle to redefine my more traditional notions of masculinity is that we have steady jobs and can conduct our struggle in circumstances of employment stability. We don't have to worry about whether there will be any money for the kids for Christmas. Sampson and Laub (1993) remind us that adult men tend to commit less crime when they are in a steady relationship, which in turn increases their probability of having a steady job, and decreases substance abuse. Less substance abuse probably also means less domestic violence. Sampson and Laub's conclusions find support in our data (Torres et al., 1996).

In the central city, the lack of steady work, along with the tantalizing profits to be made in the dope game, are the main threat to healthy male-female relationships. Long prison terms from the war on drugs threaten to disrupt these relationships even more and wreak havoc on the lives of central-city men and women and their families for a long time. The destructive roles of frat boy, bossman, stud, and gentleman are reinforced, not undermined, by the lack of jobs and corresponding participation of men in the violent and sexist dope game.

Despite these barriers, many former male gang members are struggling to negotiate a decent life with a woman. For many the future will lead to stability; for others extra-marital affairs, and breakup; still others may never settle down. On the one hand, real change will not come about without improved economic and social conditions for the central city. But on the other hand, neither will it occur without a determined struggle against values that treat women as less then men, treat minorities as less than whites, and that put money ahead of everything. I think this means a merger of sorts is needed between the values of feminism and africology, and the creation of some new, if unusual, political alliances.

The main point of this chapter is that the struggle of central-city gang men and women is our struggle as well.

9

Hypermasculinity and Prison Violence

HANS TOCH

In a recent book, Victor Hassine (1996), a long-term prison denizen, described what he called the "Inmate's Dilemma." He writes that,

> In the life of an inmate, if you catch someone stealing from you, you're compelled to deal with it physically. . . . If someone steals from you and you decide to report him to the guards, all that will happen is that the thief will go to the Hole for a while. Soon he'll be back in population and ready to seek revenge. Revenge in prison can take place years after its initiation. It generally occurs when you are vulnerable and the avenger happens to be around. This reality will leave you constantly looking over your shoulder. Additionally, involving the guards will get you the reputation as a "snitch," which means you will be physically challenged by inmates seeking to make a reputation or pass their own "snitch" label onto you.
>
> If you choose to ignore the theft, the man will steal from you again and tell his friends, who in turn will also steal from you. Eventually, you will be challenged for more than just minor belongings. (p. 23)

The passage illustrates a number of attributes of mainline prison violence. It points to the fact that male inmates subscribe to a normative system that holds that under certain circumstances a prisoner must respond with physical force. The prisoner must particularly do so if he is slighted or affronted or taken advantage of. Securing help is ruled out, as is the alternative of overlooking the slights or affronts or victimization to which one has been subjected. This fact is related to another attribute of prison violence, which is that failure to take action justifies future victimization. In prisons, vulnerability attracts predation and fear invites exploitation; such norms are accepted as givens by the prisoners.

To the extent to which a male officer subculture exists in prisons, some of its norms feature counterpart beliefs to those of inmates. One such assumption, for example, is that prisoners who assault guards must be "taught a lesson." A 1996 report about the New York detention system, for example, suggested that "tenets of street justice—revenge, retaliation, establishing dominance—appear to guide the behavior of at least some correction officers" (Purdy, 1996, p. 29). Documents detailing retaliatory incidents in jails "[suggested] that the prisoners had been injured in accidents, such as falling over furniture" (Purdy, 1996, p. 29). A local officer union president defended such retaliatory practices:

"We just don't go in there and beat the crap out of someone just to establish control," he said. But he said "the atmosphere is a jungle type atmosphere, it's survival" and when an officer is hit by an inmate "you have a right to defend yourself by punching him or grabbing him."

Punching is a fairly common response. Internal jail records, written by jail officers, show that on Aug. 4, an inmate in the disciplinary area approached an officer "with clutched fists" and in response, the officer "punched the inmate several times in the face." On Aug. 18, an inmate "verbally threatened and then pushed" an officer who then "responded with punches to the face and body." (Purdy, 1996, p. 29)

The same logic as that used by officers can inspire prisoner assaults on staff. In one New York incident, for example, "an inmate sliced two guards with a razor blade" (Gurnett, 1996, p. A1). The prisoner presumptively felt affronted when he was removed from a kitchen assignment following a fight, and he generated sympathy from peers. Thus, "while officers were escorting the inmate back to his cell, another prisoner apparently slipped him a blade" (Gurnett, 1996, p. A1). The friend who armed the perpetrator in this incident had seemingly decided that the humiliating experience to which his colleague was being subjected called for physical redress.

Violence and a Culture of Masculinity

Themes such as these subcultural themes are explicitly and self-consciously associated with masculinity in the minds of prisoners and staff. Worthy Men are presumed to defend their honor when it is assailed or impugned; they are obligated to "take care of their problems" and they are expected to deter victimization through demonstrations of pugnaciousness. Affronted men are expected to persevere in the face of odds (such as those in the last example) and to take uninvited risks. Unworthy (and by implication, feminine) Men are by contrast liable to ignore affronts, to show apprehensiveness when in danger, to admit helplessness, and to seek assistance. They show themselves incapable of physical retaliation when the occasion calls for it, and their demonstration of incapacity justifies victimization, which can be carried out with advertised impunity.

In cultures of masculinity, the demonstrated willingness to fight and the capacity for combat are measures of worth and of self-worth. One could cite a number of explanations for this across-the-board fact, and for its cultural permutations, including in the prison. The least answerable question is, How has male pugnaciousness become a measure of worth and self-worth? The most basic explanation is anthropologico-historical (or historico-anthropological), and has to do with gender roles and obligations in primitive societies. It would follow, for example, that hunters and defenders of villages should gain self-esteem from demonstrations of prowess at hunting and defending.

Such assumptions leave open the question of why Modern Man would follow in his ancestral footsteps, given that he can now obtain food neatly packaged, and that his spouse may do most of the obtaining. Of course, self-serving anachronisms can be perpetuated if they yield gratification to their perpetuators, and it is obvious that gender-related socialization can be the means whereby male investments are preserved (the fact that the upbringing of male children is not a male preserve suggests that women may also have investments in male aggressivity).

Subcultures of Masculinity and Violence

The shaping of gender-related attitudes is most obvious in single-sex peer groups such as fraternities, locker rooms, and gangs, including delinquent gangs. In such settings the prevailing indices of esteem and self-esteem clearly coincide. The rowdiest fraternity men and toughest delinquents become heroic figures and role models for others to emulate. Caricatures of maleness are consensually touted, and (sometimes fraudulently) advertised. Credible (or even incredible) achievements in physical combat and sexual conquest are rewarded with status, esteem, and collective admiration.

In the case of predelinquents or precocious delinquents, single-sex peer groups emerge early in preadolescence, and to great effect among boys least likely to experience a rich home life and a budding scholastic career. These descriptive facts relate to the form and the content of single-sex peer influence. The form—the salience of peer esteem as a criterion of self-esteem—can derive from the fact that the group fills a vacuum, that peers are substitutes for the adult support that is absent, unwelcome, or both. The content of the normative system can evolve as a way of dealing with abject failure implicit in the sacrifice, unavailability, or unachievability of prestigious and satisfying goals (such as becoming school valedictorian). In other words, the emphasis on what can be easily achieved—such as stealing someone's lunch money—compensates for what is out of reach. As a bonus, the indices of esteem that evolve are calculated to offend authorities and adults who impugn one's self-esteem (Cohen, 1955).

The Genesis of the Male Prisoner Culture

Early books on prisons used words such as *importation, deprivation,* and *mixed model* in explaining how salient themes of the prisoner culture evolved. The word *mixed* was of course a meaningless word unless one first understood what was meant by importation and deprivation.

Deprivation theory postulated an analogue to the process whereby gang norms evolve. Imprisonment involves rejections from conventional society. Moreover, prisons offer a quality of life redolent with restrictions, frustrations, and affronts to self-esteem. Some of the attributes of the prison environment are pettily circumscribing and gratuitously demeaning; others are reminiscent of the way children are treated by indifferent or suspicious adults. This fate of "deprivations" shared to varying degrees by all prisoners must be accommodated via adjustments that enable prisoners to salvage some semblance of pride and dignity, to the extent that the situation might permit. In the prisoner culture—as in the case of gangs—indigenous indices of esteem need to be shared and immune from encroachment. In lieu of the respect and self-respect lost through imprisonment, status has to be attained among peers and imperviousness or autonomy from staff (Clemmer, 1940; Goffman, 1961; Sykes, 1965). Both goals can be reached through displays of manly virtues. Imperviousness calls for stolidity, aloofness, and a John Wayne or Clint Eastwood facade. Status calls for demonstrations of bravery or fearlessness, toughness, physical prowess, and loyalty to one's kind. It is not coincidental in this connection that prisons have been single-sex and predominantly male. Indices of inmate esteem and self-esteem thus gravitated toward norms of the sort that evolve in all-male groups—in other words, toward caricatures of masculinity. (In female prisons, subcultures evolved caricatures of femininity, which lie beyond the scope of this chapter.) The fact that the male prisoner cultures resemble other male cultures that accentuated masculinity norms suggested that preimprisonment concerns and experiences could affect reactions to deprivation. The term *importation* was coined to describe differences in prison adjustment by different groups of prisoners, consonant with the way these groups adjusted to life before coming to prison (Irwin, 1970; Irwin & Cressey, 1962). In most instances this meant that the outlooks and habits of the prisoners could vary with the way they went about the business of coping or offending in civilian life. But in some instances, young men had grown up in reformatories and had evolved extreme subcultural orientations. There were also groups such as gang members who brought the norms of delinquent gangs into the prison.

Reformatory graduates—or "state-raised youths," as they were called (by Irwin, 1970)—proved especially problematic and troublesome. Such youths approached peers with a dog-eat-dog perspective, testing for vulnerability and fears they could exploit. They tended to dwell on the threat of rape, had no sense of fair play, and perpetrated violence in groups. Gang members similarly had a proclivity for group-based aggression and engaged in illicit pursuits (such as drug trading) that carried the potential of violence.

The youngest offenders were most prone to violent encounters with fellow inmates, disproportionately resistant to authority, and sensitive to "disrespect" from prison staff. This chip-on-the-shoulder stance increased the probability of incidents of conflict between officers and prisoners. Counterpart sentiments among younger staff (e.g., "never take guff from a convict") similarly increased this probability.

The Hypermasculine Worldview

The perspective of young prisoners—and of some young officers—neatly conforms to the stance of hypermasculinity described in the psychological literature. The state-raised youth, especially, resembles the evolving portrait of the so-called macho man (Mosher & Tompkins, 1988):

> Head held high, daring anyone to match his bravery, toughness, and callousness, the young macho celebrates his pride and arrogant contempt for the weak and submissive inferior. Like any warrior, he assumes power, pride, and glory as his entitlement; the vanquished reap the fear, distress, and shame that once was his.
>
> Intolerant of any ambiguity in the dichotomous classification mandated by the criterion of his ideals, he understands the world is divided into the strong and the weak, the masculine and the feminine, the emotionally callous and those who weep, the proud and the shamed, the brave and the cowardly, the excitement-seekers and those basking in safe and dubious enjoyment. He understands; his ideology of *machismo* tells him so. (p. 69)

The ideology of hypermasculinity illuminates an important theme in prison violence, which is that the fearful—those showing apprehension—are inviting targets of predation. Two objectives can be achieved when one assaults a man who is fearful: (a) one shows contempt for the man's demeaning "femininity," while (b) one reassures oneself that one is different (i.e., nonfearful) from one's target. As Mosher and Tompkins (1988) point out, "fear is a deadly affect for successful warfare, being the most serious enemy within. It is assigned to the enemies to be defeated. . . . A man must not weep, but rather make his enemy cry out in surrender" (p. 63).

Though Real Men are never supposed to show fear, or any other "unmanly" emotion (such as mushy compassion), violence allows for the display of feelings such as retaliatory rage. In the words of Mosher and Tompkins (1988),

> The "inferior feminine" emotion of distress is, thus, transformed into the "manly" emotion of anger. The rule becomes: "Big boys don't cry"; they have temper tantrums.
>
> The rules of the script are liable to be nonconscious, but, if conscious, the rules might be, "Don't cry, be tough, have contempt for those who cry" and "Don't cry, get mad, and make them cry instead." (p. 67)

In the hypermasculine world, character contests occur in which status is conferred on those who best live up to the prescriptions of the masculine script. This frequently entails systematic peer "testing" of bravery and willingness to engage in combat when one is affronted or threatened:

> Gaining admission to a male peer group in a subculture of macho youths requires fighting your way in. A place in the pecking order is pugilistically promoted. You have to have "heart."
>
> Although victory is sought, it is more important to demonstrate courage and toughness through the willingness to fight. (Mosher & Tompkins, 1998, p. 72)

New prisoners are especially subjected to hypermasculine character contests, and these create scenarios such as the Prisoner's Dilemma described by Hassine. Gresham Sykes (1965), in his classic *The Society of Captives,* points to a Catch-22 aspect of these contests that makes the prison world perpetually unsafe. He writes,

> An important aspect of this disturbingly problematical world is the fact that the inmate is acutely aware that sooner or later he will be "tested"—that someone will "push" him to see how far they can go and that he must be prepared to fight for the safety of his person and his possessions. If he should fail, he will thereafter be an object of contempt, constantly in danger of being attacked by other inmates who view him as an obvious victim, as a man who cannot or will not defend his rights. And yet if he succeeds, he may well become a target for the prisoner who wishes to prove himself, who seeks to enhance his own prestige by defeating the man with a reputation for toughness. (pp. 77-78)

Violence and the Hypermasculine Life Cycle

Hypermasculinity and violence reach their zenith at relatively young ages, and research suggests that both behaviors nowadays tend to reach their statistical peaks much earlier than they have in the past (Blumstein, 1995). But sooner or later, hypermasculine men must age and must face their decreased capacity and propensity for violence. This process of aging, according to Mosher and Tompkins, creates reliable and lawful. transitions in the perspectives or scripts of hypermasculine men. These transitions have particular relevance for the long-term prisoner, who faces an average of 10 to 15 years in confinement.

Mosher and Tompkins (1988) see the young hypermasculine man following a *counteractive script*. Counteraction means that "challenges by male adversaries require escalating violence to be more manly. . . . The rule: escalate anger, daring, callousness until dominance is established" (p. 79). "Experiencing the invulnerability of youth, the young macho relies on his strength, dominance, toughness, callousness, aggressiveness, violence, virility and physicality" (p. 80).

But "as physicality declines, . . . the macho man becomes vulnerable to the shameful discovery that he is not as fearless and as free of distress as he has claimed" (p. 81). This discovery, according to Mosher and Tompkins (1988), leads to the *defensive script*, "which is often a sub-stance-abusing script. Alcohol and other drugs are simultaneously 'manly,' and excuses for the 'unmanly.' " But unwanted unmanly (or feminine) feelings are experienced by the macho man when he is not anesthetized, and lead to states of depression, pessimism, and hopeless-ness. A residual solution can be fantasy, in which the man "believes that he can save the meaning of his life by heroically losing it" (p. 81).

Such fantasies culminate in what Mosher and Tompkins call the *pseudo-reparative script,* embodied by the motto "death before dishonor." The script presupposes some variation on the "hero's death," which "can rescue a failing macho and transform the meaning of his life from failure-at-living to that of a *real man.* Songs will be sung around the campfire, myths bear tribute to his courage and stoic acceptance of his manly fate" (p. 82).

The enactment of one such scenario is vividly described in a *New York Times* article about Clinton Prison (Purdy, 1995). The inmate in question had spent many years in confinement, where he had proved exceedingly troublesome. The incident at issue had been videotaped:

> The inmate, Felix George, who had been treated for psychiatric problems, was suspected of cutting himself, starting fires and storing urine and feces in his cell, according to prison documents. He refused to leave his cell, and officers wearing gas masks can be seen on the videotape spraying tear gas, and then hitting his hands with batons and riot shields to break his grip on the bars.
>
> The videotape shows him being driven across the prison yard to the hospital, held down in the back of a station wagon by an officer's legs. When he yells out, an officer is seen wrenching his head back and holding his hand over his mouth.

At the hospital, the officers stripped him naked and put him in a shower. He was then put face down on the floor, wet and naked, with his hands cuffed behind his back, his feet shackled and an officer's knee pressed against his back. On the videotape, he continuously yelled; "My name is Felix George. They're going to kill me." He then shouted his prison identification number. After his injuries were treated at the hospital he was left alone and naked in a cell.

Three days later, he was found dead, toilet paper stuffed in his mouth and up his nostrils. An independent board of doctors has ruled his death a suicide.

Addressing Violence in the Prison

Mosher and Tompkins (1988) suggest that hypermasculine men who approach maturity may be ripe for psychotherapy, which enables them to discover that "inferior, feminine affects are rewarding and acceptable," and leads them "to consider the rules for how to be a man—a *mensch*—without being a macho man" (p. 82). The task is daunting, but becomes less daunting over time, with the demonstrated failure of the hypermasculine approach to life in general, and prison life in particular.

Mosher and Tompkins (1988) see the outcome of change in the aging macho as a *reparative script,* which "would require the macho to embrace life, and, thus, to embrace the culturally proscribed feminine gender script." The implication of this prescription is that,

To integrate a truly reparative script, the macho must question his identity and ideology and magnify the suppressed affects here-to-fore pejoratively assigned as "inferior and feminine." The longed for loving, pacific, relaxed communion with "inferior, emotional" fellow humans can indeed be reparative of the macho script. (p. 82)

Bo Lozoff (1995), an ex-offender who operates a prisoner assistance program, has written that the hypermasculine convict code has become a "cowardly rule of silence" that is inhumane and should be supplanted (p. 32). He writes that

a new convict code must be an ideal that speaks to the best in us rather than the worst. . . . If conformist life on the streets has become "Use people and love things," then the convict code should proclaim, "Use things and love people," and prison life should be an example of it. . . . We need a code that allows people the maximum opportunity to become human beings, not one which keeps us and them stuck in the worst parts of ourselves and our past. (p. 70)

Such ruminations, in relation to prisons and prisoners, sound utopian. But in corrections, hypermasculinity is a recipe for bankruptcy and no-win stalemates. Segregation sentences for young prisoners become draconian over time. The punishing experience engenders bitterness and cements recalcitrance. It attenuates what residual hold the inmates have on reality, driving them to the brink (or over the brink) of mental illness. Hypermasculine men occupy segregation cells long after their aggressivity is attenuated and their reputation still deserved. However, their conceptions of integrity force prisoners to stage displays of hollow, unconvincing rage. Their counterparts—the guards—follow repressive scripts that become similarly autonomous. Hypermasculine nightmares evolve in the shape of super-maximum or "maxi-maxi" settings. In such settings there is often no human contact between captors and captives, and no escape from destructive and self-destructive games.

Yet de-escalation is theoretically possible, as is reparation of the sort that Mosher and Tompkins prescribe. Experiments that neatly fit the bill have been carried out in the Scottish Prison Service, starting with a pioneer effort (the Berlinnie Unit) in 1973. Long-term segregees are placed into intensive, community-centered treatment settings, in which staff work closely and intimately with the prisoners. The object is to prepare the inmates to recapture their humanity and to rejoin the prison mainstream (Scottish Prison Service, 1994).

The work is staff-intensive, and it is costly, because much damage has to be undone. But salvaging human beings who would otherwise be lost, and who would often stay segregated for life, makes the investment cost-effective. Reparative work also can be exciting for the staff and a stimulus for innovativeness. There are training benefits in working in such programs, and there is much to be learned in the process.

At earlier stages of the hypermasculine career, the challenge lies in preventing the evolution of obdurate subcultures. A first step taken by the Scottish Prison Service is that of working with prisoners coming into the system, to promote constructive adjustment to the prison. Several months of counseling and charitable work are combined into an orientation ("induction") experience. Thereafter, efforts are made to promote environments in which prisoners can openly relate to staff. Prison careers end with reintegration experiences for the long-term prisoner who is close to release into the community. This effort includes democratized, collaborative living arrangements that provide rehearsals of interpersonal skills (Toch, 1995).

The political climate in the United States today may be inhospitable to the reparative script exemplified by the Scottish experiment. Hypermasculine themes are prevalent in society, and "feminine" sentiments, such as compassion and relatedness, are dismissed as "liberal" (a term of opprobrium). But cultures can and do change, and we may yet reach a point where we can de-escalate our hypermasculine model of corrections. Prisoners are unlikely to relinquish the model—as a subcultural stance—unless we do so first. We will not control violence as long as we model it—as long as we do unto violent offenders what violent offenders do unto their victims and peers.

PART FOUR

MASCULINITIES
AND ORGANIZATIONAL VIOLENCE

10

Dow Corning and the
Silicone Breast Implant Debacle

A Case of Corporate Crime Against Women

CONSTANCE L. CHAPPLE

Setting the Stage for Crime to Occur

Dow Corning has been the leading manufacturer of silicone breast implants since 1960. Silicone breast implants had been marketed since the early 1960s for breast augmentation and postmastectomy surgery uses. Silicone breast implants were considered to be, by the medical industry and the government, medical devices much like bedpans, leg braces, or orthopedic shoes (Estrin, 1990). When the Food and Drug Administration (FDA) stepped in and banned their use in 1992, the implants, in various forms, had been on the market for 32 years, and millions of women had received them (Springen & Hager, 1995). The implants existed unregulated by the government until 1976, when the FDA imposed guidelines on the manufacture and sale of all medical devices. This crackdown was prompted by the horror stories told concerning the Dalkon Shield, manufactured by A. H. Robins (Minz, 1985). The Dalkon Shield, a intrauterine device used for contraception, had also been classified a medical device and was subject to no governmental regulation. Neither the Dalkon Shield

AUTHOR'S NOTE: I am indebted to Travis Hirschi and Neil Vance, without whose guidance this chapter would never have been written.

nor the silicone breast implant were subject to governmental scrutiny. They underwent minimal testing and were marketed as revolutionary devices enhancing the lives of millions of women. After the silicone breast implants had been used for a number of years, women started to complain of discomfort regarding their implants. In the mid-1970s, Dow Corning switched to a more liquid silicone gel that would make the implants softer (Smart, 1991). However, the new gel was prone to rupture and could more easily pass through the implant's permeable border than the rigid gel previously used. For many women the implants ruptured, sending silicone in a sticky, oozing mass throughout their bodies. Upon investigation into the manufacturing processes of the leading manufacturer of silicone breast implants, Dow Corning, these women discovered internal Dow Corning memos indicating that in-house tests revealed significant health risks correlated with silicone exposure (Smart, 1991). Many of these tests undertaken by Dow Corning were performed before 1976, when the FDA began to regulate the implants. As a result, Dow Corning was under no legal obligation to report these findings. Many of the women reporting adverse reactions to their implants have chosen to sue Dow Corning for negligence and fraud regarding its manufacture and sale of unsafe products. To understand how such an incredible tale of pain and suffering could occur, the social and cultural context in which the manufacture and sale of silicone breast implants took place must be examined.

Dow Corning, as the manufacturer of silicone breast implants, was embedded in a social matrix of hegemonic masculinity, state negligence, and corporate wrongdoing. The unethical, and perhaps illegal, practices of Dow Corning emerged from this sociocultural domain. Dow Corning, due to its placement in this sociocultural domain, never learned that their injurious practices were unethical or immoral. Within this context, the practices constituted business as usual. Concepts of "hegemonic masculinity" (Connell, 1987) and the social construction of women as the "Other" (de Beauvoir, 1952) created a corporate and political environment in which the health and safety of female life is compromised. From this standpoint, the construction of this kind of masculinity contributed both to the crimes against women committed by Dow Corning and to the dismissal of the rights of women by the FDA. This hegemonic masculinity precluded social morality; a blind-eyed hunger for profit took the place of ideals of right and wrong behavior. But first, the history of the FDA and Dow Corning must be explained.

The History of Medical Device Regulation

To explore fully the legal liabilities concerning Dow Corning's breast implants, one must relate the history of medical device regulation in the United States. In 1906, Congress enacted the Pure Food and Drug Act to prohibit the "distribution of adulterated or misbranded food and drugs in interstate commerce" (Estrin, 1990, p. 35). Ostensibly, this was to put the "snake oil" conmen out of business. The legislation did nothing to regulate medical devices, and, as a result, bogus devices proliferated in the market (Estrin, 1990, p. 35). In 1938, Congress expressly extended governmental regulatory power over medical devices in the revised Food, Drug and Cosmetic Act. However, the actual regulation was minimal and continued unchanged until 1976 (Estrin, 1990, p. 35).

In the 1960s (interestingly coincident with silicone breast implants' entrance on the market), the public began pushing for greater federal regulation of medical devices. It was not until the Dalkon Shield disaster more than a decade later (in 1976) that Congress felt the need to give the FDA greater regulatory power over medical devices. Before the technological revolution in post-World War II America, medical devices needed little regulation. The devices might be ineffectual, but were rarely harmful. However, technology changed all that with the advent of heart valves, pacemakers, implants, prosthetic devices, and IUDs. The 1938 Act gave the FDA "reactive" power over medical device regulation. The FDA had to prove that a device was unsafe after it was on the market (and being sold to consumers) in order to pull it off the market. At this point in history, no premarket safety testing was required for medical devices. Also, the FDA was limited in its regulatory powers to interstate travel. Devices manufactured and sold entirely within a single state's borders were not subject to FDA regulation.

Medical device regulation changed in 1976. "The foundation for the Medical Device Amendments of 1976 was the determination by Congress that a regulatory mechanism was needed to provide the public with a reasonable assurance of the safety and effectiveness of medical devices" (Estrin, 1990, p. 36). A medical device was defined as

an instrument, apparatus, implement, machine, contrivance, implant, in vitro reagent or other similar or related article, including any component, part or accessory . . . intended to affect the structure or any function of the body of man or other animals, and which does not achieve any of its principal intended purposes through chemical action within or on the body of man or other animals and which is not dependent upon being metabolized for the achievement of any of its principal intended purposes. (p. 39)

Under these classifications, silicone breast implants were considered to be medical devices and were newly subject to premarket testing.

Dow Corning and the FDA: Decisions and Consequences

How does the history of Dow Corning's manufacture of breast implants affect the current status of silicone implants? Figure 10.1 shows a timeline of the FDA's and Dow Corning's alleged actions. Dow Corning began manufacturing silicone breast implants for cosmetic and reconstructive uses in the early 1960s. At this time the implants were considered to be medical devices, and were not bound by any premarket testing requirements. Leaked internal memos suggest that Dow Corning's own medical research teams found adverse medical effects due to silicone exposure in laboratory rats as early as the mid-1960s. Yet because the devices were not regulated, Dow Corning was not legally required to release this information. After the difficulties suffered by thousands of women using the Dalkon Shield, the FDA stepped in 1976 and began to regulate all medical devices. Medical devices were classified into Class I, II, or III, with Class I including things like bedpans, and Class III including devices like heart valves (Estrin, 1990). Dow Corning was required to meet the FDA guidelines governing all implants manufactured after 1976, which included premarket testing to ensure safety and effectiveness. However, implants manufactured before 1976 were still subject to minimal regulation.

Around 1978, an internal Dow Corning research study found a "high rate of tumors in animals exposed to silicone gel" (Smart, 1991). Although this memo was leaked in the early 1990s, patients had begun to complain as early as the 1970s to the FDA about their defective implants. In 1982, the FDA imposed even stricter safety rules for implants. As a result, Dow Corning prepared package inserts warning physicians of the risk of complications and adverse health effects. However, the package inserts were placed in surgically sealed boxes, to be opened only at the time of surgery. Doctors often overlooked the inserts or did not take time away from surgery, with the patient under anesthesia, to inform the patient of the possible adverse effects. This is a violation of the informed consent

Timeline of Dow Corning's Activities

	1960	1975	1976	1977	1984	1988	1992	1995
(above line)		Internal Memos Indicate Adverse Effects		Package Inserts Include Possible Risk of Rupture		Package Inserts Include Possible Risk of Disease		Dow Corning Files for Bankruptcy
(below line)	Dow Corning Enters the Breast Implant Field		FDA Increases Medical Device Regulation		Nevada Jury Finds Dow Corning Guilty of Fraud		FDA Bans Silicone Breast Implants; Dow Corning Quits Implant Business	

FDA's History of Medical Device Regulation

1906	Pure Food and Drug Act
1938	Food, Drug and Cosmetic Act
	FDA must prove existing devices dangerous
1976	Medical Devices Required to Premarket Test
	Class I, II, or III
	Devices manufactured before 1976 subject to differing regulation

Figure 10.1. Dow Corning's Perceived Wrongdoing

SOURCE: Part I: Smart (1991), Nichols (1995), Springen and Hager (1995); Part II: Estrin (1990)

183

laws and creates a situation in which women were not armed in their decision making with all the necessary information to come to an informed decision.

In 1987 (through information gained from leaked internal memos), Dow Corning completed a 2-year study, finding an increased risk of cancer in the rats exposed to silicone gel (Smart, 1991). This finding, along with a host of other findings suggesting greater risks to human health from silicone exposure than were currently acknowledged, was not released to the public, nor to the FDA, the governing body charged with regulating the implants and disseminating all relevant research regarding the implants. Dow Corning continued to market and sell the devices, although their safety had been questioned by the manufacturers themselves. Warnings about the effects of silicone exposure were released in the package inserts manufactured by Dow Corning. These package inserts changed from 1977 to 1988.

In 1977, the package inserts warned of possible breast tissue hardening and the possibility of implant rupture. By 1988, the warning was more grim: In 1988, the inserts warned of possible related systemic diseases (Nichols, 1995). This 1988 revised package insert was instituted due to a court decision that found Dow Corning guilty of fraud. In 1984, a San Francisco federal court jury found that Dow Corning had committed fraud in marketing its implant as safe. The plaintiff, Maria Stern, was awarded $1.5 million in punitive damages (Smart, 1991). The judge indicated that Dow Corning's own internal research had not proven that the implants were safe.

In reaction to the adverse publicity surrounding the settlement, Dow Corning revised its package inserts. This was the sanction imposed by the FDA regulating the implants; they were found to be unsafe, yet allowed to remain on the market. To understand how the implant was found to be unsafe yet allowed to remain on the market, one must look to possible collusion between the FDA regulatory panel and the American Society of Plastic and Reconstructive Surgeons (ASPRS) for an answer. The FDA, under the current guidelines, could sanction companies violating regulations regarding safe manufacture and accurate premarket testing. In the case of the FDA panel regulating silicone implants, however, the panel was staffed, in part, by plastic surgeons and industry experts (Rynbrandt & Kramer, 1995). It was difficult for this panel to sanction its own industry.

Even as late as 1991, the FDA panel unanimously voted to allow the implants to remain on the market, even when faced with voluminous evidence questioning the implant's safety (Rynbrandt & Kramer, 1995). It took women's grassroots pressure on their legislators to convince the FDA to ban the implants in 1992. Opposition to the ban was considerable from groups such as the American Medical Association (AMA) and the ASPRS. On the eve of the 1992 FDA hearings, the ASPRS launched a $4 million publicity campaign to keep the implants on the market (Rynbrandt & Kramer, 1995). Such powerful allies may explain, in part, the foot dragging by the FDA. According to an agency (FDA) spokesperson, "it's taken a long time [further regulation and/or banning], but the agency had higher priority devices to deal with" (Smart, 1991, p. 95).

In January 1992, the FDA banned silicone breast implants, indicating that Dow Corning had failed to prove that the devices were safe (Springen & Hager, 1995). Silicone breast implants are the second medical device to be banned since the FDA began regulation in 1938 (Estrin, 1990). In March 1992, Dow Corning quit the American breast implant business, citing increasing legal pressures (Springen & Hager, 1995). Dow Corning continues to "dump" its silicone breast implants overseas where the regulations are minimal. This is a practice familiar to the pharmaceutical industry, in which the manufacturer is relieved of outdated or unsafe pharmaceuticals by selling them for a profit outside the United States (Braithwaite, 1984). Finally, in May 1995, Dow Corning filed for bankruptcy to protect its assets and ensure that pending litigation and class action suits would be paid (Springen & Hager, 1995). However, the $4.25 billion awarded in the class action suit brought by over 70,000 women against Dow Corning has yet to be disbursed (Hogue, 1995).

Complications Regarding Implants: Stories of Pain and Suffering

In determining the priority of pending cases, the FDA should have contacted the women claiming harm from the silicone breast implants. These women suffer from a host of ailments that many doctors believe can be attributed, at least in part, to their ruptured silicone implants (Bruning, 1995). Many of the ailments from which these women suffer are idiopathic, meaning that they appear to have few organic explanations (Bruning, 1995). The ailments are also diverse and seemingly unconnected, which makes a linkage to silicone exposure all the more problematic. However, some side effects of silicone breast implants are known and documented, although occurring in the minority of cases. Conditions such as capsular contracture, in which the body reacts to the implantation of a foreign object by surrounding the object with antibodies and, later, scar tissue that makes the tissue around the implant contract and harden, is the most common complaint regarding the implants (Bruning, 1995). Capsular contracture may cause discomfort due to the tissue tightening and is thought to occur in 10% to 40% of implantation cases (Bruning, 1995).

In addition to capsular contracture, there is the commonplace occurrence of "gel bleed." According to the manufacturers of the silicone breast implants, it is customary for a certain amount of silicone to "bleed" from the implant through the implant's permeable border and into the body. This amount is thought to be inconsequential and, according to many breast implant proponents, the exposure is thought to be benign (Bruning, 1995). Thus, in effect, the implant's manufacturers admit to the potential for silicone leaks but dismiss the possible adverse effects of silicone exposure. Dow Corning, in its current official stance, contends that no links have been substantiated that tie silicone gel exposure to increased risk for cancer and systemic disorders (Smart, 1992). According to Robert Rylee, Dow Corning's health care manager, silicone exposure from leaking implants is harmless and the "reaction is benign. It is picked up by the lymph system and either secreted or stored" (Smart, 1991, p. 98). Although the results of many tests of the adverse effect of silicone exposure are far from conclusive, these complications were considered to be reasonable and seemingly inconsequential.

This is the story of Susie Pellum (Hogue, 1995). Ms. Pellum desired larger, more beautiful breasts, and so in 1986 she underwent surgery to have her breasts augmented with silicone implants. At first she was ecstatic; within 5 years her breasts were rock hard (remember the 1977 package disclaimers). Six years after that, purple rashes began to appear on her back and arms. She began to feel fatigued and believed she might be suffering from scleroderma, an autoimmune disorder (Hogue, 1995). In 1993, fearful that it was her implants that were making her ill, she had them removed. Upon removal, the surgeon found that the implants were covered with what was described as "pond scum" (Hogue, 1995). The permeable holes in the implants' covering had allowed microscopic bacteria, as well as body fluids, to enter the implants. Ms. Pellum is involved in the $4.25 billion class action suit against Dow Corning.

Other women tell similar stories. One of the leaders in the silicone implant ban effort is Sybil Goldrich (Smart, 1991). Ms. Goldrich received her silicone implants following a bilateral mastectomy in 1983. Ensuing complications caused her to replace the implants four times before abandoning them. Since their rupture and removal, Goldrich has been plagued with numerous ailments and ultimately has had to have her uterus and ovaries removed. Doctors also found that the silicone had migrated to her liver. She blames the implants for her ailments. Contrary to Dr. Rylee's (Dow Corning's health care manager) beliefs, Goldrich claims there is "no way to detoxify from this substance" (Smart, 1991, p. 98). Because both Pellum and Goldrich received implants before the revised package inserts warning of systemic disease links in 1988, they were not warned of the risk of systemic disease due to silicone gel exposure. Although stories such as these are admittedly a small percentage, given the millions of women who received implants while they were on the market, literally tens of thousands of women now are suffering because of their decisions (Bruning, 1995, p. 56). It is devastatingly unfortunate that silicone breast implants were such a low priority for the FDA.

Past Lessons Ignored

It is remarkable that Dow Corning did not regulate itself given the adverse publicity suffered by A. H. Robins, the manufacturer of the Dalkon Shield. The similarities between the two companies are haunting. Hugh G. Davis was the co-inventor of the Dalkon Shield, an intrauterine device, in 1964 (Mokhibar, 1988). The device was designed like a disk with barbs at the edges to prevent slippage. This was to alleviate the problems associated with other IUDs on the market: cramping, bleeding, and pain. Some doctors, concerned with the IUD's gruesome shape and risk of complications, refused to use the "revolutionary" device (Mokhibar, 1988). Regardless of public perception and the negative reactions within the medical community, A. H. Robins, which bought the patent for the shield and employed Davis, began a mass marketing plan in 1970. Again, remember the minimal regulation regarding medical devices at this time—the FDA had to prove that devices already on the market were unsafe in order to pull them from the market (Perry & Dawson, 1985).

The manufacturers had no obligation to premarket test their product. Yet, to the contrary, Davis reported studies that not only indicated that the IUD was safe, but also the most effective birth control device on the market with a failure rate (pregnancy) of 1.1%. Subsequent research, revising Davis's previous shoddy research, found both claims to be false. The failure rate was more appropriately around 4.4%, and, in fact, the Dalkon Shield carried great risk for spontaneous and septic abortions as well as uterine wall puncture (Mokhibar, 1988). Only 6 weeks after the release of the Dalkon Shield onto the market, doctors began to complain that their patients reported great pain induced upon insertion of the IUD. This too was against the claims of the A. H. Robins Company, which touted its ease of insertion.

According to officials at Robins, if difficulty of insertion is noted, it must be an individual problem (translation—the woman's body is at fault). However, the problems associated with the shield were not hidden any longer. Many women suffered horrible consequences due to the design of the Shield (infection, miscarriage, deformed fetuses, hemorrhaging), and several women died from infections caused by their defective IUDs. By 1976, the FDA was drawn into the legal fray as women began to sue Robins for damages. As stated earlier, the Dalkon Shield controversy prompted the FDA to impose greater regulations on medical devices (Minz, 1985).

Finally, in 1984, Robins settled the cases pending against them for a total of more than $17 million. Consequently, in 1985, Robins filed for bankruptcy to protect its assets, much like Dow Corning would do 10 years in the future. The FDA did not ban the Dalkon Shield, however, but merely recalled it. If A. H. Robins's problems preceded Dow Corning's, why did Dow Corning not learn a lesson from A. H. Robins, thus saving itself virtually millions of dollars and thousands of women pain and suffering? To explain how the silicone breast implant debacle could have occurred, it is crucial to understand the sociocultural milieu in which these actions and decisions were made. Explanations of hegemonic masculinity, state negligence, and corporate wrongdoing will provide illumination.

Hegemonic Masculinity and the Construction of the "Other"

R. W. Connell (1987) developed the concept of "hegemonic masculinity" in his book, *Gender and Power*. This ideal of masculinity is thought to be represented in the power exerted by men against the less powerful (women). According to Connell, this form of masculinity is embedded in sociohistorical relations of institutions such as the state, the economy, religion, the family, and the media (Connell, 1987). This particular form of masculinity is constructed as the dominant form of masculinity at any one historical moment, and is opposed to other variations of masculinity (e.g., homosexuality) and to femininity. This notion of masculinity presumes an idealized form of masculinity and may reinforce "practices toward authority, control, competitive individualism, independence, aggressiveness, and the capacity for violence" (Messerschmidt, 1993). This normative model of masculinity enforces the virtues and rights of white, male heterosexuality, perhaps by the use of force (Walklate, 1995). Thus, men engendering hegemonic masculinity defend their privileged power positions against the threats of the subordinated "Other." The purveyors of hegemonic masculinity, in theory, will oppress non-hegemonic masculinities and femininity similarly. It is the relation of hegemonic masculinity to the social construction of the "Other" that most concerns the discussion surrounding the practices of Dow Corning.

It is from the standpoint of hegemony that the powerful determine the characteristics of the less powerful. It is from this standpoint that notions of femininity are constructed as the "Other." According to de Beauvoir (1952) in *The Second Sex,* the definition of man as the normative center and woman as outside the center denies women their personhood and constructs their identity only in relation to the identities of men. By denying women their subjectivity, hegemonic masculinity creates an Other who is dehumanized and easily dominated, thus ensuring the reign of masculinity in its present (hegemonic) form.

Hegemonic masculinity has oppressed women in a variety of ways. Radical feminists (Dworkin, 1987; MacKinnon, 1983; Tong, 1989) suggest that under conditions of male power all women are subjugated and victimized. The victimization can be sexual, in that both Dworkin (1987) and MacKinnon (1983) believe that under patriarchal rule all heterosexual sexual relations are exploitative and reducible to rape. In contrast, the subjugation can be ideological, as when men control the cultural constructions of femininity to suit their own purposes (Parker, 1995). In this instance, men construct the Other in terms of what is appropriate behavior or appearance. In this example, men determine the body images to which women aspire. This argument has been used to explain the vagaries of informed consent regarding breast implantation, given the cultural mandates of female body perfection. It is suggested that because one construction of the female body is considered the ideal, with its emphasis on the female breast, any consent women give to changing the shape of their breasts is a coerced decision, given the sociocultural milieu (Parker, 1995).

Crime against women has been explained as a situational enactment of hegemonic masculinity (Messerschmidt, 1993; Walklate, 1995) in which men assert and reinforce their form of masculinity in acts of violence against women. The violence serves to reinforce their power positions and the powerless positions of women. This line of reasoning has been used to explain both rape and domestic violence (Messerschmidt, 1993). Messerschmidt offers an interesting extension of the concept of hegemonic masculinity to corporate culture that may help explain the injurious practices of Dow Corning. Messerschmidt (1993) suggests that the practice of profitable capitalism may be antithetical to ethical business behavior. First, the institution of corporate work is highly gendered, with men overwhelmingly in positions of power and women servicing and working for them. Second, the construction of hegemonic masculinity within corporations stresses competition, status, prestige, and upward mobility, sometimes regardless of cost (Messerschmidt, 1993, p. 134). Finally, men with the least strict moral codes may be advanced up the mobility ladder within corporations in which rule breaking is legitimated. Crime is then normalized by the ideals of hegemonic masculinity, and she who is most unlike he, most dehumanized, the "Other," is the easiest target. Regardless of the location—be it political, familial, or corporate— the enactment of hegemonic masculinity can and will result in the subordination and dehumanization of women.

Feminism, the State, and Crimes of Omission

Feminist critiques would view the actions of Dow Corning as criminal; particularly, a crime against women. Few investigations have been made into the area of corporate crime against women (Gerber & Weeks, 1992). Women per se are rarely targeted for victimization by corporations; corporations are more catholic when choosing appropriate targets. However, corporate crime against women, as can be seen in the examples of the Dalkon Shield and the thalidomide disaster (Braithwaite, 1984), does occur. When women are the targets of corporate wrongdoing, they are the most compliant of victims. In a capitalistic system, women exist as consumers. They do not dominate the ranks of the rich and powerful who make the decisions in business and medicine.

Women, historically, have been subjected to medical experimentation (Anderson, 1993). Traditionally, however, minority and poor women have suffered; rarely has the experiment been performed on an misled, paying, middle- and upper-class population. In fact, the silicone implant, as well as the Dalkon Shield, disaster can be viewed as a form of institutionalized violence against women (Renzetti & Curran, 1992). Insofar as the corporations are embedded in the social structural matrix, they become institutionalized. When violence is directed from the corporation toward a selected target, the violence is institutionalized.

Again, whether one accepts the feminist critiques of institutionalized and corporate violence against women depends on whether one believes Dow Corning knowingly committed fraud. Cultural standards of beauty for women as defined by hegemonic masculinity, as well as governmental nonintervention into business affairs, set the stage for the damage sustained by thousands of women as the result of their silicone breast implants. Women, in the process, are jointly idealized and ignored. From this perspective and following the logic of Catherine MacKinnon (1983), when the state is male, female exploitation is inherent in the processes and actions of the state. This theoretical logic explains the view of the FDA during the implant debacle—it had more important cases.

Susan Caulfield and Nancy Wonders (1993) propose a theory of organizational crime as political crime when the government allows crime by institutions to occur. This is not crime of "commission," but rather crime by "omission." If the government allows crimes to continue against women, then the crime becomes political in nature.

> We argue that the state engages in political crime when it fails to define widespread and systemic harm against women as illegal, when it neglects to enforce laws that do provide some measure of protection to women, and when it provides structural support for institutional practices which clearly harm women. (Caulfield & Wonders, 1993, p. 79)

According to Caulfield and Wonders's definition, the Dow Corning implant case can be classified as a political crime, due to the inefficiency and disinterest of the government in helping to regulate the devices and to protect the women involved. The disfigurement and disease of thousands of women was not important enough to illicit speedy intervention. In fact, much regulation concerning the implants was never enforced (Rynbrandt & Kramer, 1995). Crimes against women, particularly narcissistic, consenting women seeking a body ideal, are not a high priority according to the government. As men control the capitalistic structures of business, medicine, advertising, and government, female identity is shaped by men. If men desire the big-breasted female ideal, then that image is passed on to the consumers—women. Allowing women to be used in experiments and to suffer from their voluntary implant decision reinforces the hegemony of masculinity, which dismisses female's concerns and belittles their pain and suffering.

Explanations of Corporate Wrongdoing

Is Dow Corning guilty of illegal corporate practices or simply of unethical ones? This question rests at the heart of the definition of fraud. According to definitions used by police officers in determining arrest criteria, fraud is material misrepresentation knowingly given in which the victim believed the misrepresentation, and the victim suffered a loss (personal communication, Tucson Police Department, Fraud Division, 1995). The doctors and victims involved believed the implants to be safe, because this was the information given to them by Dow Corning's salespeople. The doctors trusted the salespeople to relay the necessary information to them (Stanley, 1994). Because salespeople want to sell their product and receive higher commissions, they may be more inclined than independent research agents to provide only information beneficial to their company. Information containing possible links to cancer and systemic diseases may have been suppressed.

Due to the technical nature of the medical information disseminated, the average citizen may not be armed with the knowledge to doubt the manufacturer's and doctor's claims of the implant's safety. The salespeople were the crucial link between the doctor and the manufacturer. If the people involved in marketing and selling the silicone breast implants knowingly misrepresented the safety and efficacy of the implants, then they were committing fraud. If they were simply repeating information handed down from above, however, then the fraudulent practices may have originated higher up in the Dow Corning executive ranks. Following orders and repeating erroneous information, although potentially harmful, is not illegal.

Dow Corning had the lion's share of the implant market through the duration of its tenure as an implant manufacturer. Where else could a doctor turn to gain further evidence *before* he or she used the implants? To another implant manufacturer, as unencumbered by federal regulation as Dow Corning? Much conflicting evidence surfaced after the implants were already being used. Most women complained of implant hardening and rupture years after implantation (Bruning, 1995). Many women suffered untold agony as a result of their implants, signifying loss, as well as their financial loss in medical expenses. What remains for the definition of fraud to be complete is the question of fraudulent misrepresentation.

Is Dow Corning, or any other large corporation, ethically obligated to be socially responsible when not obligated to be legally responsible? It seems as if the executives at Dow Corning believed the answer to be no (Kelly, 1995). In this instance, Dow Corning used its consumers as unknowing research subjects. This begs the final question: Did Dow Corning knowingly release an unsafe product?

Milton Friedman, a classical economist,

> believes that corporate executives who talk about social responsibility are subverting the free-enterprise system . . . executives should be charged with the single responsibility of making money; they are misappropriating the stockholders' investments if they become involved in such activities as "pollution control" (Clinard & Yeager, 1980)

According to Friedman's description of the duties of corporate executives, the executives at Dow Corning were fulfilling their duties. Edwin K. Sutherland (1983), thought to be the first theorist of "white-collar crime," has a different definition of white-collar crime and social responsibility. According to Sutherland, "white collar crime may be defined as a crime committed by a person of respectability and high social status in the course of his occupation" (p. 7).

According to Sutherland's theory of differential association, crime (white-collar or otherwise) is learned from more experienced criminal peers. It is then a "criminogenic," peer-influenced atmosphere that normalizes corporate crime and allows it to continue (p. 240). Crime is not learned to be wrong. Crimes of the "suites" are distinguished by the social location (elite status) of those committing them, but the criminal association and learning mechanism of criminal commission is universal to all situations. According to Sutherland's depiction of white-collar offenders, it is characteristically the people in positions of power who have the ability to start the crime legitimization ball rolling. From them, others learn to commit crimes and learn that these crimes are an acceptable mode of doing business.

Gottfredson and Hirschi (1990b) examine white-collar crime and indicate that if fraud is committed within the course of one's workday, it is labeled white-collar crime because of where it takes place, not because white-collar offenses are intrinsically different from "blue-collar" offenses. For the authors, distinctions among categories of crime are useless. If fraud occurs in the workplace, then it is a crime; those engaging in fraud are criminals. The motivation of offenders in the "suites" is the same as the motivation of offenders on the streets—immediate gratification of desires. According to Gottfredson and Hirschi (1990a), the likely offender in any type of crime exhibits low self-control. The offender is likely to engage in acts that bring him or her immediate gratification of his or her desires at the expense of long-term rewards. Also following from Gottfredson and Hirschi's typology of those exhibiting low self-control, the offender is likely to be unmoved or have little regard for the pain and suffering of those victimized by the offender's actions (p. 89). According to the authors, most crime is committed overwhelmingly by men (see also Hindelang, 1979). If the enactment of hegemonic masculinity within the workplace involves acts of corporate deviance, as Messerschmidt has hypothesized, this can explain why men are disproportionately involved in white-collar crimes. Either men are enacting a form of masculinity that involves the repeated victimization of women, or they have a greater opportunity to commit crimes given their greater numbers in business relative to women. Regardless of which theory one chooses to explain white-collar deviance, it is clear that Dow Corning was involved in corporate wrongdoing (either as a learned behavior or as an expedient means to achieve an immediate desire) that increased their profits at the expense of thousands of women's health and well-being.

This brings us back to the original question: Did Dow Corning knowingly commit fraud? Did they knowingly release unsafe products to the public? The internal memos dating back to the early 1970s linking silicone exposure to cancer and systemic diseases would indicate that they did. However, one must remember that the devices were not regulated, so the unethical acts committed by burying the documents are not technically illegal, insofar as they were not committed against any federal regulations. Because so much conflicting research evidence exists, it is difficult to determine whether Dow Corning was working on knowledge gained from bad, misleading, or accurate research. However, with the recent efforts expended to cover up the past leaked documents (Rynbrandt & Kramer, 1995), it appears that something illegal did transpire. Federal court judges have since ordered the sealed documents to be opened, although Dow Corning has been characteristically slow in complying (Rynbrandt & Kramer, 1995).

Fitting the Pieces Together

To understand the actions of Dow Corning regarding the manufacture and sale of silicone breast implants, the social context in which the decisions took place must be examined. No one actor, organizational or otherwise, acts within a social vacuum. Every actor is embedded in a social structural matrix that may, in part, determine, or at least influence, the decisions made. The investigation into the practices of Dow Corning makes little sense if the patriarchal context of medicine, big business, and the state is ignored.

Connell's (1987) concept of hegemonic masculinity sheds light on the injurious practices of Dow Corning as a possible enactment of a particular form of masculine identity. Given the hegemony with which men control the avenues of power today, and particularly in the early 1960s when the implants were first introduced, it is impossible to ignore the suggestion that concepts of masculinity aided in shaping the decisions that affected millions of women. Hegemonic masculinity affords men the power to ignore "others" outside their vision. The executives at Dow Corning were determined to increase profits in their marketing of the revolutionary silicone breast implant. In this single-minded determination, the women involved were dismissed and ignored in the process. They were the "Other" variable in their profit-making equation. It is as if the women receiving the implants did not exist, except as sites to lay blame. Their complaints were manufactured, their diseases psychosomatic, and their desire for perfection pathological.

Where are women in this male-dominated process? They are the process and the end result. They are the fantasy and the research subject. It is this union of hegemonic masculinity, blind-eyed state apparatus, and unethical but profitable business practices that facilitates corporate deviance against women. The entire process has forgotten the women involved, the focus rests solely on the men. Is this an atypical scenario? A woman wants to augment her breasts, she goes to her doctor (man), asks to augment her breasts, and relies on manufacturers (men) to provide safe and effective products. If she is unsatisfied with her information or the product she receives, she can ultimately turn to the government (men) for protection against fraudulent products or to the courts (men) for redress. She is the true physical and social embodiment of the Other; her safety is dependent on the decisions of the men involved. She is socially and physically transformed in the process and is spit out in the end as a reconstituted Other.

The harm sustained by thousands of women receiving silicone breast implants is unquestionable. Currently, the women involved in court cases against Dow Corning are finding some retribution. However, did Dow Corning do anything wrong? Many say that they did not. If, as Dow Corning maintains, the implants pose an inappreciable risk of rupture and disease, are these women merely money-hungry exceptions? The history of medical device regulation is frightening at best. The government wrongly believed that the industry would regulate itself. It appears as if the pain and suffering of thousands of women was less important than protecting the interests of big business.

Why did the FDA wait so long to step in when faced with evidence questioning the safety of the implants? First, the evidence changed according to the interests funding the research. Unequivocal links between silicone exposure and disease have not been made. Second, the breast implant business was a thriving, billion-dollar enterprise. It constituted a very powerful group that resisted and ignored governmental control. Third, powerful lobbying groups, such as the AMA and the ASPRS, exerted pressure to keep the implants on the market. Ultimately, the question to be answered is, Did Dow Corning knowingly sell unsafe products? The decision is difficult to make. However, as a woman, I cannot help but ask: Would the case have been any different if men had been the majority receiving the implants? Unfortunately, I do think gender matters when considering the importance placed on human harm.

11

Engendering Violent Men

Oral Histories of Military Masculinity

TRACY XAVIA KARNER

> To be a man is to participate in social life as a man. . . . Men are not born; they are made. And men make themselves, actively constructing their masculinities within a social and historical context.
>
> Kimmel & Messner, 1992, p. 8

> Being a warrior is not an occupation but a male identity.
>
> Gibson, 1990, p. 96

The process of creating and constructing masculinity can be seen in the life stories of veterans—not only in the context of specific sex-typed behaviors of aggression and violence, but often masculinity is used to imply an evaluative relational measure. As they narrate, questions of what it means to be a man, how masculinity should be displayed, and where the appropriate social avenues for its expression are, underlie the veterans' words. The issue of masculinity and how well they, as men, measure up to the standard of manliness that they have internalized is seldom articulated directly. Gender permeates their understanding in such a subtle and taken-for-granted way that it is not untangled from their

197

worldview; indeed their whole consciousness appears textured by their masculine culture. The veterans' recollections paint a startling portrait of what it is to be male in our society—the constraints, the responsibilities, and the rewards of maleness. In exploring this portrait, masculinity appears intertwined with violence and aggressive domination.

The production of identity takes place in many ways within various contexts. Sociologists have long acknowledged the primary impact of gender, along with race and class, in dictating individual life situations, choices, and opportunities (Kimmel, 1993, p. vii). Individuals, like their stories, have structural contexts that are made known through their telling. "The culture 'speaks itself' through each individual's story" (Rosenwald & Ochberg, 1992, p. 7). Narratives are much more than simply a mirror of life events; they are embedded in temporal, geographical, political, cultural, and social fields—all of which lend shape and form to the narration. Indeed, they are "responses to the system in which they originate and thus reveal its dynamics" (Personal Narratives Group, 1989, p. 9). Life stories allow social scientists a view of individuals and the society within which the narrators act out their lives.

Individual stories and experiences, then, provide an exploratory vantage point for "how" gender works, both at the structural level and at the personal plane. It is my premise that selves are created from myriad social resources that exist prior to the individual's exposure to them. Thus family members, media ideals, educational theories, and the like, provide nascent selves with representations of appropriate behaviors and life scripts for the different social locales into which individuals are born. For instance, racial, gender, and class stereotypes are manifested in, and drawn from, numerous—often subtle—resources that map out specific social expectations critical to the formation of the self. Within these images, individuals mediate among social possibilities for the construction of self and the attendant sense of meaning that accompanies the narrative retellings of lives.

In this chapter it is my intention to use the life stories of Vietnam veterans who have been diagnosed with post-traumatic stress disorder to illuminate the processes and consequences of traditional masculinity. Identity options or maps are represented, modeled, rewarded, and enforced throughout the life course. According to Nagel (1994), identity formation can be conceived of as a "dialectic between internal identification and external ascription" (p. 10). Thus, sociologists need to focus on how gendered identities are "chosen" and negotiated to understand more fully the process of gender inculcation. Vietnam veterans provide an extreme view into male socialization patterns and options in the post-World War II era.

In the oral histories collected and analyzed here, it is the veterans' gender identity that prefigures their ideas and holds their early narratives together, creating meaning, explaining their actions, and making sense of their lives as men. By prefiguring, such a master identity as gender contains an entire cultural web of significance around which the individual constructs a self and life (Hood, 1993). Thus a gender identity can be seen as "ready made" for the recently born self. Indeed, "our first mark of identity is by gender" (Gergen, 1992, p. 129). Gender can be conceptualized as the *trajectory*—a pathway or line of development for a man's life, and Vietnam as a *transitional* event that both exacerbates the trajectory of masculinity and provides a life marker between "before combat" and "after combat" (Elder, 1985, 1986).

Vietnam Veterans With Post-Traumatic Stress Disorder

The data that form the basis of this study are drawn from intensive interviews with Vietnam combat veterans and participant observation on a PTSD (Post-Traumatic Stress Disorder) unit of a VA Hospital (see Karner, 1994). In the midwest institutional setting, one half of the inpatient population—15 veterans—were interviewed one to four times each and were observed in a variety of hospital settings. In addition, I interviewed hospital staff, sat in on staff meetings, and had access to autobiographies written by the veterans as they entered the hospital. During the study, all the patients were Vietnam veterans and one was also a Gulf War veteran. All but one of the men interviewed were white; one was African American. The veterans ranged in age from 38 to 47 years and all were from midwestern states. Only one veteran had been drafted—the majority had enlisted and many had volunteered for combat duty.

The diagnosis of post-traumatic stress disorder (PTSD) can be seen as a medicalization of deviance, where toxic behaviors become "symptoms" that legitimate and mandate medical interventions (Conrad & Schneider, 1980). As a science, psychiatry has functioned traditionally as an agent of social control (Foucault, 1973), as has the military. Sociologists conceptualize both deviance and conformity as brought about through the social bonds that individuals have with key institutions of social control (Sampson & Laub, 1993). PTSD binds together both conformity to social models of masculinity, duty, honor, and country with the deviance of violent atrocities. Dean (1992) argued that PTSD has served to expand the category of disease to include behaviors that had been seen as "normal" in the past (p. 71). Indeed, Broude (1990) found that hypermasculinity constituted the "upper end of the continuum of sex-typed behavior in men," not abnormality. Yet, within the discourse of PTSD, such toxic behaviors were reconstructed as the result of "a psychologically distressing event" (p. 120), not the consequence of cultural and military socialization processes. The medicalization of masculinity within PTSD may thus be a social response, as Robinson (1992, p. 62) suggests, for a culture in search of an explanatory narrative for the Vietnam experience.

Shifting Social Models of Masculinity

Pleck (1981, pp. 140-141) distinguishes two models for masculinity—the "traditional" and the "modern." Ironically, the men who went to Vietnam were raised in the 1950s, during the transition between the two models. The "traditional" male role validated itself through physical strength and aggression. Men were expected to show little emotional sensitivity and, especially, were socialized to avoid expressing vulnerability or weakness. In contrast, impulsivity and anger were permissible for the "traditional male." The dominance of this model began to subside after World War II with the advent of the "modern male" role, which esteemed economic achievement and organizational or bureaucratic power. However, the "modern" male was more of a middle-class notion, whereas working-class men hung on to the "traditional" model much longer.

Skolnick (1991) characterizes the male roles of the 1950s as "contradictory." She asserts that the "ideology of the strong male was at odds with the ideology of [family] togetherness" (p. 71). This was typified in media portrayals of the era. Family life was stressed, while "comic strips and television programs poked fun at emasculated, 'henpecked' males like Dagwood Bumstead" (p. 71). Thus, the gender messages of these veterans' youth were far from clear. Growing up amid ambiguous models for male behavior would, following Baffi, Kerry, Redican, and Impara (1991), contribute to greater stress and more difficulty for these men when faced with challenges to their own sense of masculinity. Similarly, in a comparison of 19th- and 20th-century mens' movements, Orr (1994, p. 6) found that the common impetus for masculine resurgence was a social landscape in which their "grip on power and privilege" was loosening. Thus, these Vietnam veterans' confusion, perhaps, mirrors the larger social narratives of their youth. As Thompson (1991, p. 3) reminds us, notions of masculinity are the expression of "deep structures" within the surrounding culture.

Cultural Idealism

Furthermore, the Vietnam veterans grew up in the social context of the 1950s, when historic, economic, and political factors in the post-World War II era created a unique period in U.S. history. The war had also produced an economic upswing that engendered a patriotic optimism in American capitalism and its promise of continued abundance, the likes of which had never been seen before. Based on military dominance, economic bounty, and political consensus, belief in a distinctive American way of life permeated 1950s society (Hodgson, 1976).

> The long-held dream of a fulfilling family life in a comfortable home seemed at last to be coming true for millions of people; not everyone was affluent or middle class, but it was assumed that those left out would eventually get their share. (Skolnick, 1991, p. 50)

The events and the values of this decade served as a backdrop to the experiences that shaped the gender identities of the men who went to Vietnam.

The Height of the Traditional Family

Growing up in the post-World War II United States, these men were consequently presented with an idealized nuclear family and separate spheres of interaction and identity for men and women. Coontz (1992, pp. 24-26) asserts that "the 1950s was a profamily period if there ever was one." She contends that the fifties were also unlike any previous decade with regard to the promotion of the nuclear family. Far from being the last decade of *the* traditional family, it was the *only* such decade. During this unique time, gender roles were tightly enforced, most pointedly within the family (Segal, 1990, p. 8).

A separation of gendered worlds requisitioned the absence of male adults from child care, which left young boys to identify with an *image* of male adulthood, rather than the *presence* of a paternal individual (Kaplan, 1988, p. 132). These rigid distinctions between gender cultures, coupled with the notion that masculinity is often considered a "relational construct"—that is, more about what one should *not* do, than what one should do (Herek, 1987, p. 73), also increased the social pressure to conform, albeit to an absent and idealized model.

World War II had played out the American belief in what Slotkin (1985) terms our cultural "regeneration through violence" mythology. A new, brighter day had dawned not only after the war but *because* of the war. War movies of the era "always pointed to how battles portrayed in the film were responsible for America's world power, affluence, and the good life" (Gibson, 1989, p. 30). War was what "good men" did for the benefit of the "greater social good," and that righteous, just wars made society stronger, were the messages of the day.

The veterans in this study spent their youth within this post-World War II culture. Amid the cultural heroism, the political consensus, and the economic boom, these men absorbed the social narratives of the time. Their own stories of childhood reflected and "spoke" this culture. Paramount in their personal narratives was the desire to achieve an acceptance as a "man." Many of their accounts seemed prefigured with generalizations about gendered behavior that would identify them as manly.

Learning to Be Men

Creating one's gender identity is a lifelong process. With each change in age, environment, or situation, an individual must learn "new tasks, attitudes, and shift from past preferences and behaviors to new ones" (Stoll, 1974, p. 77). Often, these transformations in life are periods of challenge and personal growth, and childhood is a continuum of such successive shifts. Indeed, though they had embarked on the trajectory of masculinity their significant relationships, both within the family and outside of it, mediated their individual and structural backgrounds to some extent (Sampson & Laub, 1993). The Vietnam veterans' narratives reveal a shifting sense of self and conflicted masculinity, patterned after their own fathers and honed to comply with their peers. Socioculturally, these men were given idealized images of stereotyped lives to which no one in their experience had ever lived up.

The veterans' narratives unfolded in an episodic manner. They did not have threads of coherence sewn through their stories that might relate experiences from childhood to Vietnam and through to their present lives. Their childhood recollections were held and expressed in discrete representative stories that could be located by age and historical year into a life span, but there seemed little reflection on how each story or experience affected their later lives.[1] This contrasted with their narratives of the years after Vietnam, which were full of contemplation and deliberation.

Though these veterans began their childhood retelling with thematic glosses of normalcy, its loss, and premature adulthood and restriction, we explored their recollections in greater detail. As often occurs when questioning specific aspects of a gloss, the summary childhood image begins to fragment. No longer holding a concise representation of those childhood days, the gloss can be seen as a protective veil. It contains all the memories of childhood in a tight retelling statement that explains only the distance of the previous events from the veteran's current situation. The retelling statement was meant to review certain experiences contained within specific years of their lives that left the telling self (the veteran) and the listener with a generalized acceptance of the statement and no need to attend to it further.

In exploring the foundations of masculinity and violence in the lives of these veterans, I questioned them about all aspects of their youth. Throughout the narratives, the themes of desiring manhood and the need to prove one's progress toward its attainment were clear themes that ran through many components of their early lives. Preforming masculinity, in the form of the traditional mold of strength and aggression, was a continual process. Idealized manhood was thought to be just within your grasp—if you strived hard enough. And "hard enough" was always a receding target, always held to question, and measured against cinematic representations of men. These social structures provided the structural context for learning gender.

More specifically, children first observed gender roles being modeled within the family. The veterans whose representations are included here portrayed growing up with passive, victim mothers and angry, violent fathers who were often alcoholics. The veterans were brought up within a cultural context that emphasized an ideal of the traditional nuclear family but that, in reality, harbored all sorts of unexpected emotional mayhem. This family setting provided their first or primary social environment. The lessons about personhood and maleness that they learned within their families were also replicated and reinforced in their other social spheres.

Idealized Fathers and Violent Men

The specific role fathers play in gender identity acquisition is still debated in the psychological literature, though their influence is widely accepted as formative. "Disagreements arise over whether the acquisition of sex-identity and sex-typed behaviors is a function of identification or imitation and over whether reinforcement and punishment or cognitively based autonomous motivation promote the development of sex-identity and sex-typing" (Broude, 1990, p. 107). Fathers were the young boys' primary models of male adulthood. Indeed, families constituted the fundamental setting for learning "how to do gender" (Kramer, 1991, p. 167). Both male models for identification and peer group reinforcement claim a significant role in these veterans' narratives.

Fathers were mentioned more often and with greater feeling than any other family member. They were remembered for their traditional paternal role of provider and disciplinarian as well as the central focus of the family structure. Memories and retellings of fathers were often contradictory and confusing. It seemed as though many of these veterans had yet to decide whether the fathers who raised them were the idealized "good fathers" of their youthful ideas or something quite the opposite. However, fathers occupied a central role in the remembrance of their childhoods. This finding is counter to Jackson's (1990, p. 88) notion that men tend to idealize and overemphasize their mothers and omit discussions of their fathers in autobiographical work. The content of veterans' stories was consistent with Kaplan's (1988, p. 132) assessment that fathers were more often present in the household as an image rather than an actual presence. Many veterans commented that their fathers were seldom home. Moreover, their daily life was structured by their fathers' occupations and work schedules, which gave an added impact to the paternal influence. For the veterans, like Kurt,[2] who grew up without their father (and Tommy and Larry who grew up with stepfathers), the absence seemed to have had just as distinct repercussions.

The 1950s orientation toward opposing gender roles seemed strikingly consistent within the remembrances of these veterans. In their narratives, the internalized gender models for the behavior of adult males and, specifically, fathers can be read. The veterans represented the cultural expectations and rigid stereotypes of their youth in their retellings by the information they initially volunteered. This cultural model may also have affected the way in which the memories were structured—fathers were remembered for their "traditional" behaviors, whereas the memories of their fathers engaging in less idealized behaviors may have been buried deeper or at least not volunteered. The "good father" retelling statement was always offered first, as Walter's narrative illustrated: "My dad and I, I remember as a little kid, we were real close. I remember him coming

home from work from the mines and he had a candy bar for me or
something like that."
    However, as Walter continued to describe his father, he let us know that
the "good father" was only the father of his early youth.

> He was a chemist and he was a truck driver. He would work extra even in the
> mines so we'd have a place to live, a nice house. And . . . he'd take me out to
> target shoot a .22 rifle and different things, you know. And all of a sudden, he
> got in the bar business, and everything, life changed.

With further discussion, Walter continued to loosen the idealized version
of his father with which he had begun.

> And a lot of times he would stay after the bar's long closed and drank with
> people. And you know, I remember how, his violent temper stuff, and his
> violence towards me, I mean, he'd hit me real hard with his fists or slapped me
> or hit me with a belt.

As they unfolded, the veterans' oral narratives portrayed a contradictory and less idealized view of their fathers. Many of these fathers were
violent, strict, authoritarian men with alcohol problems who believed hard
work was the best way to raise their sons. Hillman (1991, p. 201) suggests
that these "destructive" fathers destroy their sons' idealized view of not
only their fathers, but of themselves as well. These narratives revealed
the son's continuing struggle to balance between an idealized view and
his lived experience. When questioned, the initial retelling statements
revealed memories of childhood wounds, hurts, and injustices.
    David, who identified his father as a "plasterer for trade" and an
"ex-marine [who] served in World War II," also began with a retelling
gloss. "My dad was a hard worker, and loved his beer when he come home,
us kids got along with dad. He would wrestle with us and play. My dad
had a crew cut as long as I can remember." Later, David volunteered that
his father was both physically and verbally abusive when he was drinking.
"I was scared of my dad. I loved him but hated him too." Throughout the
interview, David continued to describe his relationship with his father in
more detail.

> I mean he'd beat us with, once he grabbed a frying pan, an iron frying pan and
> hit me over the head and I seen stars and I just slid to the floor and knocked

me out, then another time I did something wrong and he'd put me over a stump, a tree stump and whip me with a weeping willow branch and those sting, boy.

John and Ramsey, however, had dispensed completely with the idealized father in their narratives. Recollections of their fathers were filled with blunt, violent, negative images. Nevertheless, their representations of their fathers were still consistent with activities traditionally associated with men. Perhaps, though, their portraits revealed some of the more disagreeable aspects of stereotypical masculine behavior. As Pleck (1981, p. 147) points out, some characteristics prescribed by sex roles are dysfunctional.

He would take a light cord and beat the hell out of me . . . Oh, I know I really dreaded getting a whipping, because if I didn't fit in to all that church bunch, sit just exactly right, I knew that when I got home I was getting a light cord used on me, that or a brush. Took my pants off and then use the light cord, had welts all over me with blood, you know and that's how angry my dad got. (Ramsey)

Similar to Ramsey's, John's narrative painted a painful portrait.

He was an alcoholic, an abusive alcoholic. Not only physically but mentally and verbally. . . . It didn't really matter what I was doing, whatever it was it seemed to irritate him, you know . . . I was scared of him. . . . He was an alcoholic, [I] never knew what kind of mood he was gonna be in and I was afraid to say anything for fear of saying the wrong thing and that carried through, basically through my childhood, up until I was old enough to get out and get on my own to break that connection, and you know, try and live my life without him, 'cause I didn't like the memories. I didn't like the beatings. I didn't like his attitude. I didn't like the way he treated my mother, nor any of my sisters. So I tried to isolate myself from him as much as I possibly could.

Of all the veterans with whom I spoke, only Tommy did not remember suffering at the hand of an abusive parent.

Growing up with fathers who had served or continued to serve their country, these young boys were also given a heroic picture of military duty. In the years following the "good war"—World War II—military service was seen as a natural rite of passage from boyhood to manhood. War movies of the era portrayed "war as a crucial ritual transition from male adolescence into manhood" (Gibson, 1990, p. 91). Men who had served held a place of social esteem and were rewarded for their contribution to "the American way of life" and to "keeping America free." Nationally, this social gratitude and status was operationalized with "broad readjustment benefits" made available to *all* returning veterans (Dean, 1992, p. 73). Unlike the social myth of military men as heroic, stalwart protectors of society, however, many of these fathers were remembered as violent, unhappy men, many of whom had problems with alcoholism. Their sons grew up with the idealized picture of the good soldier "doing his duty for God and country" while often simultaneously experiencing a reality of physically and emotionally abusive veteran fathers. The father's violence and anger (or lack of it) seemed to set the emotional tone of the home. Traditionally, women were responsible for the domestic sphere of family interaction: nurturing, guiding, and teaching. Yet all of these traditionally female duties can easily be overshadowed by fear of the father, and especially his drinking or violence. However completely the "good father" image was embraced by these men, their fathers had provided a dominant male role model that still continued to impact their sons' lives.

Good Mothers and Weak Women

The impact of mothers on these men's lives seemed much less apparent than that of their fathers. In the autobiographies as well as the interviews, the veterans had little to say about their mothers, almost as though they had been invisible or not important enough to be included among the memories assembled to tell their life stories. Within the nuclear family mythology, motherhood was greatly revered, yet women were denigrated (Skolnick, 1991, p. 72). Like recollections of their fathers, remembrances of the mothers revolved around their traditional gender tasks and attributes. In contrast to descriptions of the father, mothers more often retained the "good mother" image. Even after further interview questions about their mothers, such retelling statements that merely glossed over the memories were not demystified; in most cases, the idealized image was maintained. Mothers were not represented with as much complexity or ambivalence as the fathers. They were remembered for their emotional warmth, their unconditional love, or their gender-appropriate dependencies. Consistent with his research on men and masculinity, Jackson (1990) finds that in most autobiographical works by men "often the mother is idealized," and is seen as a "self-sacrificing, passive victim" (p. 88) whose sole orientation is her son. For instance, Bill said his mother was, "a good person, typical mother." Bill's statement perhaps exemplified the casual attitude that these men had toward their mothers. She was there but taken for granted, remembered more as a role than as a person. In answering detailed questions, narratives of the mother often turned to her attempts to mediate the father's alcoholism and physical abuse, at times by taking it upon herself. "She'd try to protect the kids," John remembered,

> and dad would just turn around and smack the shit out of her just as soon as he would one of us kids, you know. . . . I couldn't understand why mother would sit there and take it, for the love of me I could never understand it.

In Larry's case, his mother would let him stay home from school after one of his father's late night tirades. He explained, "if an episode like that happened, mother kept me home from school so I could rest."

Other veterans expressed a subtle resentment toward their mothers for their father's violence. Much like the "good father/bad father" motif, the narratives of their mothers contained both the "idealized" and the "weak" mother. The "weak mother" was never equal to the "bad father's" violence; she could not protect herself or her children. She was just a "bruised and battered housewife," John summarized. "I started to resent my mother a little 'cause I didn't understand why she would subject herself and us kids to that kind of an environment, you know." Chris's memory was similar: "My mother was a very husband-oriented person. . . . The husband runs the house. . . . It was always the tyrannical father, the tyrant father, [and] the dutiful mother and wife."

Along with family, friends, play groups, fights, competitive sports, jobs, and parties frequently came to the forefront when discussing their youth. The veterans spoke of these childhood occurrences much more personally, with greater detail, than stories of more common life events, as though they found more of themselves originating in the informal interactions. Socialization theories hold that these "extrafamilial social factors, such as peers, school, books, television, or films" have a profound and pervasive influence on the formation of gender identity (Lisak, 1991, p. 245).

Warfare and Violence as Play

Like many young boys of their era, these veterans had grown up doing "boy" stuff that was symbolically embedded within motifs of war and violence. "Yeah I played with toy soldiers and stuff. Yeah, . . . with guys too, we'd have wars and stuff. . . . I remembered I had a Japanese helmet, a original one" (David). Gaining prominence in the play of the home-front children during the war (Tuttle, 1993, pp. 134-138), reenacting World War II continued to be an integral part of growing up male in the 1950s. Some fathers had brought home souvenirs, as David mentioned above. In addition, most of the veterans remembered fathers or uncles often sitting around telling "war stories" that the young boys emulated in play. John explained that he knew about war and soldiering from a variety of sources: "watching them on TV, watching old war movies . . . that and reading comic books about them. . . . G.I. Joe type stuff." Other veterans remembered watching the "battle flicks." Marty said he used to "eat that stuff up." Mangum also enjoyed war movies, "especially the ones with Audie Murphy." David recollected seeing the movies with his father, who watched "[be]cause he's an ex-marine."

From these veterans' narratives it seemed apparent that the images and lessons of World War II, with its mystique of the good American warrior and its association with masculinity, were prevalent in their early youth. These "melodramatic portrayals of men performing virile, courageous deeds designed to protect helpless civilians from some sort of aggressor" were common for young boys as male role-play simulations (Donald, 1992, pp. 125-126). Indeed, Cancian (1990, p. 66) quotes one veteran as saying, "I've been in basic training since I was six years old." In American society, combat training and masculine socialization are never separated from each other (Arkin & Dobrofsky, 1990, p. 72). Indeed as Gibson (90, p. 96) points out, *warrior* is a male identity, not an occupation, and in the 1950s it was *the* heroic male identity.

As they grew, war games turned to interpersonal violence in schoolyard fighting and competitive sports, traditional testing grounds for adolescent masculinity. Trujillo (1991) suggests that "perhaps no single institution in American culture has influenced our sense of masculinity more than sport." It is thought that competition, he continues, "builds manly character, develops physical fitness, realizes order, promotes justice, and even prepares young men for war," which is accomplished through "sanctioned aggression, (para)militarism, the technology of violence, and other patriarchal values" (p. 292). These veterans began their warrior training early. Sports and fighting helped create the self they were desirous to achieve. Larry found fighting improved his self-esteem: "I had some confrontations with a bully one time, used to be scared of them until I found out their mouth worked more than their brawn."

Other veterans chose organized sports to cultivate their sense of masculinity. Such sports are both a "gendered institution"—organized in accord with gender norms, and also an "engendering institution"—contributing and reproducing gender relations (Messner, 1992a, pp. 173-174). Donald (1992) asserts that "the closest substitutes for war are contact sports such as football or boxing" (p. 135). These athletic accomplishments were recollected fondly. David remembered his wrestling exploits with pride: "I was undefeated in my weight class in high school." He also ran track. Similarly, Marty had been successful in sports: "I played probably nine years of organized football, and I was recruited highly by several colleges." Chris played football until his family moved and he left school. Bill recalled the most extensive involvement in sports, beginning with baseball and swimming as a child and basketball as a teenager.

Military Manhood

> Really being right out of high school . . . I didn't have any qualifications for anything and so my uncle said, "So what are you gonna do, just stay here and mooch off of me?" and I said, "No I'll find something," and he said, "Well, why don't you go in the army and get it over with?" So that's where I went. . . . *That'll grow you up real fast.* (John, emphasis added)

The military did "grow" these veterans up "real fast"; their experience in Vietnam, especially, changed them in fundamental ways. Unlike narratives of childhood, recollections of military life and Vietnam do not assume a shared social referent. Combat was an unshared experience that necessitated elaborate, lengthy tales. However, some of the veterans did use introductory glosses, at times appearing to test the response of the listener. In individual interviews the men often started with positive comments. Tommy began by stating that he "loved it." Likewise, Kurt said "it was fun." In contrast, when they were in a group setting with other veterans, Vietnam was described in generally negative terms, as a "bloody mess," "useless," or "a waste." Thus, Vietnam retelling statements took the form of brief evaluative comments. These assertions were not intended to convey a shared sense of a common experience as the childhood retelling statements had been. Rather, they held the experience of Vietnam separate—unique to those who actually participated in combat, but also as different for each individual combatant. Depending on the job assignment and the branch of the service, veterans were likely to have had very distinctive circumstances during their tours. Mangum, who spent his tour as a "river rat" shuttling troops on a tango boat, saw different parts of the war than did John or Tommy, who were Army Rangers, working in the field. Different memories and experiences of Vietnam were expected even among the veterans themselves. "There was no *one* Vietnam combat experience" (Shafer, 1990, p. 82, emphasis added).

"A Good Way to Be a Man"

Several factors played a role in these veteran's decisions to enter the military. Of the 15 men interviewed, only Bill was drafted. All of the others made a conscious choice to join the service. Tommy, for example, dropped out of school specifically to go into the army to fight in Vietnam.

> It's just the way they [returning Vietnam veterans] looked . . . a thousand yard stare and stuff, stare and uh the way they treated people and acted. And I thought, "I need to be like that." They were, they'd changed. Life for them had changed. Vietnam had changed them. I seen great men that I respected, that went as kids. . . . And I thought that'd be great. And I was already patriotic as hell. (Tommy)

Though Tommy's focus in joining the service specifically to go to Vietnam was not universal in this sample, his need to uphold family honor or to prove worthy of family pride was shared by others.

Within the veterans' recollections, family honor and pride took two forms. One was the need to carry on traditions of the male family members' previous military participation. Lewis (1985) suggests that understandings of war are generated most commonly through conversation and the "responsibility for explaining and justifying the necessity of war devolved upon close male kin, predominately the father" (p. 43). Ramsey wrote in his autobiography, "I felt patriotic and wanted to serve my country just as my father and grandfather before me." David echoed these same sentiments while explaining why he entered the service: "[be]cause like my grandpa was in World War I, my Dad was in World War II." Some, like Dan and John, even enlisted in the same branch of the service in which their fathers and grandfathers had served. The majority of these men had fathers who had served during World War II, which added another dimension to, and reinforced, their perception of military life, patriotism, and family honor. Since there was "evidence enough in the form of medals, honors, recognition, jobs, education, and success for those who served, popular expectations have reinforced the military's role as patriarch under whose influence and discipline a doubtless man emerges" (Arkin & Dobrofsky, 1990, p. 70). And World War II veterans had garnered the greatest amount of social rewards for their service. As Dean (1992) asserts, they were "the *exception,* not the *rule* in the history of American veterans" (p. 73). They were welcomed back with broad readjustment benefits for all veterans, not just the disabled.[3] Furthermore, the veterans' personal sacrifice of combat duty was seen as directly responsible for the society's new abundance (Gibson, 1989, p. 30). The World War II veteran fathers had reaped the benefits of a grateful society. This was the heroic and rewarded stance of military service that they modeled for their sons.

Larry explained the impact of the era: "The 50s and the 60s were patriotic, Americans was patriotic . . . they looked up to the uniform." The veterans of World War II had come home as national heroes, and these Vietnam enlistees had grown up with "hero-fathers" who by virtue of having participated in a unique historical event—fighting the "good war"—presented a difficult standard of family honor to follow. John had grown up with the men of his family telling war stories, so when he joined the service and was assigned to a desk job in Kentucky, he was frustrated because he "wanted to be fighting somewhere, anywhere—I wanted a war to go to." His desk job would not give him the credentials of battle needed to enter into the circle of men with whom he had grown up, so he volunteered for Vietnam. John felt that he needed to "go and see what the war's like and say, well yeah, I killed one of them."

Competing With the Fathers

The other aspect of family pride, besides maintaining male traditions, was the need to prove themselves in comparison to their fathers' military careers. Gibson (1989) suggests a motive for this competition:

> Experiencing the failure of the father-son relationship as his own fault, the boy's growth toward manhood becomes problematic. In the face of an ostensibly powerful father, the son feels he is "not good enough" to merit the father's love and attention. (p. 25)

On the other hand, van der Kolk (1988) concludes that such "lack of paternal attention and respect leaves the next generation of males with a lifelong search for acceptance and, often, revenge" (p. 180). Larry expressed a desire for acceptance and recognition from his father in his choice to join the Marine Corps. His father had served in the Navy, so Larry entered the Marine Corps "just to show him I could do something better than him."

> Well, when the Korean war was going on, I heard a lot of publicity about the Marine Corps. They was the baddest, meanest on the block and that's what I wanted to be . . . [a] macho man at seventeen . . . and the Marines had the best uniform. They was the meanest, first to fight, and highly respected and that's what I wanted. *Plus, it was gonna show my Dad that I could do it.* (Larry)

The military provided a way to measure themselves against their fathers, who represented their cultural, and personal, archetype of achieved manhood. Through their service they hoped to join their fathers as symbolic brothers in the "brotherhood" of the military and warfare (Gibson, 1989, p. 25). As Larry elaborated, "It was a good way to be a man."

Another reason mentioned for enlistment concerned employment, also a prerequisite for the attainment of male adulthood. For some, entering the military was a career choice. The veterans of this study where from working-class homes, making them "most susceptible to the military's promises of opportunities for training, travel, and a better future" (Dittmar & Michaud, 1990, p. 14). In this way the traditional work ethic for men, "which equates masculinity with productivity, occupation, and breadwinning," could also be realized through military service (Arkin & Dobrofsky, 1990, p. 70). Thus, military life seemed to be a step toward the "good job" that would enable the veteran to realize the American lifestyle. This strategy had worked well for World War II veterans who had been able to use their military experience to increase their career opportunities (Elder, 1986). One's occupation is the primary vehicle for accomplishing one's goals for the future (Kaplan, 1988, p. 133). The military had seemed a logical path to self-supporting adulthood.

The Mystique of Heroic Combat

Even though the veterans had different reasons for joining the service—wanting to go to war, carrying on the family tradition, proving oneself, or looking for employment—they all shared a belief in the "mystique" of the military. Marty described the military way as glamorous:

> I thought that that was pretty darn glamorous to go into the Marine Corps, the toughest unit they've got, and to go to the war front. . . . If one would just simply watch "Victory at Sea," or anything that kids that was in my slot grew up watching, war was shown as a very glorifying and admirable thing to participate in. (Marty)

Larry had also been influenced by war films, especially the newsreels of the Korean conflict. He distinctly remembered seeing "some pictures of dress blues and such" and how the Marines were "the first to go in before war is declared." War movies of the era "imply that the soldiers' victories will be well respected since they have both defended their society and embody the society's highest ideals" (Gibson, 1990, p. 91). It was while watching newsreels that Larry decided the Marine Corps was the "best" and he wanted to be the best. Walter, much like Larry, was also intrigued with the image of a military man in uniform: "I'd seen some TV shows, John Wayne stuff, and I always figured there was a marching band and I figured I'd go in the Marines in a nice uniform and medals and stuff." Walter continued, "But yeah, I thought it would be a lot different. I'd come home and be a really tough guy and . . . heroic, you know. But it wasn't nothing like that."

When they spoke of their image of the military and their decisions to enlist, they sounded like young men seeking social acceptance. When Tommy remembered as a child seeing veterans returning, he saw them as "great men" and he wanted to be like them. Larry, sizing up the different military branches, decided that the Marine Corps was "the meanest, first to fight, and highly respected, and that's what I wanted." Both Tommy and Larry looked for available social images of accepted and respected men and attempted to fit themselves into those images. Walter's assessment that he would return from military service as a "hero" was another venture to appropriate a manly role for himself.

Organizational Masculinity

In general, the veterans remembered their training as challenging. David said his was "rough" with "hard times," whereas Chris recalled working like he had "never worked before." Kurt and Larry both pointed out that their branch, the Marine Corps, had the "worst training" and was more "brutal" than the other boot camps. Ironically, as they spoke of the demands of boot camp and the harsh treatment by the drill instructors, an incongruous note of pride emerged in their narratives. For Bill it was a kind of stoicism: "I had made up my mind to the fact that I had to do it, people before me had did it, and people behind me would have to [so] go on and get it over." John, however, "enjoyed" the challenge of it, "doing something with everybody moaning and groaning and bitching and shit" while he smiled. "It was fun," John summarized. Marty "liked it, I just liked it, I liked the Marine Corps, I liked everything about it." He also took great pride in being the only 17-year-old in his platoon, excelling alongside of the older guys. They welcomed the opportunity to test themselves and prove their worthiness as *men.*

Shatan (1989) identifies the completion of basic training socialization as the recruit's acceptance of military reality. By this point, the recruits have come to embody the "siege mentality and the paranoid position of combat: permanent hypervigilance, reflex obedience, and instant tactical response—to any threat, real or imagined" (p. 130). In short, they had become soldiers. When they left boot camp, their identity reformation was seemingly completed—they had become military *men*—tough, invincible, and ready to fight. Their childhood self was long gone. Bill spoke about going home on leave before leaving for Vietnam with "no hair but almost a soldier." David also elaborated on his new self-identity in his autobiography. "I went home on leave for thirty days, was really proud of myself for making it through boot camp, here I was home on leave with my uniform [and] felt proud, and everyone was proud of me too." The adulthood that they had sought to achieve or escape from had been bestowed upon them with a uniform, the label of soldier, and the training process. These young men had, at this point, taken on the idealized, heroic role of masculinity that the military fashioned and that matched the glossy, cinematic images of manhood they had grown up seeking.

Larry wrote that he had thought he "was a real tough guy" when he finished boot camp. Chris was a bit more direct in his recollection. His new identity had a combat purpose and a sense of invincibility. "What they did is they took a seventeen-year-old kid and put him through all this training and turn[ed] me into what I deem to be a *perfect killing machine.*" Chris continued to elaborate, "we thought we were ten feet tall and bulletproof and we were ready to kill red commie bastards zipper-faced gooks." After boot camp, Chris said, "I was in physical shape you wouldn't believe. I think I could have went bear hunting with a twig." They had been given, and took on, the mantle of manhood at 17 and 18 years of age because they had succeeded in heightening their physical prowess, followed orders promptly, and honed their anger and aggression toward appropriate targets. Having symbolically become their fathers' peers, they were competing among other men for respect and purpose. Yet this transformation was confined to their roles within the military, which in many ways still shielded them, much as their family of origin had, from many of the responsibilities of adulthood. Outside the military these traits probably would not have constituted adulthood. Yet this was the military identity that saw them through Vietnam.

A Family of Men

Separated from their family of origin and disillusioned with the military authority, *family* was refigured in the field as a homosocial institution. The newfound "family" of their individual squads and buddies was critical to their survival. With the military recast as an obstacle to their success or survival, the men around them took on an increasing importance. The essential elements of warfare were "men and the bonds of trust, respect and loyalty that bind them together on the battlefield" (Shafer, 1990, p. 88). This "Vietnam family" provided the context for learning how to "stay alive," but it also constituted a socialization unit for learning a whole new culture of male adulthood. Indeed, this "family" served as a significant informal mechanism for social control in combat. Having gone to Vietnam to become men, these veterans had initially taken on the military identity of soldier with its attendant discourse of protocol and heroism. When that identity was seen as faulty, these veterans looked to the "hard-core vets" who had been in Vietnam a few months longer than they had as role models for survival. After settling into the nonroutine of life in the bush and learning the rules of Vietnam warfare, they looked to each other for camaraderie and strategies for coping as well as understanding their experiences. This "Vietnam family" functioned as a social structure from which to learn and to participate in constructing their own Vietnam identity of male adulthood. Leed (1989, p. 175) suggests that by reconstructing the family in war, outside the patriarchal model that includes women, male socialization becomes both homoerotic and narcissistic. He also states that in war, "men learn to love each other, forming solidarities and brotherhoods" that cut across boundaries of race, class, and age that usually divide them. John, recalled that he had found a place to belong: "We'd sit around and smoke and bullshit about our missions, bragging mostly, but it made me feel like I belonged for the first time in my life I felt that I belonged and was accepted as who I really was."

The socialization of each other within this family of men was a symbolic reproduction of themselves as warriors (Gibson, 1989, p. 26). This "rebirth" into a family devoid of women corrected their original birth as boys. They had been reborn of men through violence, sweat, fear, anger into this exclusive masculine rite. The narrator in the movie *Platoon* said that in Vietnam he had become "the child of two fathers," referring to two "older" members of his squad. And in this process of rebirth and regeneration, these men had become part of "some classic male experience" (Broyles, 1990, p. 30). As Pleck (1981) points out, however, "male bonding is not a vehicle for male-male emotional relationships, but rather is a substitute for them" (p. 150). The squad camaraderie may have refigured the family into the war context with very deep survival ties, but the emotional ties it elicited were much closer to the surface.

Like all families, the "Vietnam family" had rules within which socialization took place. Specific actions were promoted and encouraged and others prohibited. Much unlike other family settings, however, these rules were enforced or rationalized with combat survival issues. Maintaining the balance between bonding and being combat ready and dependable to the other family members provided a clear example of these rules. Chris explained how the "rules" mediated this contradiction of closeness and readiness when it came to communication between "family" members:

> Oh, we told each other everything. . . . As it turned out, you know, they were my sounding post just as I was their sounding post and it was, one or the other of them would come to me and be upset, or boohooing about a girlfriend calling and I'd tell him, ahh shut up and go to work. I mean, you know, I don't want to hear this shit. . . . I told them leave that shit back here because I don't want you to try to cover my ass thinking about your girlfriend back in Ohio.

Thus, Chris'began by expressing closeness in the totality of their communication, but then illustrated that emotional topics were not appropriate because they might interfere with one's ability in combat. Jackson (1990) outlined the emotional structure of all male bonds as "one of defensive confirmation through the use of joking and jeering at the expense of feared others" (p. 172). In Chris's narrative, it was girlfriends and feelings of caring or loss that constituted the feared others. Larry also recalled similar "talking rules" that mirror the same defensive structure:

> When you was over there you was a macho figure, that was all you was taught to be, a macho figure, you know, nothing can hurt you, you're scared of nothing, no feelings, no pain, you know, just kill, okay? And everybody has got that feeling so you don't relate to the next guy, "Hey man, you know I'm

really scared that this is happening," you know what I'm saying, that this is happening, you know. You don't say that to the next guy because in return he would probably laugh at you, you know, or call you a wimp or puss or whatever and then it gets around and everybody points a finger at this guy, you know, well he's a wimp or he's a puss or queer or whatever.

By focusing on combat issues, the "Vietnam family" suppressed emotional expression while simultaneously engendering the notion of open communication by the shared purpose of survival. As Broyles (1990) romantically explained, "A comrade in war is a man you can trust with anything because you trust him with your life" (p. 32). Yet this trust of one's life, as Pleck suggests, was a substitute for emotional trust. "You had to shut off emotion," Larry elaborated, "so you can do your job." Using taunts of inadequate masculinity (wimp, puss, faggot, girl), the need to maintain a "macho" image was seen as important for combat readiness. The individual's desire to emulate the "macho figure" was used to enhance the larger goals of warfare, which maintained the focus on the group demands by playing on each man's esteem needs while simultaneously distancing him from his emotional life. Traditionally, an estrangement from one's emotions has been a common practice in the socialization of males (Pleck, 1981, pp. 148-150). It is important to note that this socialization pattern was weighted with life-and-death implications in Vietnam. In this context, masculine behavior was not just an issue of manliness, but was perceived as essential for survival.

In this family of men, drinking and partying were unofficial male bonding rituals (Donald, 1992, p. 132). Alcohol and drug use were another vehicle for group camaraderie that also helped suppress emotions. Mangum recalled that the military often supplied "all the beer you could drink" when they would come back after finishing maneuvers. David also mentioned "every three or four months" being pulled "back to the rear and we'd have . . . all the beer we can drink and we'd party." In fact, all of the men who were interviewed mentioned either alcohol or drugs as their main form of recreation in-country. Many of these men had never tasted alcohol before going into the service and some, like Ramsey, did not begin drinking until after they had been in Vietnam for a while. In his autobiography, Kurt recounted the first time he ever tasted a beer, when he went to China Beach on his first day off. "How beautiful. All I did was run and jump in the water. How good it felt. This is my first time I drank a beer. How good it tasted. And I drank more and more until I couldn't stand up. What a hangover I had the next day." Kurt's narrative of his initial introduction to drinking also expressed the "rules" for drinking behavior. Drinking was a social activity in which the level of consumption was expected to be extreme. Culturally, "boys are initiated into the community of men by their ability to drink" (Fejes, 1992, p. 14). Ramsey said he routinely "overdosed" on beer while in Vietnam, whereas Mangum remembered drinking continuously and steadily his whole tour. Quantity and "holding" one's liquor were important.

Drug use was also quite common among the men interviewed; the most esteemed characteristic was to have used or tried everything available. For the veterans who recounted their drug experiences, quantity and variety were the key points in their stories. For example, John described his use as "excessive," claiming to have "used heroin, LSD, Mescaline, THC, grass, and anything I could get my hands on." Both drinking and drug use seemed to have also provided a forum for the expression of bravado. Quantity was esteemed for both alcohol and drug consumption. However, the variety of drugs available exponentially increased the possibilities for achieving quantity of consumption.

Drinking has a social tradition for American males that provided a another layer of masculine expectations that drug use also did not seem to have. Drinking in American culture, especially when combined with our cowboy and warrior motifs, has routinely been a context for proving and achieving a level of manliness. Beer is a symbol of male group solidarity. "The well known saying that you cannot trust a man who does not drink" reflects the social importance of drinking for male bonding and group solidarity (Strate, 1992, p. 88). World War II films and oral narratives, the traditions of their fathers, focused on drinking (and womanizing) as male rites of passage as well (Rosenberg, 1993, p. 50). This context and culture link notions of quantity of consumption and physical competition as the mode of such achievements. Many veterans had stories of drinking and fighting and "cleaning out" bars. Chris enjoyed explaining:

> They enjoyed a good fight as much as I did and so we had fun and once we found out that neither one of us was going to give up and leave, we'd just sit down and get drunk together, but you know my nose may be sitting over here but we'd be sitting there singing and drinking.

Most of these fights were with other servicemen, from either other branches or other squads. Larry spoke of his participation in this kind of competition to prove themselves "bad ass Marines." Larry considered this just the military way of keeping its combatants ready. A Marine was "always wanting to prove himself against another man . . . that's basically the way the Marines are," Larry explained. Drinking and competing were both activities to manifest a sense of manhood, but they also cemented the bonds of the "family" group. One drank with those one was close to and brawled with outsiders. Drinking practices drew the lines of "family" most distinctly.

Besides setting the stage for group boundary definitions, drinking also kept the men's minds off their daily combat experiences. Ramsey found that whenever he tried to sleep, his mind would go over the events of the day so he would "drink as many as it would take to get sleepy." For Mangum, drinking was the only way he could calm down enough to get to sleep. Others chose drugs to cope with difficult events. In his autobiography, John, after recounting a particularly troubling mission, added, "it wasn't long after this that I started to smoke heroin." This suppression of the day-to-day reality of their experience of Vietnam—the unfamiliarity, the horror, and the fear—appear in one form or another as a common refrain in all the narratives. Shatan (1989) calls this the "militarization of feeling" (p. 144) where the soldier was socialized to avoid all emotions except aggression.

Thus, the drinking and drug use served to bolster notions of masculinity and group boundaries, but they also had very specific combat uses as well. David said that he had always been afraid that he would fall asleep during an ambush and that was why he had begun taking liquid speed into the field with him. "After you been humping in 120 degrees, 130 degrees all day in the heat and then you got to stay up all night for an ambush. . . . So I started taking like little bottles of liquid speed." David explained, "I'd always have a few of those on me so if I got picked after humping all day in the bush for night ambush 'cause I learned right away in Nam . . . you better not go to sleep." Kurt also told of using speed for night ambushes and then relaxing with marijuana:

> It came in exact same size bottles as Vicks Formula 44 cough syrup and it had a red devil on it. . . . You drank the whole bottle and it kept you up for a day and a half. . . . But when it started wearing off, it was just like people tearing you apart. So you smoked a couple of joints to mellow out.

These combat functions for drinking (sleep) and drug use (staying awake) further tied notions of masculine behavior to basic survival. The socialization practices within these Vietnam families of men legitimized the "rules" by tying them to life-and-death issues. This essential importance of learning and of behaving appropriately enhanced the internalization of these "rules" by the individual men. In addition, most of the "rules" revolved around the expression and representation of a masculine self. Thus, the "family" behavior acquired in Vietnam reinforced the need and expectation to be masculine at such a deep level that after combat these Vietnam survival skills had become indistinguishable from their sense of selves as men.

The culture of survival and the family structure of their peers created the context within which these young men defined and sought to achieve adulthood. This engendered a tightly woven correlation between the necessity of acquiring certain notions of manhood and masculine behavior and the likely and continuous possibility of imminent death. Once this basis was formed and these skills learned, these men had a whole new understanding of the job they were sent to do. The identity of a Vietnam combat soldier that these men constructed for themselves was in part bounded by these contexts. Understanding this provides a fundamental sensitivity to the specific resources available to these men while in Vietnam. Each man, then, to some degree appropriated these social and cultural influences, mediating them to create his own sense of self and to make sense of his experience. Issues of survival, notions of masculine behavior, and the refigured family groupings found in Vietnam can thus be comprehended as the external, or perhaps the public, structures within which certain aspects of the self were shaped.

A more internal process was also in play, however. These men had to learn to participate in unusual and, at times, unimaginable practices. Even though the military and Vietnam had created a context that legitimated and necessitated killing, dismemberment, and the handling of dead bodies, individuals still had to construct their own meaning and justification for engaging in behavior that had previously not been an acceptable part of their lives. Most of these men were not prepared for the latent effects of combat on their own core sense of self. They were especially unprepared for the prospect that they might enjoy the power and exhilaration that these activities produced. These veterans also did not expect to have to numb their own emotions in order to kill.

They went to Vietnam with notions of World War II heroism and military models of masculinity. Seeking manhood, they were frequently confronted with events that were incongruous with their previous images. This was the psychological battleground for each soldier—balancing somewhere between the image and the event.

His conscience has established an image of the ideal, a man who will acquit himself in whatever situation with independence and dignity. His inner history henceforth in combat will be the struggle to live up to this ideal. . . . The ideal of acquitting himself like a man come to appear utopian when he is confronted with certain situations. (Gray, 1967, p. 187)

The Job and the Sport of Combat

It's scary to be out there in a jungle knowing that there's lord knows how many enemy soldiers out there. Your job is to find them before they find you and do it without getting killed. . . . It's a very exciting thing. (John)

The actual duty of combat had a variety of effects on these men. One effect was a constant fear for their own safety and the safety of those who depended on them. Fear was a stressful and taxing emotion, especially when there was no release from it. The stress was so great for some that they could no longer think about it and had to refigure combat as a "job."

Well, when we were out there for the first five or six months, after that you just didn't care, you didn't care about nothing, that's because all you had to do is say, "I'm not gonna worry about tomorrow, just let me make it through today," if you make it okay, if you don't that's it, just a job to fit, and you know what job you have to do when you went out there, and you did your job and that's it. (Mangum)

There was no "behind the lines"; there was no "front line" and no "rear." The war was everywhere, all the time. David described some of his anxiety: it "was really stressful was being on guard at night. I mean you're in a goddamned jungle and there's all these weird noises and stuff. You're sitting there trying hardly not to breathe or move and just sitting like a statue." David concluded, "that was really stressful . . . but I think it was seeing people killed or wounded was very stressful." As David's memories related, stress came from the anticipation of danger as well as witnessing its consequences. To endure such stress, the men developed different coping mechanisms. For Larry, fear became a "rush" that he interpreted as "fun." "When you're scared," Larry elaborated, "you don't realize how your sight is affected or how your ears are affected, your hearing or your smell—I mean it is really elevated." All the men interviewed spoke of a keen sense of hypervigilance their entire tour of duty. While Larry had made sense of his fear by seeing the "fun" in the experience, others contextualized it as part of the "game" of combat.

Games were an important part of American male culture that influenced the way the Vietnam war was viewed (Fiddick, 1989, p. 86). Broyles (1990) wrote that "war is a brutal, deadly game, but a game, the best there is. And men love games" (p. 31). War was the ultimate game. Much like the sports of their youth, the activity of combat involved learning and practicing skills, executing maneuvers, teamwork, and competition. Donald (1992, p. 135) found that the sports metaphor for combat was common in the World War II films that these men grew up with. Of course, the stakes in combat "games" were much higher than the baseball or basketball of their early days, which for some added an enticing layer of excitement and exhilaration. "It was all a big game and when we left them dead, then I was the winner," Chris recalled, "the only way I could have fun was to play the game." Chris was not alone in his assessment; many soldiers develop a "feeling of satisfaction in killing" (Bradshaw, Ohlde, & Horne, 1993, p. 466)[4]. John spoke at length about the elation of combat in terms of the power it afforded him:

[It's] that feeling of power of who lives and who don't . . . everything comes so automatic to you . . . its just like you're programmed to do it almost. Basically you are from your training and everything you think at that certain time that you know, it's either you shoot at him or it's you and since you got the element of surprise he knows it's him, and watching the expression on their face . . . 'cause they'll look exactly right at your hand, they'll watch you squeeze the trigger and they know, they know it's coming.

The power of life and death came with the territory—it was part of the job. But it was a significant part. In his essay, "Why Men Love War," Broyles (1990) explained the attraction:

As anyone who has fired a bazooka or a M-60 machine gun knows, there is something to that power in your finger, the soft, seductive touch of the trigger. It's like a magic sword, a grunt's Excalibur: all you do is move that finger so imperceptibly, just a wish flashing across your mind like a shadow, not even a full brain synapse, and *poof!* in a blast of sound and energy and light a truck or a house or even people disappear, everything flying and settling back into dust. (p. 34)

Killing became an erotic power "rush." Shatan (1989) suggests that "automatic weapons symbolize both merciless conquest and the squandering of virility in masturbatory fashion. Eroticism and destruction are blended in an orgasmic thrill of violence" (p. 131). Veterans from many wars have told stories of their physical responses to combat. Lawson (1989, pp. 60-62) chronicled several stories of "sexual aggression," stating that the firing of a weapon often becomes a surrogate penis. VA staff members spoke about this sexualization of combat, but none of the veterans interviewed shared tales of this nature.[5] However, perhaps their discussions of the power associated with killing were a veiled way of talking about the exhilaration, sexual or otherwise, that the experience elicited.

An integral part of the sports metaphor is the preoccupation with winning. Donald (1992) faults the American fixation on winning as one of "the most serious and most potentially dangerous of all the absurd notions" (p. 135) that our culture offers young men. In Vietnam, score was kept through body counts and marking confirmed kills on weapons and helicopters. This "primary measure" of Vietnam "inflicted a terrible psychic and emotional toll on the nineteen-year-olds ordered to get the body counts" (Shafer, 1990, p. 85). Often they were sent out specifically to "get" a certain body count. The counts also served as a competitive device among squads—those with higher body counts would be rewarded by the military administration. Just as body counts kept track of who was winning, personal competence and skill were acknowledged by the number of days one survived. "The line between life and death was gossamer thin" (Broyles, 1990, p. 35). Excellence was manifested by how close one could come to death and by the coldness with which one could execute another's. "I kind of considered myself an expert, I guess you could say I had a doctor's degree in jungle warfare," John said. "We never triggered any land mines, found a lot of them, but that was part of the *game*—you find it before it hurts you" (emphasis added). This orientation to war as a sport to be won encouraged an aggressive level of behavior under the guise of gamesmanship by attempting to minimize the consequences and risks while celebrating the glory of winning. And it was manly.

Boose (1993) suggests that this is what the American public saw on the television news—"an image of wanton boys, killing for their sport" (p. 100). A major problem was that they did not always win; they got wounded and their friends died. "When I first went over there," Larry recalled, "it seemed like a game to me until I started losing friends . . . [then] it was deathly real."

Violence and Anger as Control

Although this notion of combat as a game provided a means of coping with the constant fear, it did not alleviate it. Anger was an attempt to do that. Larry explained anger as the natural response to the chaotic nature of combat. "How do you get control of something when you're confused?" Larry mused, "get angry and mad and take control." Indeed, anger seemed a common response to the situation in which they found themselves. Many veterans remembered spending most of their tour in a rage: angry at the government, at the military, and at their own mortality. "When I was in 'Nam," David recalled, "I was just P.O.'d every day." This generalized anger was echoed in Mangum's memory: "I was mad at the world and I said we's losing all these lives fighting over eight acres of rice paddy." Anger and rage provided a useful response to the horror and the bewilderment of warfare in Vietnam. Indeed, as one of the VA psychologists pointed out, anger was one of the few emotions that had survival value. "Because anger, over there, motivated these guys to take some action. It wasn't the anger by itself but it was the fact that anger was accompanied by some behavior—some survival behavior" (staff psychologist.1).

Other responses to loss, such as sadness or mourning, were not acceptable in combat situations. "The ability to watch one's comrades die and yet appear to suffer no emotional trauma is shown to be a valued commodity in most war pictures" (Donald, 1992, p. 131). These men had been well socialized not to exhibit grief, from "boys don't cry" taunts of childhood to the macho G.I.s of the cinema. They all reported learning to "shut off" their emotions to survive in Vietnam. Herman (1992) explains that individuals who have been through traumatic events are "continually buffeted by terror and rage" that are qualitatively different from common feelings of fear and anger, in that they "overwhelm the ordinary capacity to bear feelings" (p. 42). Dan described his process as a misplacement of self. "You steer your conscious of what's going [on] around you. I'd already partially misplaced myself anyway . . . I wasn't feeling anyway, but the trauma of the deal was, I don't know, carrying somebody's blood on you like that . . . gives me a headache. But it didn't stop there."

Kurt also explained, "That's why we always said it don't mean nothin'." Larry related that "you [had] to shut off emotion like that so you can do your job." However, it was only the socially unacceptable emotions that were "shut off" and, in place of mourning, the manly outlet for the losses suffered was anger. In World War II films, this anger often led to "dedicating the next kill to the deceased comrade" or "generally raising the level of mayhem" (Donald, 1992, p. 133). Shatan (1989) suggests that within combat, "male grief is 'hardened' into ceremonial vengeance:

scapegoating supplants mourning and unshed tears shed blood" (p. 136). These themes were evidenced within the veterans' narratives of Vietnam.

Anger also had other effects for these men. When anger was introduced into the game of combat, the competition became even more abhorrent than the "normal" or acceptable level of warfare, and violence became gratuitous. After honing his combat skills so that his "reaction was instinct," Larry found that "then the fear and anger would come and the payoff—the payoff was bad and there's not any white or black about it . . . the gray area got you hurt, you had to be one hundred percent killer or one hundred percent patsy." Many of these men told of participating in a state of violent anger in "borderline criminal acts," as Chris called them. Though they felt "in control" with their violence, they were, in contrast, controlled by their conditioning (Anisfield, 1989, p. 114).

The distinctions that they made between legitimate and illegitimate combat seemed to be about necessity and excess. Also, these excessive actions usually took place in direct response to the loss of someone very close to them or to some other event that reminded them of the frailty of their existence. Dan said that at one point, he went "kill crazy" and tried to kill every Vietnamese with whom he came into contact. It was almost as if there was a breaking point for each man—an occurrence that was just more than he could cope with in a rational or measured way. David recounted his transformation: "I just wanted to get everyone I could . . . that was the animal in me coming out, the hatred and the rage." Van der Kolk (1988, p. 178) suggests that retaliatory violence was related to the depth of connection that the soldier felt for his buddy. If they had unfulfilling or disrupted early family relationships, they were more likely to form "intensely dependent" attachments in the combat setting. Given this bond, they would experience the death of friends as extensions of themselves.

> Vietnam veterans with PTSD had felt particularly close to their combat units, and most had wanted revenge and had committed atrocities after a buddy was killed in action: they reacted to the death of a friend as a narcissistic injury rather than as an object loss. (van der Kolk, 1988, p. 178)

Tommy's story echoed van der Kolk's assessment. Tommy's team had been involved in a booby-trapped 500-pound bomb explosion. Everyone was killed but him and his closest friend, though both were badly wounded. Tommy, with scrap metal in his chest and most of the right side of his face and his right eye gone, carried his friend for 5 days until they were picked up on Highway One and taken to a medivac hospital. His friend died of shock after being in the hospital for 2 days. Herman (1992) supposed that "clinging together under prolonged conditions of danger, the combat group develops a shared fantasy that their mutual loyalty and devotion can protect them from harm." Thus, separation from each other, especially by death, shatters their protected myth of safety. "Me and him have been through basic—all the way through everything together—real tight," Tommy explained, "and he laid down and died on me . . . really fucked up my day though but—Gotta live—ha!" After a long recuperation in the hospital that included several reconstructive surgeries, Tommy opted to return to combat for a second tour.

> I went back to Vietnam for revenge—to kill as many as them sons-o'bitches as I could and I got good at it. I killed a lot of them . . . I loved to kill the sons-o'bitches . . . [the] more gooks I could kill, the better I felt. . . . Got every damn one I could.

Tommy continued his one-man attempt to avenge the death of his friend during his second and third tours. By continually "dealing death," many veterans, like Tommy, were attempting to deny their own mortality (Shatan, 1989, p. 138). Tommy's last wound finally prevented him from returning to Vietnam for a fourth time, even though he said he would have liked to. He told of doing assassination work, killing whole villages by lining the villagers up and shooting down the row, about getting "every damn one" he could in his own private fury. His killing was no longer connected to doing any sort of "job" in Vietnam; it had become an exercise in rage.

Chris also characterized his behavior after the loss of two of his team members as "revenge mode." Chris felt that "the only good gook was a dead gook," and he "lived by the philosophy of kill them all and let God sort out the good ones." Chris explained, "I was having fun. . . . Yes, I enjoyed killing them little commie bastards . . . because they killed my two friends. I was getting even with them. . . . At that point, I was getting even with them and loved every minute of it." To illustrate what Chris considered the extremity of his actions, he mentioned this event:

> I walked up to some male and his wife and two kids standing on the side of the road and took a .45 and put it tight between his eyes and pulled the trigger with his wife and kids watching, that borders me right on murder. . . . He hadn't

done nothing. He wasn't carrying no weapons. He was just standing there. He just looked at me wrong.

Like Chris, Ramsey also retaliated with violence. After his friend's helicopter was shot down, Ramsey said he found himself "wanting to kill somebody." His whole helicopter crew agreed to go and look for someone to kill that day. After, Ramsey remembered feeling "good." "I felt different after, after I seen my tracers hitting those bodies and those bodies hitting the ground. . . . Yeah I felt, yeah! I felt good." He tried to explain: "It's a euphoria. You like to kill after you get your first kill. I've heard it's a wonderful thing, you know. . . . I remember the feeling of accomplishment, you know, getting, getting, getting some revenge, you know, feeling good."

Killing gave each of these men a sense of power and control in an otherwise chaotic, dangerous situation. In addition, they received admiration and respect from the men around them. The more "cold-blooded" the kill, the more "macho" the individual soldier was seen to be. John described the response he got after his first kill that "kind of felt like murder" as a sense of awe. "They just looked like they were in shock," John recalled. "It was like, Goddamn this guy's for real—this is Mr. cold-hearted macho Rambo man." When his squad got back to the base camp, John was treated like a hero and his actions were held up for emulation. There appeared to have been widespread acceptance of, and even esteem for, extreme violence among the men and very few sanctions against it. "I can do anything I want to," John retold his Vietnam attitude, "and I'm not gonna get in trouble."

This construction of revenge-oriented ceremonial violence also fit the common pattern of the victim becoming the victimizer. Lashing out at their own fear and victimization by the enemy, they become the aggressor by killing to excess or participating in gratuitous violence. As a VA staff psychologist explained,

[It's] a very frightening thing and one can't afford to stay in one's helplessness in that kind of [combat] setting. You have to respond. So what they would do is go from that extreme of being a victim to being the extreme aggressor. . . . When you do that you pass on your victimization to the next guy.

In contrast, however, some men's killing sprees were preceded by the embarrassment of hesitation. Walter recounted how he had hesitated the first time he came under fire. He was the machine gunner on a troop carrier late in the war that was taking a Vietnamese troop into combat. Walter remembered being so unable to perform his duties that the crew chief threatened to kill him.

Everything opened up on us. And my driver started screaming at me, and my crew chief started screaming at me. He said, "Shoot," you know "Shoot." And I just couldn't pull the trigger. . . . He's telling me to shoot. He's screaming at me and I couldn't shoot. And all of the sudden, I felt this jolt so he must have kicked me or punched. I can't remember what, but there's this jolt. And he's screaming at me, "Shoot," you know, or be killed.

After this incident, Walter spent the rest of his tour and later life trying to re-prove the manhood that had eluded him that day. Aggression in combat was not only a way to protect their lives, but their masculinity as well (Levy, 1992, p. 184). John, who wanted to go to war to say "Yeah, I killed one of them," similarly froze the first time he had a Vietnamese soldier in his rifle site. After the firefight, John's team labeled him as a coward. John's next act was to kill a wounded POW at point-blank range to regain his status as a man who could kill. John continued to maintain his manhood by always "taking as many shoots as possible." After going to Vietnam specifically to see "if I was capable of doing it or if I would chicken out, break down or . . . I had to know, I had to know myself," John found that he was "capable of a whole lot than what I had originally thought I was capable of doing in given circumstances and situations." As Pleck (1981) theorized, violations of sex role norms, in this case military duty, led to overcompensation through a hyperconformity to the expected behavior. Both Walter and John felt compelled to go beyond the behaviors of others to gain the mantle of manhood. In their moment of hesitation, their masculinity had become suspect.

Sometimes it was the extreme nature of the situation itself that these men remembered as their turning point from combat soldier to enraged avenger. Bill related the distinct moment when he developed his "hatred" and began participating in "homicidal things and then justifying things." For Bill it started when he had to shoot a young boy who had a satchel charge strapped to his back. The horror of the event and its discontinuity with the idealized image of a warrior was often more than the veteran could handle. One day Larry found himself "hacking off" the arm of a dead Vietnamese and shooting the dead boy's mother point-blank. David's first confirmed kill turned out to be a Vietnamese woman who had walked into his team's ambush. These men had previously been able to maintain a sense of themselves as good combatants or perhaps as victims of the situation that necessitated unusual talents to survive while they lived in the violent chaos of Vietnam. These veterans found themselves taking part in activities completely alien to their earlier notions of right and wrong, even for combat behavior. None of their fathers had told war stories of killing women or children. The heroic films of World War II portrayed idealized soldiers who protected and served—"a Noble Warrior" (Norden, 1990, p. 218). Women and children looked up to them and they protected them. Vietnam gave these men a decidedly different view of war and themselves. Ramsey pondered, "I feel like I *was,* I feel like I *am* a murderer." Larry questioned the broader context: "we're supposed to be the good guys and we're acting like Hitlers."

Vietnam continued the contradictory images of masculinity that these men had witnessed in their families of origin. Behaviors that were "macho" simultaneously made it possible to perform the "unmanly" acts of killing women and children, dismembering bodies, and other previously unimagined horrors of warfare. This was the incongruity that many veterans could not reconcile and that they had often tried to erase from their memories and current identities. The manhood required for an ethic of warfare and of survival in Vietnam consisted of rage, violence, and inhumane atrocities that were processually detached from previous notions of morality. In their pursuit of manhood, these men exceeded the goal and found themselves suspended in a state of hypermasculinity that did not leave them upon their return home (Karner, 1995).

These veterans returned home with their combat instincts for immediate violent response intact. They had just spent time in an environment in which all problems were solved with aggression and were still "dependent on violence" (Levy, 1992, p. 197). The war lessons about alertness, constant danger, families of men, betrayal of organizations, denial of loss, and violence that they learned in Vietnam did not translate well to their stateside, postmilitary lives.

The Consequences of Maleness

These veterans' years after Vietnam were troubled with failures and futility that created a sense of desperation for many of them. They wanted to be accepted as men, and yet felt deceived and victimized by those in positions of leadership in the military and government. After exploring, and failing at, other avenues of traditional and toxic behaviors for resolution of their manhood (see Karner, 1996b), these men entered therapy. In the therapeutic community they found narrative resources for creating sense in their lives and a discourse that gave voice to their experiences. Terms like *flashbacks, intrusive thoughts, stressor events,* and *survivor guilt* gave the veterans labels for things that had happened that they had not previously understood. Mangum recounted, "I thought I was losing my mind." Many veterans had believed that they were just "crazy." "For a long time," Ramsey revealed, "I honestly convinced myself that I was just a sick, losing-my-mind type of person."

Idealized Heroic Masculinity

These veterans' lives seem foretold, constrained, and problematized by their own internalized views of what it means to be a man. Their quest for manhood initially led them to the military and into combat, which in turn left them with a continuing need to find acceptance as men, which has led them to participate in what I have elsewhere called "toxic masculinity"— aspects of the gendered culture that influenced the veterans' behaviors in detrimental and pernicious ways (Karner, 1996a). Themes of manhood were intrinsically interwoven in the narratives—not only in terms of specific behaviors, but often as an implicit measure of evaluation. The veterans' experience raises questions about what it meant to be a man, how masculinity should be displayed, and where there were appropriate social avenues for its expression. The veterans' perceptions of their own lives were shaped by the cultural images around them to the point that they could not see beyond them; they seemed unaware that their gender ideals could have been socially constructed, and thus not absolute.

The internalized manhood that the veterans sought has not fulfilled its promise in their minds—they went to war, seemingly the ultimate sacrifice and the very embodiment of the masculine, and did not return heros. This betrayal and disillusionment has had distinct negative life consequences for the veterans. The aftermath of investing heavily (and for the most part, unconsciously) in an ideological belief of heroic, warrior masculinity that leads one to participate in harmful, toxic behaviors is clearly heard in their narratives.

Notes

1. Often, they dismissed childhood with general assessments of "pretty good" or an "average childhood." Childhood was the forgotten, long-ago part to their lives, the time

before Vietnam that had slipped away from them as so distinct and distant. Whereas Vietnam retellings were lengthy explanations, childhood was glossed over. One explanation for the dearth of narrative attention to their childhoods may be that all people experience some sort of childhood, but not everyone experiences wartime combat. The veterans easily narrated the events and circumstances that they felt were unique to them, while skimming over those experiences that seemed more general. Childhood, for the most part, fell into the latter category. Kurt summarized, "We got along pretty good . . . that's basically my childhood and everything. It was pretty good. I enjoyed it." Like Kurt's comments, most often childhood was condensed to idyllic phrases. "I remember living out in the country, the horses I used to ride, the chickens which I was scared of, the mama sow that chased me because I was playing with her babies, and milking cows or attempting to milk" (Bill.a). Others mentioned material issues. "I had a good life on the farm," Ramsey wrote in his autobiography, "My parents provided well for us. We eventually had good clothes and good shoes and ate well." Larry also focused the sum total of his youth with an assessment of class: "We didn't have a lot of things other people had, but then again, we weren't going hungry or nothing. We always had food and a roof over our head, clothes on our back." Dan, however, was able to blend both the material and the emotional into his brief overview: "My childhood was a good childhood. My family was close. We did a lot of things together, lower-income family, not a lot of money."

2. Veterans are referred to by pseudonyms of their own choosing and all identifying aspects of their narratives have been changed to protect their confidentiality. Also, the different forms of data utilized within this research study are denoted as follows: excerpts from my field notes are labeled (FN); veteran quotes from the interviews are cited with their pseudonym; material from their autobiographies is distinguished with an *a* after their pseudonym—for example, (Ramsey.a).

3. This was not the case for all other American veterans, from the Civil War through Vietnam. In addition, the economic prosperity of the post-World War II era was also unprecedented, which allowed for more benefits than were available during the recession of the mid-1970s. Laufer and Gallops (1985) assert that service in Vietnam resulted in an extremely high economic and physical toll on those who served. Furthermore, Sampson and Laub (1996) find that Vietnam veterans' difficulties were related more to the lack of economic opportunity through a comprehensive G.I. Bill than to actual combat experience itself.

4. Ironically, perceiving combat experiences as meaningful and positive is seen to mediate the negative consequences of stressful events (Aldwin, Levenson, & Spiro, 1994; Bradshaw, Ohlde, & Horne, 1991).

5. This, of course, may be due to the fact that I was a younger female and such discussions could have been embarrassing. I also did not focus questions directly on sexual issues. This topical omission in the narratives could be the sole result of the lack of direct questions as well.

References

Adler, C., & Polk, K. (1996). Masculinity and child homicide. In Masculinities, social relations, and crime [Special issue]. *British Journal of Criminology, 36*(3).

Aldwin, C. M., Levenson, M. R., & Spiro, A., III. (1994). Vulnerability and resilience to combat exposure: Can stress have lifelong effects? *Psychology and Aging, 9*(1), 34-44.

Allen, N. H. (1983). Homicide followed by suicide: Los Angeles, 1970-1979. *Suicide and Life Threatening Behavior, 13,* 155-165.

Alves, M. (1985). *State and opposition in military Brazil.* Austin: University of Texas Press.

Amir, M. (1971). *Patterns of forcible rape.* Chicago: University of Chicago Press.

Anderson, C. (1994). *Keeping youth sports safe and fun.* St. Paul: Minnesota Children's Trust Fund.

Anderson, E. (1990). *Streetwise: Race, class, and change in an urban community.* Chicago: University of Chicago Press.

Anderson, M. L. (1993). *Thinking about women* (3rd ed.). New York: Macmillan.

Anisfield, N. (1989). Sexist subscript in Vietnam narratives. *Vietnam Generation, 1*(3-4), 109-114.

Arendt, H. (1964). *Eichmann in Jerusalem: A report on the banality of evil.* New York: Viking.

Arendt, H. (1970). *On violence.* London: Penguin.

Arkin, W., & Dobrofsky, L. R. (1990). Military socialization and masculinity. In F. M. Cancian & J. W. Gibson (Eds.), *Making war making peace: The social foundations of violent conflict* (pp. 68-78). Belmont, CA: Wadsworth.

Ayers, E. L. (1984). *Vengeance and justice: Crime and punishment in the nineteenth century American south.* New York: Oxford University Press.

233

Bachman, R. (1994). *Violence against women: A National Crime Victimization Survey Report.* Washington, DC: Bureau of Justice Statistics.

Baffi, C. R., Kerry, J., Redican, M. K. S., & Impara, J. C. (1991). Gender role identity, gender role stress, and health behaviors: An exploratory study of selected college males. *Health Values, 15*(1), 9-18.

Baker, P. (1984, June). The domestication of politics: Women and American political society, 1780-1920. *American Historical Society, 89,* pp. 620-647.

Barnes, H. E. (1925). Representative biological theories of society. *Sociological Review, 18,* 120-130, 182-194, 294-300.

Barrett, M. (1980). *Women's oppression today: The Marxist/feminist encounter.* London: Verso.

Barry, K. 1981. *Female sexual slavery.* Englewood Cliffs, NJ: Prentice Hall.

Baskin, D., Sommers, I., & Fagan, J. (1993). The political economy of female violent street crime. *Fordham Urban Law Journal, 20*(Spring), 401-417.

Bavolek, S. J. (1994). *Child centered coaching: Instructors training manual.* Park City, UT: Family Nurturing Center.

Beddoe, D. (1979). *Welsh convict women.* Barry, Wales: Stewart Williams.

Bederman, G. (1995). *Manliness and civilization: A cultural history of gender and race in the United States, 1880-1917.* Chicago: University of Chicago Press.

Benedict, J. R. (1996, December 27). College protects athletes, not students. *New York Times,* p. A39.

Berger, P., & Luckmann, T. (1966). *The social construction of reality: A treatise in the sociology of knowledge.* Garden City, NY: Anchor.

Berman, A. L. (1979). Dyadic death: Murder-suicide. *Suicide and Life Threatening Behavior, 9*(1), 15-23.

Bierstedt, R. (1981). *American sociological theory: A critical history.* New York: Academic Press.

Birrell, S., & Cole, C. L. (Eds.). (1994). *Women, sports, and culture.* Champaign, IL: Human Kinetics.

Blumstein, A. (1995, August). Violence by young people: Why the deadly nexus? *National Institute of Justice Journal,* pp. 2-9.

BNM (Archdiocese of Sao Paulo). (1986). *Torture in Brazil.* New York: Vintage.

Boose, L. E. (1993). Techno-muscularity and the "boy eternal": From the quagmire to the Gulf. In M. Cooke & A. Woollacott (Eds.), *Gendering war talk* (pp. 67-106). Princeton, NJ: Princeton University Press.

Bourdieu, P. (1993). *The field of cultural reproduction.* Cambridge, UK: Polity Press.

Bourgois, P. (1995). *In search of respect: Selling crack in el barrio.* Cambridge, UK: Cambridge University Press.

Bourgois, P., & Dunlap, E. (1993). Exorcising sex—for crack: An ethnographic prespective from Harlem. In M. Ratner (Ed.), *The crack pipe as pimp* (pp. 97-132). Lexington, MA: Lexington Books.

Bowker, L. H. (1983). *Beating wife-beating.* Lexington, MA: Lexington Books.

Bowker, L. H. (1985). The effects of national development on the position of married women in the Third World: The case of wife beating. *International Journal of Comparative and Applied Criminal Justice, 9,* 1-13.

Bowker, L. H. (1986a). *Ending the violence: A guidebook based on the experiences of 1,000 battered wives.* Holmes Beach, FL: Learning Publications.

Bowker, L. H. (1986b). The meaning of wife beating. *Currents, 4*(2), 37-43.

Bowker, L. H. (1994). Existing community-based alternatives will not deter serious woman batterers. *Sociological Imagination, 52,* 50-62.

Box, S. (1983). *Power, crime and mystification.* New York: Tavistock.

Bradshaw, S. L., Ohlde, C. D., & Horne, J. B. (1991). The love of war: Vietnam and the traumatized veteran. *Bulletin of the Menninger Clinic, 55,* 96-103.

Bradshaw, S. L., Ohlde, C. D., & Horne, J. B. (1993). Combat and personality change. *Bulletin of the Menninger Clinic, 57,* 466-478.

Braithwaite, J. (1984). *Corporate crime in the pharmaceutical industry.* London: Routledge & Kegan Paul.

Bretl, D. J., & Cantor, J. (1988). The portrayal of men and women in U.S. television commercials: A recent content analysis and trends over 15 years. *Sex Roles, 18,* 595-609.

Brittan, A. (1989). *Masculinity and power.* Oxford, UK: Basil Blackwell.

Broude, G. J. (1990). Protest masculinity: A further look at the causes and the concept. *Ethos, 18*(1), 103-122.

Brown, R. M. (1975). *Strain of violence: Historical studies of American violence and vigilantism.* New York: Oxford University Press.

Browne, A. (1987). *When battered women kill.* New York: Free Press.

Brownmiller, S. (1976). *Against our will: Men, women and rape.* New York: Penguin.

Broyles, W., Jr. (1990). Why men love war. In F. M. Cancian & J. W. Gibson (Eds.), *Making war making peace: The social foundations of violent conflict* (pp. 29-37). Belmont CA: Wadsworth.

Brundage, W. F. (1993). *Lynching in the New South: Georgia and Virginia, 1880-1930.* Chicago: University of Illinois Press.

Bruning, N. (1995). *Breast implants: Everything you need to know* (2nd rev. ed.). Alameda, CA: Hunter House.

Bureau of Justice Statistics. (1988). *Profile of state prison inmates, 1986.* Washington, DC: U.S. Department of Justice.

Bureau of Justice Statistics. (1995a). *Jails and jail inmates 1993-1994.* Washington, DC: U.S. Department of Justice.

Bureau of Justice Statistics. (1995b). *Prisoners in 1994.* Washington, DC: U.S. Department of Justice.

Burkhart, K. (1973). *Women in prison.* Garden City, NY: Doubleday.

Burt, M. R. (1991). Rape myths and acquaintance rape. In A. Parrot & L. Bechhoffer (Eds.), *Acquaintance rape: The hidden crime* (pp. 26-40). New York: John Wiley.

Campbell, A. (1993). *Men, women, and aggression.* New York: Basic Books.

Camper, D. (1992, April 13). Adolescents at risk [Editorial Notebook]. *New York Times,* p. 18.

Cancian, F. M. (1990). A conversation on war, peace, and gender. In F. M. Cancian & J. W. Gibson (Eds.), *Making war making peace: The social foundations of violent conflict* (pp. 64-67). Belmont, CA: Wadsworth.

Caputi, J. (1993). The sexual politics of murder. In P. Bart & E. G. Moran (Eds.), *Violence against women: The bloody footprints* (pp. 5-25). Newbury Park, CA: Sage.

Carmen, E., Crane, B., Dunnicliff, M., Holochuck, S., Prescott, L., Rieker, P., Stefan, S., & Stromberg, N. (1996). *Massachusetts Department of Mental Health Task Force on the restraint and seclusion of persons who have been physically or sexually abused: Report and recommendations.* Boston: Massachusetts Department of Mental Health.

Caulfield, S., & Wonders, N. (1993). Personal and political: Violence against women and the role of the state. In K. Tunnell (Ed.), *Political crime in contemporary America* (pp. 79-100). New York: Garland.

Cazenave, N. A. (1981). Black men in America: A quest for manhood. In H. P. McAdoo (Ed.), *Black families* (pp. 176-185). Beverly Hills, CA: Sage.

Chambliss, W. J. (1973). The saints and the roughnecks. *Society, 11,* 24-31.

Chesney-Lind, M., & Rodriguez, N. (1983). Women under lock and key. *The Prison Journal, 63,* 47-65.

Chesney-Lind, M., & Shelden, R. G. (1992). *Girls, delinquency, and the juvenile justice system.* Pacific Grove, CA: Brooks/Cole.

Clay, N. (1991, August 27). Ex-football player felt above the law (Commentary). *USA Today,* p. 8C.

Clemmer, D. (1940). *The prison community.* New York: Holt, Rinehart & Winston.

Clinard, M. B., & Yeager, P. C. (1980). *Corporate crime.* New York: Free Press.

Cohen, A. K. (1955). *Delinquent boys: The culture of the gang.* Glencoe, IL: Free Press.

Cohen, E. (1954). *Human behaviour in the concentration camp.* London: Jonathan Cape.

Cohen, G. L. (Ed.). (1993). *Women in sport: Issues and controversies.* Newbury Park, CA: Sage.

Connell, R. W. (1987). *Gender and power.* Palo Alto, CA: Stanford University Press.

Connell, R. W. (1995). *Masculinities.* Berkeley: University of California Press.

Conrad, P., & Schneider, J. W. (1980). *Deviance and medicalization: From badness to sickness.* St. Louis, MO: C. V. Mosby.

Coontz, S. (1992). *The way we never were: American families and the nostalgia trap.* New York: Basic Books.

Cooper, M. (1996, December 31). Employee of store where woman was found slain is sought in inquiry. *New York Times,* p. B3.

Craig, G. (1995, April 8). Videotaped frisks anger women inmates. *Rochester Democrat and Chronicle,* pp. 1A, 8A.

Craig, G. (1996a, March 23). Advocates say nude filming shows need for new laws. *Rochester Democrat and Chronicle,* pp. A1, A6.

Craig, G. (1996b, August 17). A "huge problem" in men guarding women. *Rochester Democrat and Chronicle,* pp. A1, A6.

Cullen, J. (1992). "I's a man now": Gender and African American Men. In C. Clinton & N. Silber (Eds.), *Divided houses: Gender and the Civil War* (pp. 76-91). New York: Oxford University Press.

Currens, S. (1991). Homicide followed by suicide—Kentucky, 1985-1990. *Journal of the American Medical Association, 266,* 2062-2063.

Curriden, M. (1993, September 20). Prison scandal in Georgia: Guards traded favors for sex. *National Law Journal,* p. 8.

Curry, G. D. (1995). *Responding to female gang involvement.* Paper presented at the meeting of the American Society of Criminology, Boston.

Curry, T. J. (1991). Fraternal bonding in the locker room: A profeminist analysis of talk about competition and women. *Sociology of Sport Journal, 8,* 135-191.

D'Emilio, J., & Freedman, E. B. (1988). *Intimate matters: A history of sexuality in America.* New York: Harper & Row.

Daly, M., & Wilson, M. (1988). *Homicide.* New York: Aldine de Gruyter.

A damaging remedy. (1992, April 13). *New York Times* [Editorial], p. 13.

Davis, A. (1983). *Women, race, and class.* New York: Vintage.

Davis, N. (1990, April). *Alternatives to prostitution.* Paper presented at meeting of the Pacific Sociological Association, Spokane, WA.

Dawson, J. M., & Langan, P. A. (1994). *Murder in families* (U.S. Department of Justice, Bureau of Justice Statistics Special Report). Washington, DC: Government Printing Office.

Dean, E. T., Jr. (1992). The myth of the troubled and scorned Vietnam veteran. *Journal of American Studies, 226*(1), 59-74.

de Beauvoir, S. (1952). *The second sex.* New York: Knopf.

Decker, S., & Van Winkle, B. (1996). *Life in the gang: Family, friends, and violence.* New York: Cambridge University Press.

Dittmar, L., & Michaud, G. (1990). America's war films: Marching toward denial. In L. Dittmar & G. Michaud (Eds.), *From Hanoi to Hollywood: The Vietnam war in American film* (pp. 1-18). New Brunswick, NJ: Rutgers University Press.

Dobash, R. E., & Dobash, R. (1979). *Violence against wives.* New York: Free Press.

Dobash, R. E., & Dobash, R. (1992). *Women, violence and social change.* New York: Routledge.

Donald, R. R. (1992). Masculinity and machismo in Hollywood's war films. In S. Craig (Ed.), *Men, masculinity, and the media* (pp. 124-136). Newbury Park, CA: Sage.

Doolittle, J., & Pepper, R. (1974). Children's TV ad content: 1974. *Journal of Broadcasting, 19,* 131-151.

Dorpat, T. L. (1966). Suicide in murderers. *Psychiatry Digest,* (7), 51-55.

Dowd Hall, J. (1979). *Revolt against chivalry: Jessie Daniel Ames and the women's campaign against lynching.* New York: Columbia University Press.

Dowd Hall, J. (1983). "The mind that burns in each body": Women, rape, and racial violence. In A. Snitow, C. Stansill, & S. Thompson (Eds.), *Powers of desire: The politics of sexuality* (pp. 328-349). New York: Monthly Review Press.

Dworkin, A. (1987). *Intercourse.* New York: Free Press.

Edgell, S. (1980). *Middle-class couples.* London: George Allen & Unwin.

Edwards, S. (1984). *Women on trial.* Manchester, UK: Manchester University Press.

Egger, S. A. (1984). A working definition of serial murder and the reduction of linkage blindness. *Journal of Police Science and Administration, 12,* 348-357.

Eiss, H. (Ed.). (1994). *Images of the child.* Bowling Green, OH: Bowling Green State University Press.

Elder, G. H., Jr. (1985). Perspectives on the life course. In G. Elder, Jr. (Ed.), *Life course dynamics* (pp. 23-49). Ithaca, NY: Cornell University Press.

Elder, G. H., Jr. (1986). Military times and turning points in men's lives. *Developmental Psychology, 22,* 233-245.

England, P., & Farkas, G. (1986). *Households, employment, and gender: A social, economic, and demographic view.* New York: Aldine de Gruyter.

Enloe, C. (1989). *Bananas, beaches and bases: Making feminist sense of international politics.* Berkeley: University of California Press.

Erbe, S. (1984). Prostitutes: Victims of men's exploitation and abuse. *Law and Inequality: Journal of Theory and Practice, 2,* 607-623.

Estrin, N. F. (1990). *The medical device industry: Science, technology, and regulation in a competitive environment* (pp. 35-71). New York: Marcel Dekker.

Fagan, J. (1990). Social processes of delinquency and drug use among urban gangs. In C. R. Huff (Ed.), *Gangs in America.* Newbury Park, CA: Sage.

Fagan, J., & Chin, K.-L. (1991). Social processes of initiation into crack. In R. Dembo (Ed.), *Drugs and crime* (pp. 109-138). Lanham, MD: University Press of America.

Fagan, J. A., Stewart, D. K., & Hansen, K. (1993). Violent men or violent husbands? Background factors and situational correlates. In D. Finkelhor, R. J. Gelles, G. T. Hotaling, & M. A. Straus (Eds.), *The dark side of families* (pp. 49-67). Newbury Park, CA: Sage.

Farr, K. A. (1988). Dominance bonding through the good old boys sociability group. *Sex Roles, 18,* 259-277.

Fejes, F. J. (1992). Masculinity as fact: A review of empirical mass communication research on masculinity. In S. Craig (Ed.), *Men, masculinity, and the media* (pp. 9-22). Newbury Park, CA: Sage.

Feld, S. L., & Straus, M. A. (1990). Escalation and desistance of wife assault in marriage. In M. A. Straus & R. J. Gelles (Eds.), *Physical violence in American families* (pp. 489-505). New Brunswick, NJ: Transaction Books.

Fernandes, H. R. (1979). *Política e Suguração.* São Paulo: Editora Alfa-Omega.

Fiddick, T. (1989). Beyond the domino theory: The Vietnam war and metaphors of sport. *Journal of American Culture, 12*(4), 79-87.

Fine, G. A. (1987). *With the boys: Little League baseball and preadolescent behavior.* Chicago: University of Chicago Press.

Fink, D. (1992). *Agrarian women: Wives and mothers in rural Nebraska 1880-1940.* Chapel Hill: University of North Carolina Press.

Finkelhor, D., & Yllo, K. (1985). *License to rape: Sexual abuse of wives.* New York: Holt, Rinehart & Winston.

Flanders, L. (1997). Promise keepers, media sleepers: Reporters take a men's movement at face value. *Extra!, 30*(1), 6-8.

Follingstad, D. R., Laughlin, J. E., Polek, D. S., Rutledge, L. L., & Hause, E. S. (1991). Identification of patterns of wife abuse. *Journal of Interpersonal Violence, 6,* 187-204.

Foner, E. (1988). *Reconstruction: America's unfinished revolution, 1863-1877*. New York: Harper & Row.

Foucault, M. (1973). *Madness and civilization: A history of insanity in the age of reason*. New York: Vintage Books. (Original work published 1965)

Foucault, M. (1981). *The history of sexuality* (Vol. 1). Harmondsworth, UK: Pelican.

Fox-Genovese, E. (1988). *Within the plantation household: Black and white women of the Old South*. Chapel Hill: University of North Carolina Press.

Fraiman, S. (1994). Geometries of race and gender: Eve Segwick, Spike Lee, and Charlayne Hunter-Gault. *Feminist Studies, 20*(1), 67-84.

Frankenberg, R. (1993). *White women, race matters: The social construction of whiteness*. Minneapolis: University of Minnesota Press.

Franklin, C. W., II, & Pillow, W. (1994). The black male acceptance of the Prince Charming ideal. In R. Staples (Ed.), *The black family: Essays and studies* (5th ed., pp. 97-103). Belmont, CA: Wadsworth.

Fullilove, M., Lown, A., & Fullilove, R. (1992). Crack hos and skeezers: Traumatic experiences of women crack users. *The Journal of Sex Research, 29*(2), 275-287.

Genovese, E. (1974). *Roll, Jordan, roll: The world the slaves made*. New York: Random House.

Geoghegan, I. (1996, June 30). Boy "forced to rape his dead mother." *Guardian Weekly*, p. 5.

Gerber, J., & Weeks, S. (1992). Women as victims of corporate crime: A call for research on a neglected topic. *Deviant Behavior: An Interdisciplinary Journal, 13*, 325-347.

Gerbner, G. (1994). Television violence: The power and the peril. In G. Dines & J. Humez (Eds.), *Gender, race, and class in media*. Thousand Oaks, CA: Sage.

Gergen, M. (1992). Life stories: Pieces of a dream. In G. Rosenwald & R. Ochberg (Eds.), *Storied lives* (pp. 127-144). New Haven, CT: Yale University Press.

Gibson, J. W. (1989). Paramilitary fantasy culture and the cosmogonic mythology of primeval chaos and order. *Vietnam Generation, 1*(3-4), 12-32.

Gibson, J. W. (1990). American paramilitary culture and the reconstitution of the Vietnam war. In F. M. Cancian & J. W. Gibson (Eds.), *Making war making peace: The social foundations of violent conflict* (pp. 86-99). Belmont, CA: Wadsworth.

Giddens, A. (1976). *New rules of sociological method: A positive critique of interpretive sociologies*. New York: Basic Books.

Giddens, A. (1984). *The constitution of society: Outline of the theory of structuration*. Berkeley: University of California Press.

Giddens, A. (1989). A reply to my critics. In D. Held & J. B. Thompson (Eds.), *Social theory of modern societies: Anthony Giddens and his critics* (pp. 249-301). New York: Cambridge University Press.

Gidycz, C. A., Coble, C. N., Latham, L., & Layman, M. J. (1993). Sexual assault experience in adulthood and prior victimization experiences: A prospective analysis. *Psychology of Women Quarterly, 17*, 151-168.

Ginzburg, R. (1988). *100 years of lynchings* Baltimore, MD: Black Classic Press.

Goffman, E. (1959). *The presentation of self in everyday life*. Garden City, NY: Anchor.

Goffman, E. (1961). *Asylums: Essays on the social situation of mental patients and other inmates*. Garden City, NY: Anchor.

Gondolf, E. W. (1988). Who are those guys? Toward a behavioral typology of batterers. *Violence and Victims, 3,* 187-203.

Gordon, L. (1988). *Heroes of their own lives: The politics and history of family violence*. New York: Penguin.

Gottfredson, M. R., & Hirschi, T. (1990a). The nature of criminality: Low self control. In *A general theory of crime* (pp. 85-122). Palo Alto, CA: Stanford University Press.

Gottfredson, M. R., & Hirschi, T. (1990b). White collar crime. In *A general theory of crime* (pp. 180-201). Palo Alto, CA: Stanford University Press.

Gray, J. G. (1967). *The warriors: Reflections on men in battle*. New York: Harper & Row.

Grossman, D. (1995). *On killing*. Boston: Little, Brown.

Groth, A. N. (1979). *Men who rape*. New York: Plenum.

Guber, S. S., & Berry, J. (1993). *Marketing to and through kids*. New York: McGraw-Hill.

Gurnett, K. (1996, January 15). Two guards slashed at Coxsackie state prison. *Albany Times Union*, pp. A1, A2.

Hagedorn, J. M. (1988). *People and folks: Gangs, crime, and the underclass in a rustbelt city*. Chicago: Lakeview Press.

Hagedorn, J. M. (1994). Homeboys, dope fiends, legits, and new jacks: Adult gang members, drugs, and work. *Criminology, 32,* 197-219.

Hagedorn, J. M. (1996). The emperor's new clothes: Theory and method in gang research. *New Inquiry for a Creative Sociology, 24*(2), 111-122.

Hall, D., Bronstein, H. H., Crimmins, S., Spunt, B., & Langley, S. (1996). *Homicide by women*. New York: New York State Division of Criminal Justice Services.

Hanmer, J. (1996). Women and violence: Commonalities and diversities. In B. Fawcett, B. Featherstone, J. Hearn, & C. Toft (Eds.), *Violence and gender relations: Theories and interventions* (pp. 7-21). Thousand Oaks, CA: Sage.

Hannerz, U. (1969). *Soulside: Inquiries into ghetto culture and community*. New York: Columbia University Press.

Haritos-Fatouros, M., & Huggins, M. (1997). Being "hung out to dry": Case studies of torturers and killers in authoritarian Brazil. (Available from M. Haritos-Fatouros, Department of Psychology, University of Thessaloniki, Thessaloniki, Greece)

Harrell, A. V. (1991). *Evaluation of court-ordered treatment for domestic violence offenders. Final report submitted to the State Justice Institute*. Washington, DC: Urban Institute.

Harris, S. M. (1994). Black male masculinity and same sex friendships. In R. Staples (Ed.), *The black family: Essays and studies* (5th ed., pp. 82-89). Belmont, CA: Wadsworth.

Harris, T. (1984). *Exorcising blackness*. Bloomington: Indiana University Press.

Hassine, V. (1996). *Life without parole: Living in prison today*. Los Angeles: Roxbury.

Hatty, S. (1989). Violence against prostitute women: Social and legal dilemmas. *Australian Journal of Social Issues, 24*(4), 235-248.

Hearn, J. (1996). Men's violence to known women: Historical, everyday and theoretical constructions by men. In B. Fawcett, B. Featherstone, J. Hearn, & C. Toft (Eds.), *Violence and gender relations: Theories and interventions* (pp. 22-37). Thousand Oaks, CA: Sage.

Herek, G. M. (1987). On heterosexual masculinity: Some psychical consequences of the social construction of gender and sexuality. In M. Kimmel (Ed.), *Changing men: New directions in research on men and masculinity* (pp. 68-82). Newbury Park, CA: Sage.

Herman, J. L. (1992). *Trauma and recovery.* New York: Basic Books.

Hester, M., Kelly, L., & Radford, J. (Eds.). (1996). *Women, violence and male power: Feminist activism, research and practice.* Philadelphia: Open University Press.

Hillbrand, M., & Pallone, N. J. (Eds.). (1994). *The psychology of aggression: Engines, measurement, control.* New York: Haworth.

Hillman, J. (1991). Fathers and sons. In K. Thompson (Ed.), *To be a man: In search of the deep masculine* (pp. 201-202). Los Angeles: Tarcher.

Hindelang, M. (1979). Sex differences in criminal activity. *Social Problems, 27*(2), 143-156.

Hodes, M. E. (1991). *Sex across the color line: White women and black men in the nineteenth century American South.* Unpublished doctoral dissertation, Princeton University.

Hodgson, G. (1976). *America in our time.* New York: Vintage.

Hoffer, E. (1966). *The true believers: Thoughts on the nature of mass movements.* New York: Harper.

Hofmann, R. (1986a, March 17). Rape and the college athlete. *Philadelphia Daily News,* p. 96 (Part I).

Hofmann, R. (1986b, March 18). Rape and the college athlete. *Philadelphia Daily News,* p. 84 (Part II).

Hogue, R. A. (1995, July 26). Sisters in silicone: Women share breast-implant frustrations. *Arizona Republic/Phoenix Gazette,* p. 1.

Holloway, T. H. (1993). *Policing Rio de Janeiro: Repression and resistance in a nineteenth century city.* Palo Alto, CA: Stanford University Press.

Holtzworth-Munroe, A., & Stuart, G. L. (1994). Typologies of male batterers: Three subtypes and the differences among them. *Psychological Bulletin, 116,* 476-497.

Homophobia persists in media. (1994). *Fans of Women's Sports, 3*(1), 4-5.

Hood, J. C. (1993). Introduction. In J. Hood (Ed.), *Men, work, and family* (pp. 1-7). Newbury Park, CA: Sage.

Horton, J. O. (1993). *Free people of color: Inside the African American community.* Washington, DC: Smithsonian Institution Press.

Hotaling, G. T., & Sugarman, D. B. (1990). A risk marker analysis of assaulted wives. *Journal of Family Violence, 5,* 1-13.

Huggins, M. K., & Haritos-Fatouros, M. (1995). *Tortured consciousness: Brazilian police secrets and moralities about violence.* (Available from M. Huggins, Department of Sociology, Union College, Schenectady, NY 12308)

Huggins, M. K. (in press-a). From bureaucratic consolidation to structural devolution: Police death squads in Brazil. *Policing and Society.*

Huggins, M. K. (in press-b). *Political policing: The United States and Latin America.* Durham, NC: Duke University Press.

Huling, T. (1991). *New York groups call on state lawmakers to release women in prison.* New York: Correctional Association of New York.

Huling, T. (1996). Drug mules. In P. Green (Ed.), *Drug couriers: A new perspective.* London: Quartet Books.

Hull, A. (1988, May 29). A Greek tragedy. *St. Petersburg Times,* pp. 1F, 6F.

Hunter, S. K. (1989). *Alternatives to prostitution.* Paper prepared for the Third National Workshop on Female Offenders, Pittsburgh, PA.

Inciardi, J., Lockwood, D., & Pottieger, A. E. (1993). *Women and crack-cocaine.* New York: Macmillan.

Irwin, J. (1970). *The felon.* Berkeley: University of California Press.

Irwin, J., & Cressey, D. R. (1962). Thieves, convicts, and the inmate culture. *Social Problems, 10,* 142-155.

Jackson, D. (1990). *Unmasking masculinity: A critical autobiography.* London: Unwin Hyman.

Jaeger, R. W. (1992, September 23). Attack on wrestler "a joke." *Wisconsin State Journal,* pp. 1D-2D.

Jaffe, P. (1996, June). *Domestic violence and child custody disputes: Critical issues for mental health and legal professionals in assessment and decision-making.* Paper presented at the First National Conference on Children Exposed to Family Violence, Austin, TX.

James, J. (1976). Motivations for entrance into prostitution. In L. Crites (Ed.), *The female offender.* Lexington, MA: Lexington Books.

James, J., & Meyerding, J. (1978). Early sexual experience as a factor in prostitution. *Archives of Sexual Behavior, 7*(1), 31-42.

Janis, I. L. (1982). *Groupthink* (2nd ed.). Boston: Houghton Mifflin.

Jansen, S. C., & Sabo, D. F. (1994). The sport/war metaphor: Hegemonic masculinity, the Persian Gulf war, and the New World Order. *Sociology of Sport Journal, 11,* 1-17.

Jefferson, T. (1996). Introduction. In Masculinities, social relations, and crime [Special issue]. *British Journal of Criminology, 36*(3).

Jenkins, P. (1994). *Using murder: The social construction of serial homicide.* New York: Aldine de Gruyter.

Joe, K. (1996). The life and times of Asian American women drug users: An ethnographic study. *Journal of Drug Issues, 26*(1), 125-142.

Johnson, J. H. (1970). *Race relations and miscegenation in the South, 1776-1860.* Amherst: University of Massachusetts Press.

Johnson, M. M. (1988). *Strong mothers, weak wives.* Berkeley: University of California Press.

Joint Select Committee on the Condition of Affairs in the Late Insurrectionary States. (1871). *Report and testimony on the condition of affairs in the late insurrectionary states* (42d Cong., 2d Sess.) (13 vols.). Washington, DC: Government Printing Office.

Jones, A. (1994). *Next time she'll be dead.* Boston: Beacon.

Jones, J. (1986). *Labor of love, labor of sorrow: Black women, work, and the family from slavery to the present.* New York: Vintage.

Jordan, W. D. (1968). *White over black: American attitudes toward the Negro, 1550-1812.* Williamsburg, VA: University of North Carolina Press.

Kalmuss, D., & Straus, M. (1982). Wife's marital dependency and wife abuse. *Journal of Marriage and Family, 44,* 277-286.

Kaplan, A. G. (1988). How normal is normal development? Some connections between adult development and the roots of abuse and victimization. In M. Straus (Ed.), *Abuse and victimization across the life span* (pp. 127-139). Baltimore, MD: Johns Hopkins University Press.

Karner, T. X. (1994). *Masculinity, trauma, and identity: Life narratives of Vietnam veterans with post traumatic stress disorder.* Unpublished doctoral dissertation, University of Kansas.

Karner, T. X. (1995). Medicalizing masculinity: Post traumatic stress disorder in Vietnam veterans. *Masculinities, 3*(4), 23-65.

Karner, T. X. (1996a, August). *A crisis of masculinity: Gender and trauma in Vietnam veteran post-war narratives.* Paper presented at the American Sociological Association Meetings, New York City.

Karner, T. X. (1996b). Fathers, sons, and Vietnam: Masculinity and betrayal in the life narratives of Vietnam veterans with post traumatic stress disorder. *American Studies Journal, 37*(1), 63-94.

Katz, J. (1988). *Seductions of crime.* New York: Basic Books.

Katz, J. (1994). Advertising and the construction of violent white masculinity." In G. Dines & J. Humez (Eds.), *Gender, race, and class in media* (pp. 133-141). Thousand Oaks, CA: Sage.

Kelly, L. (1996). When does the speaking profit us? In M. Hester, L. Kelly, & J. Radford (Eds.), *Women, violence and male power: Feminist activism, research and practice* (pp. 34-49). Philadelphia: Open University Press.

Kelly, M. (1995, July/August). Dow Corning's one percent disaster: A quick lesson in being rationally right, ethically wrong, and bankrupt. *Business Ethics,* p. 10.

Kemper, T. D. (1987). How many emotions are there? Wedding the social and autonomic components. *American Journal of Sociology, 93,* 263-289.

Kersten, J. (1996). Culture, masculinities and violence against women. In Masculinities, social relations, and crime [Special issue]. *British Journal of Criminology, 36*(3).

Kim, E.-K. (1996, August 26). Sheriff says he'll have chain gangs for women. *Tuscaloosa News,* p. 1A.

Kimmel, M. S. (1987). Men's responses to feminism at the turn of the century. *Gender and Society, 1*(3), 261-283.

Kimmel, M. S. (1993). Foreword. In J. Hood (Ed.), *Men, work, and family* (pp. vii-viii). Newbury Park, CA: Sage.

Kimmel, M. S., & Messner, M. A. (1992). Introduction. In M. S. Kimmel & M. A. Messner (Eds.), *Men's lives* (pp. 1-12). New York: Macmillan.

Klein, M. W. (1995). *The American street gang: Its nature, prevalence, and control.* New York: Oxford University Press.

Kline, S. (1993). *Out of the garden.* London: Verso.

Koss, M. P., Gidycz, C. A., & Wisniewski, N. (1987). The scope of rape: Incidence and prevalence of sexual aggression and victimization in a national sample of higher education students. *Journal of Consulting and Clinical Psychology, 55,* 162-170.

Kramer, L. (1991). *The sociology of gender.* New York: St. Martin's.

Lang, D. (1969). *Casualties of war.* New York: McGraw-Hill.

The last laugh. (1994a). *Women in Higher Education, 3*(8), 12.

The last laugh. (1994b). *Women in Higher Education, 3*(9), 12.

Laufer, R. S., & Gallops, M. S. (1985). Life-course effects of Vietnam combat and abusive violence: Marital patterns. *Journal of Marriage and the Family, 47,* 839-853.

Lawson, J. (1989). "She's a pretty woman . . . for a gook": The misogyny of the Vietnam war. *Journal of American Culture, 12*(3), 55-65.

Leed, E. J. (1989). Violence, death, and masculinity. *Vietnam Generation, 1*(3-4), 168-189.

Lengyel, O. (1947). *Five chimneys: The story of Auschwitz.* Chicago: Ziff-Davis.

Lenskyj, H. (1990). Power and play: Gender and sexuality issues in sport and physical activity. *International Review for the Sociology of Sport, 25,* 235-245.

Lenskyj, H. (1992). Sexual harassment: Female athletes' experiences and coaches' responsibilities. *Science Periodical on Research and Technology in Sport, 12*(6), 1-5.

Levin, J., & Fox, J. A. (1990). Mass murder: America's growing menace. In N. Weiner, M. A. Zahn, & R. Sagi (Eds.), *Violence: Patterns, causes, public policy* (pp. 65-69). San Diego, CA: Harcourt Brace Jovanovich.

Levy, C. J. (1992). ARVN as faggots: Inverted warfare in Vietnam. In M. S. Kimmel & M. A. Messner (Eds.), *Men's lives* (pp. 183-198). New York: Macmillan.

Lewis, L. B. (1985). *The tainted war: Culture and identity in Vietnam war narratives.* Westport, CT: Greenwood.

Liddle, A. M. (1996). State, masculinities and law: Some comments on gender and english state-formation. In Masculinities, social relations, and crime [Special issue]. *British Journal of Criminology, 36*(3).

Liebow, E. (1967). *Tally's corner.* Boston: Little, Brown.

Lifton, R. J. (1986). *The Nazi doctors: Medical killing and the psychology of genocide.* New York: Basic Books.

Lisak, D. (1991). Sexual aggression, masculinity, and fathers. *Signs: Journal of Women in Culture and Society, 16,* 238-262.

Lopez, S. (1993, July 8). Fifth guard arrested on sex charge. *Albuquerque Journal,* pp. A1, A2.

Lopreato, J. (1988). *Human nature and biocultural evolution.* Boston: Allen & Unwin.

Lorber, J. (1994). *Paradoxes of gender.* New Haven, CT: Yale University Press.

Lozoff, B. (1995, July-August). Revising the convict code—One step further. *Prison Life,* pp. 32, 69-70.

MacKenzie, D., Elis, L. A., Simpson, S. S., & Skroban, S. B. (1994). *Female offenders in boot camp prisons.* College Park: University of Maryland, Institute of Criminal Justice and Criminology.

MacKinnon, C. (1983). Feminism, Marxism, method and the state: Toward a feminist jurisprudence. *Signs: Journal of Women in Culture and Society, 8*(Summer), 635-658.

MacKinnon, C. (1987). Feminism, Marxism, method and the state: Toward a feminist jurisprudence. In S. Harding (Ed.), *Feminism and methodology* (pp. 135-156). Indianapolis: Indiana University Press.

Macklin, M. C., & Kolbe, R. H. (1984). Sex role stereotyping in children's advertising: Current and past trends. *Journal of Advertising, 13*(2), 34-42.

Maguire, K., & Pastore, A. L. (Eds.). (1994). *Sourcebook of criminal justice statistics.* Washington, DC: U.S. Department of Justice.

Maher, L., & Curtis, R. (1992). Women on the edge: Crack cocaine and the changing contexts of street-level sex work in New York City. *Crime, Law and Social Change, 18,* 221-258.

Mailer, N. (1964). *An American dream.* New York: Dell.

Majors, R., & Billson, J. M. (1992). *Cool pose: The dilemmas of black manhood in America.* New York: Simon & Schuster.

Mann, C. (1984). *Female crime and delinquency.* University: University of Alabama Press.

Maran, R. (1996). After the Beijing Women's Conference: What will be done? *Social Justice, 23*(1-2), 352-367.

Margolick, D. (1990, June 1). At the bar. *New York Times,* p. B6.

Martin, P. Y., & Hummer, R. A. (1989). Fraternities and rape on campus. *Gender and Society, 4,* 457-473.

Maryanski, A. (1994). The pursuit of human nature in sociobiology and evolutionary sociology. *Sociological Perspectives, 37,* 375-398.

Marzuk, P. M., Tardiff, K., & Hirsch, C. S. (1992). The epidemiology of murder-suicide. *Journal of the American Medical Association, 267,* 3179-3183.

Mauer, M. (1994). *Americans behind bars: The international use of incarceration, 1992-1993.* Washington, DC: The Sentencing Project.

Maxfield, M. G. (1989). Circumstances in supplementary homicide reports: Variety and validity. *Criminology, 27,* 671-695.

McCall, N. (1994). *Makes me wanna holler.* New York: Random House.

McClellan, D. S. (1994). Disparity in the discipline of male and female inmates in Texas prisons. *Women and Criminal Justice, 5*(2), 71-97.

McCloskey, L. A., Figueredo, A. J., & Koss, M. P. (1995). The effects of systemic family violence on children's mental health. *Child Development, 66,* 1239-1261.

McNeal, J. U. (1987). *Children as consumers: Insights and implications.* Lexington, MA: Lexington Books.

McNelly, R. L., & Mann, C. R. (1990). Domestic violence is a human issue. *Journal of Interpersonal Violence, 5,* 129-132.

McNelly, R. L., & Robinson-Simpson, G. (1987). The truth about domestic violence: A falsely framed issue. *Social Work, 32,* 485-490.

Mercy, J. A., & Saltzman, L. (1989). Fatal violence among spouses in the United States, 1976-1985 *American Journal of Public Health, 79,* 595-599.

Merton, R. K. (1938). Social structure and anomie. *American Sociological Review, 3,* 672-682.

Messerschimdt, J. W. (1986). *Capitalism, patriarchy, and crime.* Totowa, NJ: Rowman & Littlefield.

Messerschimdt, J. W. (1993). *Masculinities and crime: Critique and reconceptualization of theory.* Totowa, NJ: Rowman & Littlefield.

Messerschmidt, J. W. (1996). Structured action theory: Understanding the interrelation of gender, race, class, and crime. In B. D. MacLean & D. Milovanovic (Eds.), *Thinking critically about crime* (pp. 67-74). Vancouver, BC: Collective Press.

Messerschmidt, J. W. (1997). Gender, race, class and crime in the making. Thousand Oaks, CA: Sage.

Messner, M. A. (1992a). Boyhood, organized sports, and the construction of masculinity. In M. S. Kimmel & M. A. Messner (Eds.), *Men's lives* (pp. 161-175). New York: Macmillan.

Messner, M. A. (1992b). *Power at play: Sports and the problem of masculinity.* Boston: Beacon.

Messner, M. A., & Sabo, D. F. (Eds.). (1990). *Sport, men, and the gender order: Critical feminist perspectives.* Champaign, IL: Human Kinetics.

Meyer, M. (1992, November 9). Coercing sex behind bars: Hawaii's prison scandal. *Newsweek,* pp. 23-25.

Miedzian, M. (1992). *Boys will be boys: Breaking the link between masculinity and violence.* Garden City, NY: Doubleday.

Milgram, S. (1969). *Obedience to authority.* New York: Harper & Row.

Milkie, M. A. (1994). Social world approach to cultural studies: Mass media and gender in the adolescent peer group. *Journal of Contemporary Ethnography, 23*(3), 354-380.

Miller, J., & Schwartz, M. (1995). Rape myths and violence against street prostitutes. *Deviant Behavior, 16*(1), 1-23.

Miller, W. (1958). Lower class culture as a generating milieu of gang delinquency. *Journal of Social Issues, 14,* 5-19.

Millett, K. (1969). *Sexual politics.* New York: Avon Books.

Millman, J. (1980). New rules for the oldest profession: Should we change our prostitution laws? *Harvard Women's Law Journal, 3,* 1-35.

Minz, M. (1985). *At any cost: Corporate greed, women and the Dalkon Shield.* New York: Pantheon.

Moffat, M. (1989). *Coming of age in New Jersey: College and American culture.* New Brunswick, NJ: Rutgers University Press.

Mokhibar, R. (1988). Dalkon Shield. In *Corporate crime and violence: Big business power and the abuse of the public trust* (pp. 149-162). San Francisco: Sierra Club Books.

Moncrief, W., & Landry, R. (1982). Children's commercial content: A look at sexual roles and the use of animation. In B. Walker et al. (Eds.), *Educators' conference proceedings, 48* (pp. 374-377). New York: American Marketing Association.

Moore, J. W. (1978). *Homeboys: Gangs, drugs, and prison in the barrios of Los Angeles.* Philadelphia: Temple University Press.

Moore, J. W. (1991). *Going down to the barrio: Homeboys and homegirls in change.* Philadelphia: Temple University Press.

Moore, J. W., & Vigil, J. D. (1987). Chicano gangs: Group Norms and Individual Factors to Adult Criminality. *Aztalan, 18,* 27-44.

Morgan, D. H. J. (1992). *Discovering men.* New York: Routledge.

Mosher, D. L., & Tompkins, S. S. (1988). Scripting the macho man: Hypermasculine socialization and enculturation. *Journal of Sex Research, 25,* 60-84.

Nagel, J. (1994). *American Indian ethnic renewal.* Oxford, UK: Oxford University Press.

Nelson, M. B. (1994). *The stronger women get, the more men love football: Sexism and the American culture of sports.* New York: Harcourt Brace Jovanovich.

Nenadic, N. (1996). Femicide: A framework for understanding genocide. In D. Bell & R. Klein (Eds.), *Radically speaking: Feminism reclaimed* (pp. 456-464). North Melbourne, Australia: Spinifex.

Nichols, B. (1995, February 16). Dow liable in implants verdict: Jury in historic case awards couple $5.2 million. *The Dallas Morning News,* p. 1A.

Nicholson, J. (1993). *Men and women: How different are they?* New York: Oxford University Press.

Norden, M. F. (1990). Portrait of a disabled Vietnam veteran: Alex Cutter of *Cutter's Way.* In L. Dittmar & G. Michaud (Eds.), *From Hanoi to Hollywood: The Vietnam war in American film* (pp. 217-225). New Brunswick, NJ: Rutgers University Press.

O'Donnell, G. (1988). *Bureaucratic authoritarianism: Argentina, 1966-1973.* Berkeley: University of California Press.

O'Sullivan, C. S. (1991). Acquaintance gang rape on campus. In A. Parrot & L. Bechhoffer (Eds.), *Acquaintance rape: The hidden crime* (pp. 140-156). New York: John Wiley.

O'Sullivan, C. S. (1993). Fraternities and the rape culture. In E. Buchwald, P. R. Fletcher, & M. Roth (Eds.), *Transforming a rape culture* (pp. 23-30). Minneapolis: Milkweed Editions.

O'Sullivan, C. S. (1996). *Alternatives to violence: An evaluation of a batterers intervention program: Final report to the van Ameringen Foundation.* Victim Services, New York City.

O'Sullivan, C. S., & Heinz, A. (1992, April). *Implicit masculine generics: Are "youths" male?* Paper presented at the Annual Meeting of the Eastern Psychological Association, Boston.

Oliver, W. (1994). *The violent social world of black men.* Lexington, MA: Lexington Books.

Omerdic, M. (1992, June 1). Another genocide against Muslims: Let it be known and never repeated. *Preporod, 3,* p. 11.

Orr, J. R. (1994, March). *Masculinity in trouble: A comparison of the primitive masculinity movement of the late 19th century and the modern mythopoetic men's movement.* Paper presented at the Midwest Sociological Society Meetings, St. Louis, MO.

Ouellet, L. J., Wiebel, W. W., Jimenez, A. D., & Johnson, W. A. (1993). Crack cocaine and the transformation of prostitution in three Chicago neighborhoods. In M. Ratner (Ed.), *The crack pipe as pimp* (pp. 69-96). Lexington, MA: Lexington Books.

Parker, L. S. (1995). Beauty and breast implantation: How candidate selection affects autonomy and informed consent. *Hypatia, 10*(Winter), 183-202.

Parsons, T. (1951). *The social system.* Glencoe, IL: Free Press.

Parsons, T., & Shils, E. A. (Eds.). (1959). *Toward a general theory of action.* Cambridge, MA: Harvard University Press.

Patrick, D. L. (1995). [Letter to Governor John Engler, re: Crane and Scott Correctional Centers, dated March 27, 1995].

Pence, E., & Paymar, M. (1993). *Education groups for men who batter: The Duluth model.* New York: Springer.

Perl, G. (1948). *I was a doctor in Auschwitz.* New York: Arno Press.

Pérusse, D. (1994). Mate choice in modern societies: Testing evolutionary hypotheses with behavioral data. *Human Nature, 5,* 255-278.

Perry, S., & Dawson, J. (1985). *Nightmare: Women and the Dalkon Shield.* New York: Macmillan.

Personal Narratives Group. (1989). *Interpreting women's lives: Feminist theory and personal narratives.* Bloomington: Indiana University Press.

Pleck, E. (1987). *Domestic tyranny.* New York: Oxford University Press.

Pleck, J. H. (1981). *The myth of masculinity.* Cambridge: MIT Press.

Pleck, J. H., Sonenstein, F. L., Ku, L., & Burbridge, L. C. (1996). *Individual, family, and community factors modifying male adolescents' risk behavior trajectory.* Washington, DC: Urban Institute.

Polk, K. (1994). *When men kill: Scenarios of masculine violence.* Cambridge, UK: Cambridge University Press.

Purdy, M. W. (1995, December 19). An official culture of violence infests a prison. *New York Times,* pp. 1, 17.

Purdy, M. W. (1996, January 28). Who guards the guards? At Rikers, a history of beatings. *New York Times,* pp. 25, 29.

Rable, G. C. (1984). *But there was no peace: The role of violence in the politics of Reconstruction.* Athens: University of Georgia Press.

Radford, J., & Russell, D. E. H. (1992). *Femicide.* Milton Keynes, UK: Open University Press.

Rafter, N. H. (1990). *Partial justice: Women, prisons and social control.* New Brunswick, NJ: Transaction Books.

Raper, A. F. (1969). *The tragedy of lynching.* New York: Negro University Press.

Reiss, A. J., Jr., & Roth, J. A. (1993). *Understanding and preventing violence.* Washington, DC: National Academy Press.

Renzetti, C. M., & Curran, D. J. (1992). *Women, men and society* (2nd ed., pp. 219-249). Boston: Allyn & Bacon.

Riesman, D. (1950). *The lonely crowd.* New Haven, CT: Yale University Press.

Rittner, C., & Roth, J. K. (Eds.). (1993). *Different voices: Women and the holocaust.* New York: Paragon House.

Ritzer, G. (1992). *Sociological theory* (3rd ed.). New York: McGraw-Hill.

Robinson, L. S. (1992, January 20). The Vietnam syndrome. *The Nation,* pp. 60-62.

Rose, H. (1986). Women's work women's knowledge. In J. Mitchell & A. Oakley (Eds.), *What is feminism?* (pp. 161-183). Oxford, UK: Basil Blackwell.

Rosenbaum, M. (1990). The role of depression in couples involved in murder-suicide and homicide. *American Journal of Psychiatry, 147,* 1036-1039.

Rosenberg, S. D. (1993). The threshold of thrill: Life stories in the skies over Southeast Asia. In M. Cooke & A. Woollacott (Eds.), *Gendering war talk* (pp. 43-66). Princeton, NJ: Princeton University Press.

Rosenwald, G. C., & Ochberg, R. L. (1992). Introduction: Live stories, cultural politics, and self understanding. In G. Rosenwald & R. Ochberg (Eds.), *Storied lives* (pp. 1-18). New Haven, CT: Yale University Press.

Russell, D. E. H. (1990). *Rape in marriage.* Bloomington: Indiana University Press.

Russett, C. E. (1989). *Sexual science: The Victorian construction of womanhood.* Cambridge, MA: Harvard University Press.

Rynbrandt, L. J., & Kramer, R. C. (1995). Hybrid nonwomen and corporate violence: The silicone breast implant case. *Violence Against Women, 3,* 206-225.

Sabo, D. (1989). Pigskin, pain, and patriarchy. In M. Messner (Ed.), *Men's lives* (pp. 185-187). New York: Macmillan.

Sampson, R. J., & Laub, J. H. (1993). *Crime in the making: Pathways and turning points through life.* Cambridge, MA: Harvard University Press.

Sampson, R. J., & Laub, J. H. (1996). Socioeconomic achievement in the life course of disadvantaged men: Military service as a turning point, circa 1940-1965. *American Sociological Review, 61,* 347-367.

Sanday, P. R. (1992). *Fraternity gang rape.* New York: NYU Press.

Saunders, D. (1992). A typology of men who batter: Three types derived from cluster analysis. *American Journal of Orthopsychiatry, 62,* 264-275.

Saunders, D., Lynch, A. B., Grayson, M., & Linz, D. (1987). The inventory of beliefs about wife-beating: The construction and initial validation of a measure of beliefs and attitudes. *Violence and Victims, 2,* 39-57.

Schuetz, S., & Sprafkin, J. (1978). Spot messages appearing within Saturday morning television programs. In A. K. Daniels & J. Benet (Eds.), *Hearth and home, images of women in mass media.* New York: Oxford University Press.

Schwarcz, S. K., Bolan, G. A., Fullilove, M., McCright, J., Fullilove, R., Kohn, R., & Rolfs, R. T. (1992). Crack cocaine and the exchange of sex for money or drugs. *Sexually Transmitted Diseases, 19,* 7-13.

Schwarz, P. J. (1988). *Twice condemned: Slaves and the criminal laws of Virginia, 1705-1865.* Baton Rouge: Louisiana State University Press.

Scott, A. F. (1970). *The southern lady: From pedestal to politics, 1830-1930.* Chicago: University of Chicago Press.

Scottish Prison Service (1994). *Small units the Scottish Prison Service: The report of the Working Party on the Barlinnie Special Unit.* Edinburgh: Author.

Segal, L. (1990). *Slow motion: Changing masculinities, changing men.* London: Virago.

Segrave, J. O. (1994). The perfect 10: "Sportspeak" in the language of sexual relations. *Sociology of Sport Journal, 11,* 95-113.

Sewenely, A. (1993, January 6). Sex abuse charges rock women's prison. *Detroit News,* pp. B1, B7.

Shafer, D. M. (1990). The Vietnam combat experience: The human legacy. In D. M. Shafer (Ed.), *The legacy: The Vietnam war in the American imagination* (pp. 80-103). Boston: Beacon.

Shatan, C. F. (1989). Happiness is a warm gun, militarized mourning and ceremonial vengeance: Toward a psychological theory of combat and manhood in America, Part III. *Vietnam Generation, 1*(3-4), 127-151.

Shaw, C. R., & McKay, H. D. (1942). *Juvenile delinquency and urban areas.* Chicago: University of Chicago Press.

Shearing, C. (1996). Reinventing policing: Policing as governance. In O. Marenin (Ed.), *Policing change, changing police: International perspectives.* New York: Garland.

Short, J. F., & Strodtbeck, F. L. (1965). *Group process and gang delinquency.* Chicago: University of Chicago Press.

Skolnick, A. (1991). *Embattled paradise: The American family in an age of uncertainty.* New York: Basic Books.

Skovholt, T. M., Moore, D., & Haritos-Fatouros, M. (n.d.). The 180° bind: Trained for war, expected to nurture. (Available from M. Haritos-Fatouros, Department of Psychology, University of Thessaloniki, Thessaloniki, Greece)

"Slain secretary feared husband would be violent." *The Advocate Messenger,* May 11, 1990. pp. A1-A7.

Slotkin, R. (1985). *The fatal environment: The myth of the frontier in the age of industrialization, 1800-1890.* Middletown, CT: Wesleyan University Press.

Smart, C., & Smart, B. (Eds.). (1978). *Women, sexuality and social control.* London: Routledge & Kegan Paul.

Smart, T. (1991, June 10). Breast implants: What did the industry know, and when? *Business Week,* pp. 94-98.

Smart, T. (1992, January 27). This man sounded the alarm—in 1976. *Business Week,* p. 34.

Smith, E. (1997, January 7). [Letter to the Editor]. *New York Times,* p. 38.

Smith, L. J. (1994). A content analysis of gender differences in children's advertising. *Journal of Broadcasting & Electronic Media, 38*(3), 323-337.

Smith, M. D. (1990). Patriarchal ideology and wife beating: A test of a feminist hypothesis. *Violence and Victims, 5,* 257-273.

Smith-Rosenberg, C. (1985). *Disorderly conduct: Vision of gender in Victorian America.* New York: Oxford University Press.

Snell, T. L., & Morton, D. C. (1994). *Women in prison* (Special report). Washington, DC: Bureau of Justice Statistics.

Spergel, I. A. (1995). *The youth gang problem: A community approach.* New York: Oxford University Press.

Spindel, D. J. (1989). *Crime and society in North Carolina, 1663-1776.* Baton Rouge: Louisiana State University Press.

Springen, K., & Hager, M. (1995, November 13). Silicone: Juries vs. science. *Newsweek,* p. 75.

Stanko, E. A. (1994). Challenging the problem of men's individual violence. In T. Newburn & E. A. Stanko (Eds.), *Men, masculinities and crime: Just boys doing business?* (pp. 32-45). London: Routledge & Kegan Paul.

Stanley, D. (1994, December 18). Blame shifting from doctors in medical suits: Physicians are seen as at the mercy of manufacturers, hospitals. *Austin American-Statesmen.* p. B1.

Stark, E., & Flitcraft, A. (1996). *Women at risk: Domestic violence and women's health.* London: Sage.

Stato, J. (1993). Montreal gynocide. In P. Bart & E. G. Moran (Eds.), *Violence against women: The bloody footprints* (pp. 132-133). Newbury Park, CA: Sage.

Stein, B. (1996, July). Life in prison: Sexual abuse. *The Progressive,* pp. 23-24.

Steinmetz, S. (1977-1978). The battered husband syndrome. *Victimology, 2,* 499-509.

Stephenson, J. (1995). *Men are not cost-effective: Male crime in America.* New York: Harper Perennial.

Stewart, J. B. (1991). *Den of thieves.* New York: Touchstone.

Stoll, C. S. (1974). *Female and male.* Dubuque, IA: William C. Brown.

Strate, L. (1992). Beer commercials: A manual on masculinity. In S. Craig (Ed.), *Men, masculinity, and the media* (pp. 78-92). Newbury Park, CA: Sage.

Straus, M. A., & Gelles, R. (1990). Societal change and change in family violence from 1975 to 1985 as revealed by two national surveys. In D. Kelly (Ed.), *Criminal behavior* (2nd ed.; pp. 114-136). New York: St. Martin's.

Straus, M. A., Gelles, R. J., & Steinmetz, S. K. (1981). *Behind closed doors: Violence in the American family.* Newbury Park, CA: Sage.

Straus, S. (1996, Winter). Escape from Animal House: Frat boy tells all. *On the Issues,* pp. 26-28.

Studervant, S. P., & Stoltzfus, B. (1992). *Let the good times roll: Prostitution and the U.S. military in Asia.* New York: New Press.

Sullivan, P. A., & Wilson, D. J. (1993). The coach's role. In G. L. Cohen (Ed.), *Women in sport* (pp. 230-237). Newbury Park, CA: Sage.

Sutherland, E. (1924). *Criminology.* Philadelphia: J. B. Lippincott.

Sutherland, E. H. (1983). *White collar crime: The uncut version.* New Haven, CT: Yale University Press.

Sykes, G. M. (1965). *The society of captives: A study of a maximum security prison.* New York: Atheneum.

Symons, D. (1981). *The evolution of human sexuality.* New York: Oxford University Press.

Takaki, R. (1982). *Iron cages: Race and culture in nineteenth century America.* New York: Knopf.

Taves, A. (Ed.). (1989). *Religion and domestic violence in early New England: The memoirs of Abigail Abbott Bailey.* Bloomington: Indiana University Press.

Telender, R., & Sullivan, R. (1989, February 27). You reap what you sow. *Sports Illustrated,* pp. 20-26, 31.

Thompson, H. (1971). Group rape. In J. MacDonald (Ed.), *Rape offenders and their victims* (pp. 162-170). Springfield, IL: Charles C Thomas.

Thompson, K. (1991). Introduction. In K. Thompson (Ed.), *To be a man: In search of the deep masculine* (pp. i-xxi). Los Angeles: Tarcher.

Thorne, B. (1993). *Gender play: Girls and boys in schools.* New Brunswick, NJ: Rutgers University Press.

Thorpe, E. E. (1967). *Eros and freedom in southern life and thought.* Durham, NC: Seeman.

Toch, H. (1995). Inmate involvement in prison governance. *Federal Probation, 59,* 34-39.

Tolnay, S., & Beck, E. M. (1995). *A festival of violence: An analysis of southern lynchings, 1882-1930.* Chicago: University of Illinois Press.

Tomes, N. (1978). A torrent of abuse: Crimes of violence between working-class men and women in London, 1840-1875. *Journal of Social History, 11*(Spring), 328-345.

Tong, R. (1989). Radical feminism on gender and sexuality. In *Feminist theory: A comprehensive introduction* (pp. 72-139). Boulder, CO: Westview.

Torres, J., Hagedorn. J. M., & Giglio, G. (1996). *Drug use of Milwaukee gangs.* Paper presented at the meetings of the American Society of Criminology, Chicago.

Town split over teen wrestler's gang rape by teammates. (1992). *Donahue* [Transcript #3407, February 20]. New York: Multimedia Entertainment.

Tracy, K. K., & Crawford, C. B. (1992). Wife abuse: Does it have an evolutionary origin? In D. A. Counts, J. K. Brown, & J. C. Campbell (Eds.), *Sanctions and sanctuary: Cultural perspectives on the beating of wives* (pp. 19-32). Boulder, CO: Westview.

Trelease, A. W. (1971). *White terror: The Ku Klux Klan conspiracy and southern Reconstruction.* New York: Harper & Row.

Trujillo, N. (1991). Hegemonic masculinity on the mound: Media representations of Nolan Ryan and American sports culture. *Critical Studies in Mass Communication, 8,* 290-308.

Tuttle, W. M., Jr. (1993). *Daddy's gone to war: The Second World War in the lives of America's children.* New York: Oxford University Press.

Two guilty in video-rape of teen. (1992, June 13). *Daily News,* p. 20.

Udry, J. R. (1988). Biological predispositions and social control in adolescent sexual behavior. *American Sociological Review, 53,* 709-722.

Udry, J. R., Talbert, L. M., & Morris, N. M. (1986). Biosocial foundations for adolescent female sexuality. *Demography, 23,* 217-227.

U.S. Department of Justice. (1994, November). *Violence between intimates* (Rep. No. CJ-149259). Washington, DC: Bureau of Justice Statistics.

Vachss, A. (1993). *Sex crimes*. New York: Random House.

Valentine, C. A. (1968). *Culture and poverty*. Chicago: University of Chicago Press.

van der Kolk, B. A. (1988). Trauma in men: Effects on family life. In M. B. Straus (Ed.), *Abuse and victimization across the life span* (pp. 170-187). Baltimore, MD: Johns Hopkins University Press.

Verna, M. E. (1975). The female image in children's TV commercials. *Journal of Broadcasting, 19,* 301-309.

Vigil, D. (1988). *Barrio gangs*. Austin: University of Texas Press.

Walby, S. (1990). *Theorizing patriarchy*. Oxford, UK: Basil Blackwell.

Walby, S. (1992). Post-post-modernism? Theorizing social complexity. In M. Barrett & A. Phillips (Eds.), *Destabilizing theory: Contemporary feminist debates* (pp. 31-52). Palo Alto, CA: Stanford University Press.

Walker, L. (1979). *The battered woman*. New York: Harper & Row.

Walklate, S. (1995). *Gender and crime: An introduction*. London: Prentice Hall/ Harvester Wheatsheaf.

Wallace, R. A., & Wolf, A. (1995). *Contemporary sociological theory: Continuing the classical tradition* (4th ed.). Englewood Cliffs, NJ: Prentice Hall.

Warshaw, R. (1988). *I never called it rape*. New York: Harper & Row.

Wasser, S. K. (1994). Psychosocial stress and infertility: Cause or effect? *Human Nature, 5,* 293-306.

Watson, T. (1992, November 16). Ga. indictments charge abuse of female inmates. *USA Today,* p. A3.

Websdale, N. (1992). Female suffrage, male violence and law enforcement. *Social Justice, 19*(3), 82-106.

Websdale, N. (1995). Rural woman abuse: The voices of Kentucky women. *Violence Against Women, 1,* 309-338.

Welch, R. L., Huston-Stein, A., Wright, J. C., & Plehal, R. (1979). Subtle sex-role cues in children's commercials. *Journal of Communication, 29*(3), 202-209.

West, C., & Fenstermaker, S. (1993). Power, inequity and the accomplishment of gender: An ethnomethodological view. In P. England (Ed.), *Theory on gender/feminism on theory* (pp. 151-174). New York: Aldine.

West, C., & Fenstermaker, S. (1995). Doing difference. *Gender and Society, 9*(1), 8-37.

West, C., & Zimmerman, D. H. (1987). Doing gender. *Gender & Society, 1*(2), 125-151.

West, D. (1967). *Murder followed by suicide*. Cambridge, MA: Harvard University Press.

White, G. F., Katz, J., & Scarborough, K. E. (1992). The impact of professional football games upon violent assaults on women. *Violence and Victims, 7,* 157-171.

Wiegman, R. (1993). The anatomy of lynching. *Journal of the History of Sexuality, 3*(3), 445-467.

Williams, T. (1992). *Crackhouse: Notes from the end of the line*. New York: Penguin.

Wilsnack, S. C., & Beckman, L. J. (1984). *Alcohol problems in women: Antecedents, consequences, and intervention*. New York: Guilford.

Wilson, E. O. (1975). *Sociobiology: The new synthesis.* Cambridge, MA: Harvard University Press.

Wilson, J. Q., & Herrnstein, R. (1985). *Crime and human nature.* New York: Simon & Schuster.

Wilson, W. J. (1987). *The truly disadvantaged.* Chicago: University of Chicago Press.

Wilson, W. J. (1996). *When work disappears: The world of the new urban poor.* New York: Knopf.

Wilson, W. J., & Sampson, R. J. (1995). Toward a theory of race, crime, and urban inequality. In J. Hagan & R. D. Peterson (Eds.), *Crimes and inequality.* Palo Alto, CA: Stanford University Press.

Winant, H. (1995). Symposium. *Gender and Society, 9*(4), 503-506.

Wolfe, T. (1987). *The bonfire of the vanities.* New York: Bantam Books.

Wolfgang, M. E., & Ferracuti, F. (1967). *The subculture of violence: Towards an integrated theory in criminology.* London: Social Science Paperbacks.

Wright, G. C. (1990). *Racial violence in Kentucky, 1865-1940: Lynchings, mob rule, and "legal lynchings."* Baton Rouge: Louisiana State University Press.

Wright, R. (1994). *The moral animal.* New York: Pantheon.

Yllo, K., & Straus, M. (1984). Patriarchy and violence against wives: The impact of structural and normative factors. *Journal of International and Comparative Social Welfare, 1,* 1-13.

Young, B. M. (1990). *Television advertising and children.* Oxford, UK: Clarendon.

Zinn, H. (1980). *A people's history of the United States.* New York: Harper & Row.

Index

About the Contributors

Lee H. Bowker, PhD, is Professor of Sociology and Emeritus Dean of the College of Behavioral and Social Sciences at Humboldt State University. He is the author of 17 books and monographs, plus approximately 300 scientific papers, journal articles, book chapters, and published reviews. He regularly serves as an expert witness on behalf of battered women, abused children, and innocent men in criminal courts and other legal system settings. His current research interests include coaching abuse, trigger mechanisms in lethal counterviolence by long-term victims of violence, gender differences in social support on athletic teams, profiling pedophilia, and developing a general theory about masculinities, violence, domination, and predation.

Constance L. Chapple is a doctoral candidate in Sociology/Criminology at the University of Arizona with research interests in juvenile delinquency, corporate crime, criminological theory, and race and gender. She is pursuing work that addresses these overlapping areas. Her dissertation uses criminological theory to explain intimate, dating violence in a teenaged population.

Meda Chesney-Lind, PhD, is Professor of Women's Studies at the University of Hawaii at Manoa. She has served as vice president of the

American Society of Criminology and as president of the Western Society of Criminology. She is the author of over 50 monographs and papers on the subject of women and crime; her books include *Girls, Delinquency and Juvenile Justice,* which was awarded the American Society of Criminology's Michael J. Hindelang Award for the "outstanding contribution to criminology, 1992" and *The Female Offender: Girls, Women, and Crime,* published in 1997 by Sage. She has also received the Distinguished Scholar Award from the Women and Crime Division of the American Society of Criminology, the Paul Tappan Award for "outstanding contributions to the field of criminology" from the Western Society of Criminology, and the University of Hawaii Board of Regent's Medal for "Excellence in Research."

John M. Hagedorn has been doing gang research in Milwaukee for more than a decade. He is currently Principal Investigator of the Drug Posse and Homegirl Studies, a 5-year research project funded by the National Institute on Drug Abuse. He heads a collaborative research that features former gang members who interview their homeboys and homegirls and participate in all phases of the research. He has published widely on gangs and drugs. He is presently preparing a second edition of his book, *People & Folks: Gangs, Crime, and the Underclass.* His most recent book, *Forsaking Our Children: Bureaucracy and Reform in the Child Welfare System,* is based on 3 years that he spent working as a reformer in Milwaukee's social service system. The book describes the punitive nature of the child welfare bureaucracy and proposes practical short-term steps for reform. He is an Assistant Professor in the Department of Criminal Justice at the University of Illinois-Chicago.

Mika Haritos-Fatouros is Professor of Clinical Psychology and Director of Post-Graduate Studies in Clinical Psychology at the Aristotellan University of Thessaloniki, Greece. She is former Dean of the Faculty of Philosophy at Thessaloniki University. She was educated at London and Oxford Universities. She is former president of the Greek Psychological Association and an active member of the Greek Women's Movement. Her publications include 36 articles and two books, including one on the *Psychology of Torture* to be published in 1997. For the past 18 years, she has lectured throughout the United States, Europe, and Australia on the psychology and training of torturers.

Martha K. Huggins is Roger Thayer Stone Professor of Sociology at Union College in Schenectady, New York, where she has taught since 1979. She has been Visiting Professor of Sociology at the Universidade Federal de Pernambuco, the Universidade Federal da Brasília, and at the Universidade do São Paulo, all in Brazil. She conducted research in Brazil for 22 years, and has produced numerous articles on crime, on the police, and on extra-legal violence, as well as three books: *From Slavery to Vagrancy in Brazil: Crime and Social Control in the Third World* (1981), *Vigilantism and the State in Modern Latin America: Essays in Extra-legal Violence* (1991), and *Political Policing: The United States and Latin America* (in press). Her recently completed study (with Mika Haritos-Fatouros) of Brazilian police torturers will be her fourth book.

Tracy Xavia Karner is Research Assistant Professor in the Gerontology Center at the University of Kansas. She is currently working on a book tentatively titled *Retelling Vietnam: Stories of American Masculinity,* which is a historical and cultural recollection of the Vietnam war as well as an overview of the prevalent themes of socially prescribed, and personally internalized, masculine identities of in-patient combat veterans. In addition, she has published a number of articles on masculinity and Vietnam veterans with PTSD. The majority of her research focuses on issues of identity, including gender, ethnicity, and health, from a sociocultural view and a social-psychological lens.

James W. Messerschmidt (Ph.D., the Criminology Institute, University of Stockholm, Sweden) is Professor of Sociology and Chair of the Criminology Department at the University of Southern Maine. His research interests focus on the interrelation of gender, race, class, and crime. In addition to numerous articles and book chapters, he is author of *The Trial of Leonard Peltier* (1983), *Capitalism, Patriarchy, and Crime: Toward a Socialist Feminist Criminology* (1986), *Criminology* (2nd ed.), with Piers Beirne (1995), and *Masculinities and Crime: Critique and Reconceptualization of Theory* (1993).

Chris O'Sullivan, a social psychologist who conducts research on male violence as an independent scholar in New York City, is completing a book on gang rape. She received her doctorate in experimental psychology with a concentration in cognition from the University of Oklahoma, and held an NIMH postdoctoral fellowship at Michigan State University. She taught social psychology and psychology of women at the University of Kentucky and at Bucknell University. She also has a master's degree in linguistics. Her initial research was on language and cognition, then social cognition, using laboratory experimentation. When gang rapes and trials seemed to keep occurring on the campuses where she was working, she began to investigate them. She attended trials around the country, interviewing prosecutors, perpetrators, and defense attorneys, as well as studying the students around her and collecting artifacts of the fraternal culture. She has consulted with district attorneys on rape prosecution, and worked with rape crisis and domestic violence services. When she was appointed Research Director at Victim Services in New York City, she switched her focus to domestic violence. In that position, she evaluated a batterers program, conducted a needs survey of women in shelters, and documented violence during visitation through a study of women receiving assistance with orders of protection in Family Court. She also served the agency as general research advisor on service delivery, program design, and evaluation. As a consultant, she contributed to a National Institute of Justice "Issues and Practices Report" on batterers programs, conducting a national telephone survey, a site visit to programs for minority populations, and reviewing theories of domestic violence. She is a UN representative for the Association for Women in Psychology.

Sarah Sobieraj is a doctoral student in the sociology department at the State University of New York at Albany. She graduated from the State University of New York at Geneseo in 1993 with a BA in political science and from American University in 1997 with an MA in sociology. Her primary research interests involve exploring culture as an agent in the reproduction of social inequality.

Hans Toch is Distinguished Professor at the School of Criminal Justice, University at Albany, State University of New York. Among his books are *Living in Prison, Violent Men, Mosaic of Despair,* and *Corrections: A Humanistic Approach.*

Neil Websdale, PhD, is Assistant Professor of Criminal Justice at Northern Arizona University, Flagstaff. He has published a number of articles on violence against women, the criminal justice response to violence against women, and the history of policing class and gender relations. His first book is *Rural Woman Battering and the Justice System: An Ethnography,* published by Sage in 1997.